D1599844

...∕ **STAY TUNED** ∕ ...

.... / Stay Tuned /...

An Inside Look at the Making of Prime-Time Television

.../ by Richard Levinson and William Link /...

St. Martin's Press / New York

Copyright © 1981 by Richard Levinson
and William Link
For information, write: St. Martin's Press,
175 Fifth Avenue, New York, N.Y. 10010
Manufactured in the United States of America

Library of Congress Cataloging in Publication Data
Levinson, Richard.
  Stay tuned.
  1. Television broadcasting—United States.   I. Link,
William, joint author.   II. Title.
PN1992.3.U5L38   791.45'0973   80-28487
ISBN 0-312-76136-8

Design by Mina Greenstien
10 9 8 7 6 5 4 3 2 1
First Edition

"Crisis of Conscience" by Richard Levinson and William
Link is reprinted with permission from TV GUIDE ®
Magazine. Copyright © 1977 by Triangle Publications, Inc.
Radnor, Pennsylvania.

For Rosanna and Margery
And for Christine

*"When she was good she was very, very good,
but when she was bad she was horrid."*

Contents

...*/STAY TUNED/*...

Foreword

From its beginnings as a national medium in the early fifties, television has received little more than begrudging acknowledgment from established drama and cinema critics. Today the "intellectual" community pays scant notice to commercial television, preferring to affirm support for the occasional grand opera or British import on PBS. Academic halls bristle with disdain for "mass culture." The humanities, traditionally devoted to a concern for quality of life in the society, have so far failed to do much more than generalize about TV as a major social force. This cultural elitism has, on occasion, encouraged an apologetic attitude among even the more talented television writers and producers.

Two of the most gifted practitioners of the television art, Richard Levinson and William Link, humanists and intellectuals both, have refused to engage in such apology. Rather, they offer in this volume a view of the medium's inner working and a vision of its potential. Their uncompromising commitment to quality television has marked them as the premier writers-producers of drama in the industry. Their names are equated with excellence and their observations offer a welcome commentary on the nature of television itself. This book could be a significant contribution to the development of constructive dialogue among those prepared to acknowledge the serious import of popular culture. It most certainly will be a treasure for anyone interested in understanding prime-time commercial television as it exists today.

I first met Link and Levinson in 1975 while I was engaged in research. It was a time when socially relevant half-hour comedies dotted the TV schedule. Network news was at its zenith as a consequence of vigorous reporting in Vietnam and Watergate. In early 1974 TV drama presented in *The Autobiography of Miss Jane Pittman,* a story weaving sensitive emotion and social justice into a brilliant fabric. *Roots* followed three years later. Films for television, docudramas, and mini-series were examining serious issues as tens of millions of Americans watched. What the documentary of the sixties failed to do, attract audiences, the social dramas and comedies of the seventies accomplished.

It was amid these events that Link and Levinson sat down with me in a noisy and crowded Universal Studios commissary to discuss television and values. Like most artists, both men were ambiguous on the subject, unwilling to see themselves either as social reformers or molders of ideas. They were writers and producers who sought the best scripts, the most honest characters as their offering to the American public. But what the viewers of their work know and the readers of this book will perceive is that they create against the background of extremely sensitive social consciences. And as the reader will discover, their blending of craft and conscience has placed an indelible stamp on television drama in the seventies.

In March of 1969 the two men began work on their dramatic film, *My Sweet Charlie,* aired on NBC January 20, 1970. They had already addressed the student unrest of the sixties in the pilot that sold the *Lawyers* segment of *The Bold Ones. Charlie* signaled a decade of perceptive television treatment of race relations coupled with intelligent character study. Link and Levinson set a standard with this production, which earned them an Emmy for Outstanding Writing Achievement in Drama. Many of the memorable hours of drama and comedy that followed in the next ten years were indebted to their effective descriptions of human relations cast against current social conditions.

Columbo, the meat and potatoes cop, established Link and Levinson as creators-producers of high-quality series drama and earned them a second Emmy in 1972. Building upon that success the twosome moved into a totally uncharted area of social comment with *That Certain Summer.* This sympathetic, thoughtful, and effective play that dealt with homosexuality literally changed the face of commercial television. Its very lack of advocacy made it a powerful statement for diversity and freedom. It attacked stereotypes and altered perceptions among viewers and network executives alike.

Since their early days in television Link and Levinson have been concerned with violence. They sold some of it with their first successful series, *Mannix.* But, in their words, "after the spate of assassinations we decided to reduce the level of violence in our shows." *Columbo* and *Ellery Queen* were tangible evidences of this feeling reflected in series television. In 1974 they determined to approach the subject not by diminishing its use, but rather by addressing it dramatically. Their growing concern over the American fascination with violence, so often depicted on the small screen, surfaced in the first television movie docu-drama, the wrenching story of *The Execution of Private Slovik.* Again, written with an even hand, the representations of war and violence were compelling. It was a masterpiece and a model for future efforts to translate history into drama.

In that same year Link and Levinson turned to the writing and producing of their most overt "message" piece, an anti-gun drama entitled *The Gun.* This cautionary tale evoked the wrath of the National Rifle Association and embroiled the authors in potential censorship. After its initial airing by ABC it disappeared into the maw of the archives, and now is seldom seen in spite of its continued timeliness.

The two men returned to television drama in 1977 with concern about violence, a concern they now focused upon themselves as writers. The result was an engrossing film, *The Storyteller,* an examination of the role of television violence in society and the responsibilities that lie with writers, producers, and networks. It was, and remains, the only serious effort to wrestle with this issue in dramatic form. The balance that has become a hallmark of their productions drew criticism both from industry people who accused the writers of selling out to would-be censors and from TV detractors who saw the film as an apologia for the creative community. It was neither. Rather, it was an attempt to encourage thoughtful examination of a complex problem, something sorely lacking in the heated rhetoric over violence that has raged since the fifties. It is the most effective instrument for discussing the subject with college students that I have found.

After *The Storyteller* Link and Levinson departed Universal for the status of independent producers, having set a high standard for the industry both in terms of dramatic excellence and concern for social justice. Along the way their wit and craft lightened the lives of millions of viewers with *Columbo* and several other fine series. One of the best, least remembered, was the 1973 *Tenafly.* It cast a black hero in a standard detective environment, with a focus on his family life. Again, it was a first. In 1979 their love of mystery emerged in a first-rate thriller, *Murder by Natural Causes.* After the screening of this film, I heard many in the audience urge the writers to stick to this type of drama and drop the social comment.

It was the good fortune of American TV viewers that they failed to take that advice, and in 1981, little more than ten years after *My Sweet Charlie,* Link and Levinson returned to the searing effect of racial prejudice and the healing power of racial justice in *Crisis at Central High,* a sterling two-and-a-half-hour docu-drama about desegregation in 1957 Little Rock. Once again they were the conscience of an industry for both quality and content.

Just as Norman Lear is properly identified as the pioneer in quality TV comedy exhibiting a social conscience, likewise Bill Link and Dick Levinson have utilized their talents to effect maturity in the television drama, while consistently demonstrating a dedication to principle unusual in any industry. As they move into the eighties with *Crisis at Central High* and this current volume, as much as any individuals in Hollywood, they have given the audience a reason to *Stay Tuned.*

ROBERT S. ALLEY
Professor of Humanities
University of Richmond, Virginia

1 / Notes from the Wasteland

"Oh, what fun it'll be," said Alice from the other side of the mirror, "when they see me through the glass in here, and can't get at me!" But of course they *can* get at television, they've been doing it for years, and what they've seen through the glass has rarely pleased them. As the medium stumbles into the eighties it trails a wake of failed promises and richly-deserved critical abuse.

Still, the title of this book is meant to offer a glimmer, however dim, of hope. For prime-time commercial TV is not quite the "vast wasteland" deplored by Newton Minow when he coined the phrase during his tenure as Chairman of the Federal Communications Commission, and it's not always candy for the mind. As America's favorite Rorschach test, it has the odd capacity to be whatever anyone wants it to be, and its vices—or virtues—depend to a large extent on the eye of the beholder.

Minow was reacting, in 1961, against what he felt was a daily electronic bombardment of almost unbelievable banality, and much of that is still with us. But television, if it is anything, is a grab-bag, a magpie's nest of fragments—the series, the game show, the newscast, the sports event, the documentary, the variety show, the soap opera, the interview, the TV movie, the mini-series, the talk show, the special—and the two of us have seen, from our sometimes precarious position on the battlefield, a gradual improvement in at least some of these forms. Not that the airwaves aren't filled with junk. They are. But the exceptions have increased in number.

Situation comedy, for example, has evolved from *My Little Margie* and *December Bride* to the more literate (and funnier) series of Norman Lear and the MTM group. And while it's true that television's salad days gave us the brashness of Sergeant Bilko, the wild and slapdash lunacy of *Your Show of Shows,* and the gentle eccentricities of *Mr. Peepers,* programs of this quality were few and far between. Whatever one may think of *Mash, The Mary Tyler Moore Show, All in the Family, Maude,* and *One Day at a Time,* not to mention *Fernwood 2-Nite* and *Mary Hartman, Mary Hartman,* the fact is that all of these shows were on the air, cheek-to-jowl, every single week just a few years ago. And all of them could deal with story content unheard of in the days of *Mr. Ed* and *My Mother the Car,* comedies about rape, impotence, bigotry, and even death. Trafficking in controversy (sometimes known in the trade as the "issue-of-the-week gambit") is obviously no guarantee of quality, but a more open atmosphere and a wider range of choices are hardly hindrances to better work.

Paradoxically, there have been few advances in the bread-and-butter field of the dramatic series. Although *Shotgun Slade, Sea Hunt,* and *Surfside Six* gave way to *Family, Lou Grant,* and *Hill Street Blues,* there are few recent offerings that can compare with *East Side, West Side, The Defenders, Naked City,* or *The Westerner.* And the Family Hour fiasco led to early-evening pablum on the order of *Wonder Woman* and *Spider Man.*

Nevertheless, a new form of programming emerged during the past decade that has made a significant contribution to the upgrading of dramatic entertainment—the films created especially for television—and much of this book will deal with our experiences writing and producing these films.

Electronic drama had its origins in the Golden Age (or, as it is now characterized, somewhat defensively, the "so-called Golden Age") of the 1950s, when New York-based writers, including Paddy Chayevsky, Tad Mosel, Reginald Rose, William Gibson, and Rod Serling, tried their hands at the new medium and fashioned small-scale teleplays for shows such as *Studio One,* the *U.S. Steel Hour,* and *Philco Playhouse.* At their best these closet dramas, starring then relatively unknown actors (Rod Steiger, Paul Newman, Eva Marie Saint, Jack Klugman, E. G. Marshall) and directed by a cadre of talented young men (Sidney Lumet, Arthur Penn, George Roy Hill) were touching character studies *(Marty)* and socially relevant dramas *(Twelve Angry Men, Patterns, Days of Wine and Roses)* that many in the audience remember, even without their motion picture reincarnations, to this day.

But as the television industry shifted westward to Los Angeles and live TV was replaced by film, the anthologies gradually disappeared. *Playhouse 90* was the last of its breed, eventually succumbing to a ratings battle with *The Untouchables.* For many years thereafter, serious drama barely existed on television. There were exceptions, but for the most part Westerns, private detective and doctor shows, and inane sitcoms dominated the screen.

Then, in the late sixties, Universal Studios and NBC came up with a new way to package the anthology concept. They began by dispensing with the dirty word "anthology" altogether. Their research indicated that it signified an absence of continuing characters, and the conventional wisdom of the time was that the audience wanted to meet the same group, or "family," of regulars every week. Instead, these shows were called *World Premieres,* and they were shrewdly promoted as a first look at newly minted pictures made for TV. Viewers would presumably feel like first-nighters in the forecourt of the Chinese Theatre, surrounded by limousines and klieg lights—and totally unaware that they were meeting their old friend, the anthology, in a new guise. If the films did well they would alleviate a major network problem, the need for product to replace the rapidly diminishing reserves of theatrical feature films.

The first *World Premieres* were known as "long-form" programs, a term originally used to describe an elongated—some said "padded"—Western series called *The Virginian.* These early television movies were standard fare, melodramas on the order of a remake of the film version of Hemingway's "The Killers" and slick pieces of fluff such as

Fame Is the Name of the Game, a purported behind-the-scenes look at a big-city magazine. They were, in essence, overbloated series segments: the same formula stories, but with more star names and bigger budgets. And they did surprisingly well in the ratings (or predictably well, if one has a low opinion of mass taste).

An occasional work of quality managed to slip through, but it was usually an accident; the network had no interest in serious drama or a return to the Golden Age. Then ABC began to program its own ninety-minute *Movies of the Week* and CBS moved into the field. Suddenly, in this welter of what Judith Crist called "tailored-for-TV" movies, there were more and more departures, more risks taken as talented people, liberated from the constraints of series television, began to sense the possibilities of the form. Finally, in the course of any given season, there were at least a handful of individual motion pictures that required no apologies.

John J. O'Connor, the TV critic for the *New York Times,* complained in one of his columns that "commercial television has just about abandoned all pretense of artistic achievement." O'Connor is one of the few sane voices raised in favor of maintaining meaningful esthetic standards, and if by his quote he's condemning the lack in prime time of reverential (and sometimes overstuffed) productions of Ibsen, Shaw, and Chekov, he's quite correct. It's also true that many of our better playwrights have not had their work performed on the small screen. But it's our view that if the films for television are not art, many of them are certainly high-level popular entertainment. And in any given year the best television movies are better than all but a few theatrical motion pictures and plays for the legitimate stage.

Consider, by way of a case for the defense, the following television films made over the past twelve years, and keep in mind that this list is far from complete: *Deadlock, Silent Night, Lonely Night, Brian's Song, The Glass House, The Neon Ceiling, Larry, I heard the Owl Call My Name, Duel, The Law, Sunshine, The Marcus-Nelson Murders, Love Among the Ruins, The War of the Children, Tribes, The Autobiography of Miss Jane Pittman, A Death in Canaan, The Migrants, Catholics, Judge Horton and the Scottsboro Boys, The War Between the Tates, Farewell to Manzinar, A Clear and Present Danger, Fear on Trial, A Case of Rape,*

The Last Tenant, The Deadliest Season, A Question of Love, Friendly Fire, Attica, On the Minnesota Strip, and *Playing for Time.*

All of these films were made with meager budgets relative to the cost of most theatrical motion pictures, and they were completed in a fraction of the time. Many of them are still playing in syndication around the country, most have been aired overseas, and all of them, in our perhaps biased judgment, hold up as impressive enterprises that merit serious consideration.

Interestingly, attention (to paraphrase Arthur Miller, a major playwright who *has* written for television) is already being paid. More and more books and critical studies are being written, not only the expected ones about television's social, psychological and/or political ramifications, but also investigations into its esthetics, of all things. A professor of humanities told us recently, and not entirely in jest, that he sees television as the coming prestige medium. He reasons that the cultural establishment dismissed most of the motion pictures of the thirties and forties as mindless mass entertainment. Fiction and the theater were the preeminent forms, and the *films noirs* of the period were either ridiculed or overlooked. But fashions change and now the trend-setters, and particularly the young, are praising the very same films that were largely ignored when they were released. Movies are screened in museums, dissected by cineasts, beloved by the French, and have spawned a cottage industry of posters, T-shirts, and numberless books about their stars, their scripts, their productions, and, in some cases, even their wardrobe designers and makeup men.

However—again, in the opinion of our professor-theorist—the motion picture experience as we have known it is soon to become extinct. Cable TV, satellite broadcasting, cassettes, or some form of videodiscs will relegate the local movie house to a dinosaur boneheap, and the vast majority of films will be made for television and viewed in the home. Ergo, the much-maligned TV of today will take on the luster of fond remembrance, and the shows we currently underrate will be overrated in the nostalgic hindsight of the future.

It's a baroque hypothesis, but perhaps not without a grain of truth. Tomorrow's children may well hold up the Archie Bunkers, the Kojaks, and the Fonzies as icons, much as we have a collective soft spot for the heroes of our youth—the Bogarts, Cagneys, Garfields, and Edward G. Robinsons. There's no question that the study of television is on the increase in some of our high schools and universities. A TV series called *Star Trek* (long gone, but alive and kicking in reruns) has had a minimum of fifty books written about it. And many of us in the field find, to our surprise, that we are receiving a growing number of requests from scholars and educators for scripts and production information.

All of this notwithstanding, it's still considered good form in many quarters to denigrate the medium. Being omnipresent, it lacks cachet. And even those who pay lip service to its potential frequently adopt an air of condescension when they discuss its content.

Many of these detractors see very little of television's best. They are not selective viewers, and each season a good many worthwhile moments slip by without their notice. They will rush to see a film such as *An Unmarried Woman,* never knowing that *Breaking Up,* a television movie on the same subject (and aired at the same time the picture was released) examined a contemporary woman's divorce with perhaps more subtle insights and greater reality.* They will applaud a Mel Brooks film or a play by Neil Simon, unmindful of the fact that some of America's best comedy writing can be found on *All in the Family, Taxi, Barney Miller,* and, in spite of its excesses, the original version of *Saturday Night Live.*

Richard Reeves, the political columnist, has pointed out that the very people who should be most aware of the medium's impact, the community of New York and Washington journalists, seldom watch television at all. Their jobs require them to keep late hours and they never seem to have the time to sit in front of their sets with the rest of the country. For the most part their papers and magazines quarantine TV news and criticism to a back-of-the-book Siberia, and the writers assigned to cover the field are not always the most qualified—or even the most interested. Karl E. Meyer, the television critic for the

---

* Most film critics, in their Olympian remove from their television sets, were completely unaware that the theatrical feature *And Justice For All* owed a suspiciously large debt of gratitude to *The Law,* a superior (and earlier) TV treatment of many of the same materials.

Saturday Review, has said that he knows of no other form of expression in which there is a greater disparity between popular availability and critical attention. In Hollywood it's much the same. Because of an outmoded but lingering caste system, those who control the nation's films often pride themselves on their ignorance of television. They are oblivious to the fact that many of the actors, directors, and writers they employ have done their best work for the small screen.

We have no wish to be apologists for television. Far from it. We know from first-hand experience that the schedules are brutal, the budgets sparse, and the censors timid. The tyranny of the ratings is a constant irritant. And the very structure of the system itself mitigates against quality, with three networks bent on maintaining a profitable status quo as the final arbiters and only marketplace. Finally, television has a notorious appetite for material; there are simply not enough talented people to meet its demands with anything more than a journeyman's level of competence. After laboring in the vineyards for a while, one tends to think of television as the equivalent of a black hole, sucking in everything and giving no light in return.

And yet. And yet. Though it may well be heresy, we still have the desire to write and produce films for this much-abused medium. The marquee goes dark after one brief evening, the words may seem to be written in smoke, but where else on earth can so vast an audience be found? To reach so many people, and perhaps move some of them, is a powerful inducement not easily ignored.

Certainly television is, at least in part, a wasteland, and clearly much of it is candy. But, like Everest, it's very much there, and neither handwringing nor benign neglect will make it go away. For better or worse it is a significant part of most people's daily lives, and the technological changes already taking place may make it even more pervasive.

This book is an attempt to explain why at least a portion of it is the way it is. Many writers have contributed to the understanding of television—Les Brown, with his comprehensive book *Television: The Business Behind the Box,* and Bob Shanks, with *The Cool Fire,* are two notable examples; and Michael Arlen along with one or two other critics has explored the trends and foibles of the medium. But there seems to be a lack of specific information concerning what it is actually like to work in commercial television on a day-to-day basis, where ability and good intentions are in constant conflict with forces that are unknown, or often misunderstood, by the public and the press.

We are neither critics nor social scientists, and we have no particular ax to grind. We are storytellers, and we have written the following in the hope that by chronicling our adventures (and misadventures) on the other side of the tube—a strange world where even the failures are seen by viewers numbered in the tens of millions—perhaps we can shed some light on one or two corners of Pandora's box.

2 / Backstory

The term "backstory" is used in television writing to describe the events leading up to the story itself. Since it was our good fortune to be present at the beginning of the still-continuing cycle of made-for-television motion pictures, the reader may find some curiosity value in how we got to that place at that particular time.

Then again, the following may only be of interest to close friends and blood relations. But history, as the philosopher once observed, is just one damned thing after another, and with that in mind, and having given fair warning, we intend to ease our way into a flashback.

We grew up, middle-class children of radio and comic books, in the suburbs of Philadelphia during the forties and early fifties. Our tastes were formed well before the advent of television, and what we ingested by way of out-of-school influences was an eclectic mix of wonderful trash and high art, swallowed whole. Long before we met, each of us frequented countless Saturday afternoon serials; we laughed at Abbott and Costello, worshiped Disney (happily unaware that he was out of vogue with the intellectuals); collected Superman and Captain Marvel comics—turning out our own hand-drawn versions on the side—and listened to everything from *Let's Pretend* and *Jack Armstrong* to *Suspense, Escape,* and *Inner Sanctum.*

When we finally met in junior high school and began to compare notes we found, to our surprise, that we had shared virtually the same youth, and so we immediately began to share the same adolescence. We devoured books, chiefly thrillers, with an occasional Hemingway, Faulkner, or Fitzgerald thrown in for cultural diversity. Along with the rest of our generation we became addicted to J. D. Salinger and Sartre, to Camus and Kafka, but there was always time for John Dickson Carr and Ellery Queen, not to mention those famous graduates from the pulps, the Messrs. Hammett and Chandler.

Philadelphia was a major Broadway tryout town, and so we saw dozens of plays and musicals, from the ill-fated *Flahooley* to *Death of a Salesman* and *Guys and Dolls.* Our nights away from the theater—and the neighborhood movie houses—were spent avoiding homework with the likes of Jack Benny, Fred Allen, Edgar Bergen, and *Lights Out.* Hardly a classical education.

It was, nevertheless, a rich brew. L. Frank Baum, Jules Verne, and Erle Stanley Gardner. *Appointment in Samarra* and *Animal Farm. Singin' in the Rain* and *All About Eve.* In school there was *Silas Marner, Beowulf,* and Shakespeare; but between classes, in the locker room, there was also *God's Little Acre* and *I, the Jury.*

At this point wire recorders became available to the general public. They were minor by-products of America's wartime technology, gadgets that could record sound on a threadlike strand of wire. As soon as they hit the market we persuaded our parents to buy them for us (and to later buy us tape recorders) for "educational purposes." Our real purpose, as our parents no doubt surmised, was to collect some of radio's better moments, and though we were too late for Norman Corwin, Arch Oboler, and Orson Welles, we did manage to snatch *Sorry Wrong Number, Lenningen vs. the Ants,* and many others out of the ether.

But our twin recorders began to serve another purpose. In addition to preserving radio plays we decided to write some of our own, and so we started to fashion scripts, adaptations of Lord Dunsany's ghoulish *Two Bottles of Relish* and Curt Siodmak's *Donovan's Brain.* Needing actors, we gathered friends in our basements for long afternoons of recording. We improvised sound effects (dry strawberry cartons, when crunched, made perfect splintering doors) and we plundered music cues from *Scheherazade* and Miklos Rozsa's *Spellbound* album. Suddenly, in order to supply our makeshift repertory company with material, we were writers. And in manipulating our mothers into providing the massive snacks required to feed a houseful of teenagers, suddenly we were producers as well.

Influenced by the "Mrs. Hush" contest on *Truth or Consequences,* we concocted a "Mr. Mystery" contest for a school charity drive. Fascinated by Poe and O. Henry, we wrote gloomy short stories with surprise endings. Dazzled by the MGM musical films, we put on an original musical comedy in our senior year of high school. We even wrote several private eye novels, homages to Wade Miller and Ross Macdonald. Much of this literary output was mailed on an almost weekly basis to various magazine markets, from the *New Yorker* to the *Saturday Evening Post.* All of it was returned. But on rare occasions a sympathetic editor would drop us a note of encouragement amid the blizzard of rejection slips.

If there was a common thread to this experience it was the love of popular culture in all of its many forms. As our tastes became more sophisticated we broadened and deepened the range of our reading, but even the major novelists and playwrights didn't have quite the same visceral appeal as the movies, the radio, and the popular songs.

When television arrived on the scene it was not with the force of revelation; rather, it was an easily integrated part of our everyday lives—it seemed an amalgam of everything we had been doing. We studied the techniques involved and set about writing plays for the new medium, dozens of them, and shipping them off to New York with the obligatory self-addressed return envelope. None sold, of course, and we had new rejection slips to add to our mounting collection.

Purely as a matter of happenstance, we both matriculated at the same college, the University of Pennsylvania, where we intended to prepare for careers in our fathers' businesses. But while we studied we continued our collaboration, at long last selling our first short story, which was published in *Ellery Queen's Mystery Magazine.* Convinced now that we had the knack for marketing commercial fiction, we churned out an endless stream of pages, but it was a good four years before we sold our next story.

In the meantime we contributed to Penn's literary and humor magazines, founded a new campus magazine of our own (prompted, more than likely, by our need to find hospitable pages for our rejected short stories), wrote weekly film criticism for the student paper, and supplied the books and some of the lyrics for the university's annual musicals. These "Mask and Wig" productions played a theater in Philadelphia during Thanksgiving week and then toured the Eastern seaboard over the Christmas holidays. F. Scott Fitzgerald wrote that nothing has quite the same glow as a musical comedy, and as we stood in the wings on opening nights, or read the notices of the first-string critics, a future in automotive body hardware (Levinson) or waste textiles (Link) seemed profoundly unexciting. We wanted to stay in this world, or some variant of it, and for the rest of our college careers we increased the tempo of our collaboration. Even our senior thesis was a joint effort: we submitted a television script.

Within months of graduation one of us was drafted and the other enlisted in the six-month reserve program; it was a full two years before we relocated in New York as civilians once again–only to discover that the migration of television to the West Coast had trans- pired in our absence. The anthology was gone, eclipsed by the series, and most of the New York production centers had closed down. The few remaining shows could pick and choose from among the writers who wished to stay in the East; there was scant interest in newcomers without credits.

We supported ourselves by selling our short fiction to *Playboy, Hitchcock's Magazine,* and various literary periodicals. Then, on a Christmas Eve, our agent's assistant called. Shouting over the din of an office party, he informed us that one of our television scripts (an old one, no less) had just been accepted by *General Motors Presents.* Our elation was somewhat tempered by the fact that we had never heard of *General Motors Presents,* but it was patiently explained to us that the program was an hour-long anthological series originating in

Canada. Our teleplay would be broadcast from Toronto over the Canadian Broadcasting Corporation. An honest-to-God full-scale production, but with one small hitch—it wouldn't be aired in the United States.

Still, it was a beginning. We journeyed to Toronto for the rehearsals and found ourselves in a kind of time warp. Canadian television had much in common with the New York phase of live TV almost a decade earlier: young directors were flexing their muscles and new playwrights, having suddenly discovered the medium, were contributing material. We half-expected Fred Coe to gather them under his wing for production on *Philco Playhouse*.

In all, we had two of our teleplays on *General Motors Presents*. But despite the polish and professionalism of these productions they were somewhat frustrating for us because they were limited to Canadian viewers; neither our friends nor families could see them.

Our next script was an army story *(Chain of Command)* set in the American South, and we decided to bypass our friends in Canada. At our insistence it was sent by our agents to *Desilu Playhouse,* the one remaining anthological series in Hollywood. A week later we were notified that they had purchased it, and within months it was on the air. The reviews were kind and *TV Guide* listed it as one of the best shows of the season.

Had the script been rejected we would have probably remained in New York. But its acceptance forced us to make a reluctant decision: if we wanted to continue writing for the medium we would have to move, like prime-time television itself, to California. A nice place to live, as Fred Allen put it, if you happen to be an orange.

We headed west in the summer of 1959. Almost as soon as we set foot on California soil we were gainfully employed as free-lance television writers, and our anxieties about finding work quickly gave way to concerns about the nature of the work itself. Most of the shows of the time, particularly in the area of the dramatic series, required little more from a writer than a knack for coming up with "springboards," or story premises, and a rough sense of structure. Writers were tailors, cutting bolts of cloth to a rigid set of specifications. They would be provided with an existing group of characters and a format, and any flexibility within these parameters was severely limited. The key words were "jeopardy" and "conflict," and the emphasis was almost totally on plot. Much of this is still true today.

To write for television during that period was to construct scripts for such as *Bourbon Street Beat, Johnny Ringo, Sugarfoot, Hawaiian Eye, 77 Sunset Strip, Wanted Dead or Alive,* and *Black Saddle.* There were exceptions—the aforementioned *The Westerner,* with Brian Keith and an engagingly bedraggled dog, and a political series called *Slattery's People*—but both shows, as if subjected to a perverse form of Gresham's Law, quickly went off the air.

Then, too, the writer had only the most marginal involvement with his own shows. He (almost never she; the female television writer is a relatively recent phenomenon) would meet with the story editor of a given series, but seldom have any contact with the producer, the director, or the actors. Edicts would filter down to him through channels, arbitrary dos and don'ts whose origins were always shrouded in deep mystery. He might be permitted to visit the set, but he almost never had a voice in the evolution of his script from printed page to finished film. If there were creative discussions, and he happened to be present, his opinion carried little weight. To a large extent he was a necessary nuisance, to be tolerated until he completed his teleplay.*

Our initial excitement at having our work produced rapidly diminished under the conditions—and markets—that prevailed. The only pleasures were on a craft level, learning how to cope with the peculiar demands of act breaks and artificial climaxes, and finding ways to use cinematic exposition in place of windy passages of dialogue.

It was a frustrating time. Whenever we complained about the kind of shows available and our inability to gain some measure of control over our material, friends pointed out, rather bluntly, that we were writing for the boob tube. What else did we expect?

It was not all bleak, of course. Four Star Television, a creation of

---

* A TV writer would be lucky to get a form postcard, with the airdate of his show penciled in, alerting him to the upcoming broadcast.

Dick Powell, David Niven, Charles Boyer, and Tom McDermott, and one of the major suppliers of product to the networks, offered us a term contract. We accepted, and for the next two years we had the advantage of working, in our early twenties, at one of the busiest film studios in Hollywood. Our function was to serve as troubleshooters, moving from show to show, sometimes as writers, sometimes as script doctors; and the sound stages, editing rooms, carpenter shops, special effects departments, and scoring stages were open to us. Orson Welles has said that a film studio is the greatest children's toy in the world, and for a while we were diverted (and educated) by the paraphernalia of production.

But eventually the novelty wore off. However pleasant it was to loiter on the sets, or go to dailies, our work consisted in the main of scripts for *Richard Diamond, Private Eye; Michael Shayne;* and *The June Allyson Show.* We were rehashing the pop forms of our childhood, and in spite of a weekly paycheck there was little sense of personal satisfaction. Finally, following the dictum that lives should be shaken up every now and then, we asked for a release from our contract and returned to New York.

Graham Greene, in characterizing his books, came up with an ingenious bit of semantic legerdemain: He divided them into "serious" novels and "entertainments." Never mind that some of the entertainments—*Brighton Rock,* for one—were better than some of the serious books; his notion, given our current mood, seemed a useful one. We would spend half the year in New York, surrounded by theater, good restaurants, and cosmopolitan excitement; then, in the spring and summer months, we'd dally in the fleshpots of Los Angeles, grinding out enough television scripts to subsidize the plays and books we'd be writing in the East.

It was an appallingly pretentious idea. And it had its roots in a particular kind of blind spot: the belief, ours as well as others, that "good work" could only be done between the covers of a book or on a stage. It simply never occurred to us that something of merit could be conceived for television. After all, hadn't Chayevsky abandoned the medium, moving on to the greener pastures of Broadway and motion pictures? Wasn't Gore Vidal, who had written his share of TV dra-

mas, busy crafting screenplays and novels? Even Fred Coe was gone—
he had become a theatrical producer and film director.

And so we hunkered down in New York and left the television set
unplugged. But for all our noble intentions, the very first play we
wrote was a commercial thriller. It was called *Prescription: Murder,* and
one of the characters was a rather nonprepossessing police lieutenant
named Columbo.

Astonishingly, the play found a producer, and within six months it
opened in San Francisco, starring Joseph Cotten, Agnes Moorehead,
and Thomas Mitchell. It toured the country for almost half a year,
alighting in cities as diverse as Detroit and Fargo, North Dakota. But
it, too, was a frustrating experience. We were in our mid-twenties and
green behind the ears, and we discovered that we had nothing to say
about the production. The management even brushed us aside when
we suggested rewrites. The show was grossing a fortune on the road.
Why make waves? We were confused. This was the *theater,* wasn't it?
Surely writers weren't relegated to the back of the bus as they were in
television. But the play continued its tour without a single rewrite, so
we contented ourselves by making the changes we wanted for the
stock version and turned to other business.

Militantly serious now, we wrote a novel and published more short
fiction. Some of our stories were listed on the honor roll of the annual
Martha Foley collections, but the novel was to remain unpublished
for many years. During the California half of our lives we wrote for
The Rogues, The Fugitive, Dr. Kildare, The Man from U.N.C.L.E.; and,
in a relationship that lasted for several seasons, we did a number of
scripts for *The Alfred Hitchcock Show* and *Hitchcock's Hour.*

Gradually, the foolishness of this bicoastal existence became evident. When we were in New York we'd be writing teleplays for the
TV markets in California. And when we were in Los Angeles we'd
stop in the middle of a television script because we'd be seized by a
sudden idea for a short story. Also, disenchantment began to set in as
our novel made the rounds of publishing houses and brought us
rejections bearing more or less the same message: they liked it, it was
well-written, but first novels are not very profitable ventures—and

didn't we have anything with stronger female appeal, a dollop of sex, and more exotic locales? It was the beginning of the televisionization of American publishing, and Jacqueline Susann and seven-figure paperback auctions were just around the corner.

Ironically, we were starting to enjoy some of our TV assignments. Writing for *The Rogues* was pure fun; the Hitchcock shows allowed us a wide latitude in characterization and dialogue, plus the sneaky pleasures of playing games with the audience; and one of our *Dr. Kildare* scripts, a sharply critical look at funeral practices, embroiled us in a controversy with the nation's funeral directors. The network, with a typical display of corporate backbone, bowed to the pressure and never reran the episode, and our producer wryly advised us not to die until it all blew over, "or else they'll leave your bodies in the street."

It seemed, finally, an impractical eccentricity to live so far from our source of employment, and so we decided, with considerable misgivings, to return to Los Angeles on a permanent basis. Inherent in this decision was the knowledge that we were making a full commitment to television. And commit ourselves we did. We turned commercial with a vengeance. Since the creation of a series is higher on the pecking order than the writing of individual segments, we fabricated with a friend a dreadful series called *Jerico*. On our own we created *Mannix,* which ran for eight seasons. But our usual discontent began to surface. Tyrone Guthrie once wrote that Hollywood screenwriters are maintained in luxuriant anonymity. The same was true of us— although one could quibble with the "luxuriant"–and even though we had sold back-to-back series, the decision-making process remained in the hands of others.

Then we heard that Universal Studios was seeking material for their new "long-form" television movies. Along with most other freelance writers, we had worked in the hour and half-hour formats, but this was something different: two full hours in which to tell a story. One of us remembered *Prescription: Murder.* We dug the stock version from our files and instructed our agent to make a submission. Shortly thereafter we were called in for a meeting with Don Siegel, a director whose movies, particularly *Invasion of the Body Snatchers,* were cult favorites in European and American film circles. He told us he had been assigned to direct and produce a television version of our play. Were we interested? We were.

But in characteristic Hollywood fashion Siegel was suddenly pulled off the project to direct a feature film; our new producer-director was Richard Irving, a Universal executive and a veteran of the company's earliest days of television production. He apologized for the midstream change in personnel and asked if we minded relocating the setting of our script from New York to Los Angeles. Having just made this geographic transition in our own lives, we saw no reason not to inflict it on our characters, and we agreed.

Unlike some of our previous producers, Irving involved us closely with the preproduction process. We even sat in on some of the casting sessions. But when it came to finding the right actor to play the part of Lieutenant Columbo, we were prisoners of our own preconceptions. Thomas Mitchell had played the role on the stage, and played it well. He was a man in his seventies with the sly charm of a leprechaun, and so in our minds we saw an older character actor for the part. We suggested Lee J. Cobb and, remembering his work in the film version of *The Country Girl,* Bing Crosby.

When Peter Falk's name was tossed on the table we all dismissed him. He was far too young, not even in his mid-forties. But Cobb and Crosby were not available, and as the start date approached other suggestions fell by the wayside. Eventually there were no realistic alternatives and Falk was hired for the role by default. We shrugged it off. He was a more than capable actor, and although he was obviously miscast he'd somehow manage to squeak by.

When *Prescription: Murder* aired we watched it with a clinical eye to see if we had fixed most of the problems that troubled us in the stage version. But we soon forgot the internal clockwork of the piece under the spell of Falk's performance. He was an unexpected delight. He nosed around in the part like a dog sniffing out truffles, and in place of the overcoat of our play he affected one of his old raincoats, a garment more wrinkled than Methuselah. The reviews were flattering, and the all-important ratings placed the show among the top ten television motion pictures made to that date.

It was therefore not surprising that Universal offered us a contract. We thanked them and politely refused. It seemed pointless for us to tie ourselves down to what would only be a repetition of our Four Star experience, ricocheting from show to show, doctoring here and rewriting there. Besides, Universal had a reputation in the industry as a sausage factory, grinding out product at a price with no regard for style or content.

But as time passed we began to reconsider. The Hitchcock shows had been filmed at Universal, and in our view they were a cut above most of the series being made by Fox, Warner Brothers, and many of the independents. We had no complaints about the studio's handling of *Prescription: Murder.* And whether it was a sausage factory or not, Universal was still the biggest game in town as far as the two-hour television movies were concerned. There was even a rumor that the studio had a commitment from NBC for dozens more.

Perhaps, if we accepted the offer, we could eventually make a television film of our own. And if things didn't work out, our option would be dropped in twelve months and no harm done.

We crossed our fingers and signed on the dotted line.

3 / My Sweet Charlie

The Making of a Television Film

When we moved into a small office at Universal in the summer of
1967, the studio was (and still is) the largest film complex in the
world and the major supplier of American television programs. This is
not the place for a history of MCA (formerly The Music Corporation
of America), Universal's parent company. Suffice to say that it grew
from a tiny agency booking bands in Chicago into a massive leisure-
time conglomerate, with the studio as only one of its many and varied
holdings.

The phrase "world's largest" comes trippingly to the tongue when
discussing MCA. For a time it was the world's largest talent agency,
with offices scattered around the globe; it represented luminaries from
Tennessee Williams and Alfred Hitchcock to Jack Benny, James Stew-
art, and the acting profession's once and future gift to the nation's
political scene, Ronald Reagan. Its base of operations was a colonial
mansion in the heart of Beverly Hills, a mini-Tara furnished entirely
with antiques supplied by the founder of the company, a former
ophthalmologist named Jules Stein. As the structure of the motion
picture industry changed, with the old studio system in decline and
more and more independents entering the field, MCA's agents, usually
dressed in black suits and always wary of personal publicity, began to

exercise enormous power. Under the leadership of Lew Wasserman, Stein's right-hand man, the agency grew to the point where the creative community on several continents took to calling it, and not with any particular sense of affection, "The Octopus."

MCA also owned Revue, a production subsidiary that was one of Hollywood's earliest manufacturers of filmed television series. Since many of the agency's clients were employed by Revue, and since MCA was frequently negotiating with itself on behalf of these clients— allegedly giving them preference over the clients of other agencies— the Justice Department bestirred itself and ordered MCA to either divest itself of its production arm or else get out of the agency business.

It was not a difficult choice. Wasserman and his associates correctly perceived the money-making potential of huge stores of television films that could be distributed on a worldwide basis, and the doors of the Beverly Hills mansion closed forever. Everything shifted to four hundred-odd acres in the San Fernando Valley, with thirty-four sound stages and a vast back lot containing European and New York streets, a lake with a submarine (for *McHale's Navy)* and even an Arabian fort. Brooding over all of this is the house used by Hitchcock in his film *Psycho.* As a symbol, it's only a notch or two below the eyes of Dr. T. J. Eckleburg in *The Great Gatsby.*

An administration building was erected entirely in black stone, and in the opinion of some it was far more intimidating than the Hitchcock house. It served, however, a useful purpose. If a script was rejected, or a long-standing project abruptly canceled, fingers were never pointed at any executive by name. That would be impolitic. Instead, "The Black Tower didn't like it" became the standard explanation. All hostility could therefore be directed at a building and not a specific individual. When George Roy Hill learned that the studio had made unwanted changes in his film *Thoroughly Modern Millie,* he didn't punch anyone in the nose. Rather, it seemed perfectly appropriate for him to get into his airplane and buzz the Black Tower.

Our first assignment as newcomers came to us from Jennings Lang, one of the old-guard MCA agents and the head of Universal's television operation. A complex and forceful man, with a gift for invective unrivaled in an industry where it is the coin of everyday conversation, Lang was known as one of the best salesmen in the business. Part of his job was to "pitch" new product to the networks, and if they rejected his line he was sufficiently fast on his feet to manufacture new ideas on the spot, leaving their implementation to his bewildered underlings. In one notorious instance he completely forgot what he had sold; he had to be contacted on his vacation and read a list of Universal-owned motion pictures before he remembered that it was a TV version of *Destry Rides Again*.

Lang's reputation was that of a man driven to sell for the sake of selling, with no interest in considerations of quality. He had assembled a remarkably tasteful collection of paintings and sculpture, but his critics accused him of rarely permitting any of his finer sensibilities to spill over into his work. These broadsides—and the harsher they were, the more he seemed to enjoy them—never took into account the fact that he, more than most others, had changed some of the medium's basic assumptions. As the chief architect of the long-form concept, he had stretched prime-time programming from its traditional half-hour and hour lengths to ninety minutes, and finally to a full two hours with the *World Premieres*. Whatever his faults he was nothing if not colorful, and flair was in short supply among MCA's ever-cautious corporate types.

And so, on our first day at the studio, we found ourselves in his Black Tower office, listening to him insult various callers on the phone. Having vented his spleen he slammed down the receiver, turned to us pleasantly, and welcomed us to the studio. "I have something in mind for you to do," he said, leaning forward across his immaculate desk. "What we want is *The Virginian* on a train."

It was an inauspicious beginning. We had hopes of breaking away from the meat-and-potatoes of series television, and here was Lang asking for more of the same. Worse still, we even knew what he was talking about. Roughly translated, he wanted a pilot script with a train serving the function of home base—the equivalent of the eternal Western town—and a continuing group of characters. The train, of course, would be the prime gimmick and main selling point.

For the next few months we fashioned a two-hour teleplay for *Istanbul Express,* into which we shoe-horned every convention of every espionage book and movie: an art dealer working under cover for the CIA (this was pre-Watergate, so he was the hero), various exotic ladies with thick accents, a numbered Swiss bank account, Russian spies, sodium pentothal injections, and an international auction of something called "the Janisek papers." We never quite came to grips with what these papers contained, except that their value was beyond price to the enemies of the American Way of Life. They served their purpose as a Hitchcockian "McGuffin," the vaguely defined gizmo that everyone will kill for, be it the Moonstone or the Maltese Falcon.

Writing the script was fun in a simpleminded way, but, as we explained to Lang, there was a basic conceptual flaw in a series about people on a train. Characters did interesting things *before* they got on a train and *after* they disembarked. The journey itself might provide one or two stories (i.e. *The Lady Vanishes)* but it would be impossible to keep our group riding the rails for a sustained series of thirteen or twenty-six weeks.*

Istanbul Express, starring Gene Barry and Senta Berger and directed by Dick Irving, with a few days of filming on European locations, sank without a bubble the moment it was aired. It did not elicit the kind of reviews one preserves in a scrapbook.

Istanbul shared one thing in common with many of the television movies of the period: It was a pilot. From the studio's point of view this made sound economic sense. Two birds could be killed with one film—a *World Premiere* commitment would be fulfilled and the network would be presented with the prototype for a potential series. But in our opinion the best television movies were usually not pilots at all. Our favorite among the handful that had been made was a stylish melodrama called *The Borgia Stick.* By its nature it was a one-shot, meaning there was no way to extend it into a series. And it was exactly the kind of show we wanted to do.

But Universal had other plans for us. One of their recent television

---

* Years later, in an imitative attempt to duplicate the success of *The Love Boat,* NBC put a series called *Supertrain* on the air. It was a quick and expensive failure.

movies, *Fame Is the Name of the Game,* had just received a series green light from NBC. Its title had been truncated to the less unwieldy but equally meaningless *Name of the Game,* and scripts, as always, were in short supply. It was actually a rather bold departure for a series, although more in terms of form than content. Three leading men had been signed: Gene Barry, Tony Franciosa, and Robert Stack. They would almost never appear together in any one of the ninety-minute episodes of the show. Instead, each actor would have his own producer, writers, and production unit, and he would alternate with the other stars every third week. The setting was a mass-circulation news magazine empire. Thus, for the first time the so-called "umbrella" concept would be presented to the public: three rotating stars in one series.

Since we had just completed a film with Gene Barry it seemed only logical to have us write some of his *Name of the Game* segments. Dick Irving had been put in charge of the Barry unit, and he called and asked us to join his staff. With our customary display of corporate loyalty, we refused. We were not being cavalier; it was simply that we had spent the better part of our professional careers writing for one series or another, and now we wanted to move on to other areas. Irving suggested we have a talk about this with someone named Sid Sheinberg.

Apparently we had missed the most recent game of musical chairs in the Black Tower. Jennings Lang had made a lateral (or was it vertical?) shift to the theatrical features division and Sheinberg, his former assistant, was the new head of Universal television. A Texan in his early thirties and a graduate of Columbia Law School, Sheinberg had worked his way up through the business affairs department to his present position, where he now had to deal with two recalcitrant writers who wanted no part of *Name of the Game.*

We met with him in his twelfth floor office and responded to him immediately. He was tall and friendly, with thick-framed glasses and unruly black hair. The other desks in the Tower were bare (a Wasserman-inspired tradition) but Sheinberg's was cluttered with haphazard piles of scripts and papers. In a world of high-gloss executive polish he was ever-so-slightly out of place, and it was a refreshing quality. His manner was formal and almost shy; although he was our contemporary he seemed somehow older. He was also, as it transpired, quite skilled in the dark arts of manipulation—a fact we didn't fully appreciate until, on our way down in the elevator, we suddenly realized we had promised to go to work at once on *Name of the Game.*

As our contacts with Sheinberg increased, we began to have a sense of the peculiar nature of his position. His primary responsibility was to sell a product, the Universal television series, and to keep it on the air in a ferociously competitive market for as long as possible. At the same time he had to motivate—and placate—the diverse, ambitious, and self-absorbed writers, producers, actors, and directors under the studio's employ, highly intelligent men and women who were frequently unsympathetic to whatever he might have in mind for them at any given moment. All of this within the framework of a large corporation, many of whose executives coveted his job and whose physical plant had to be kept humming in a constant state of operation.

The traditional Hollywood tycoons, the L. B. Mayers, Selznicks, and Thalbergs, had an arsenal of weapons to bend obstreperous prima donnas to their wills. But that time had passed and Sheinberg had to rely almost solely on his powers of persuasion. To his credit, whether by temperament or necessity, he tended toward a hands-off approach, with little or no Monday-morning quarterbacking. He could be arbitrary on occasion, but his enthusiasm was contagious, and he was so obviously overburdened with work that people would often accede to his wishes simply because they wanted to make life easier for him.

During this time we also came to know a number of our coworkers, including George Eckstein, who was to make *Duel, Sunshine,* and *Masada;* William Sackheim, a tasteful and energetic producer who guided *The Senator, The Law,* and *Delveccio;* and a gracious gentleman named Adrian Scott. Adrian had been an important film producer during the forties *(Crossfire* being perhaps his most famous motion picture), but his political beliefs and affiliations had brought him to the attention of the House Committee on Un-American Activities. He refused to name any of his associates, and along with Dalton Trumbo, Albert Maltz, and others, he became a member of the Hollywood Ten. He served a jail sentence for contempt of Congress, was blacklisted, and had lived in England until Wasserman and Lang offered him a contract at the studio. Now, at last reinstated under his own name, he was busying himself with various projects.

Time drifted agreeably by and we settled into a comfortable rut, meeting at the studio, writing, lunching with friends at the commissary, and heading homeward in the early afternoons. It was a seductive life-style. We completed two *Name of the Game* episodes and supplied the story for another *World Premiere,* and then circumstances moved us sharply in another direction.

Herb Schlosser, the head of NBC's West Coast programming department, called us with an idea for a lawyer series. "There's been one lawyer on *Perry Mason,*" he told us, "and two lawyers on *The Defenders.* But there's never been a show with *three* lawyers!" The inherent magic of multiple attorneys escaped us, but Herb had responded favorably to a Universal legal show starring James Farentino and Burl Ives, and he had placed an order with Sheinberg for a two-hour pilot. We set about writing it for producer Roy Huggins and his associate, Jo Swerling.

The papers and newscasts of the time were filled with stories about the student protest riots at Berkeley and Columbia. Like many other Americans we were both fascinated and disturbed by the fury of the middle-class young, and as a means of trying to understand these events we incorporated some of them into our script. Thus, *The Whole World Is Watching* became the first television drama to deal with the student movement of the late sixties. Long after it aired, a spate of motion pictures on the same subject opened in the nation's movie houses, but television, with its accelerated schedules, always has the advantage of a shorter time lag. It can move with greater speed than theatrical films and present topical issues before they become yesterday's news.

Even though our pilot sold the series, which became the lawyers segment of *The Bold Ones* (another umbrella show) we realized we hadn't done a very good job. We had written a hybrid, half student revolution story and half pilot presentation, and the two parts didn't jell. Also, it struck us in retrospect that we were exploiting an important social phenomenon by using it as window dressing to sell a series. We learned other creative lessons as well: Television can usually deal with an intimate personal story better than a large-scale event. Our film had its throngs of jeering students, its smashed windows, folk singers, and pot parties—all very cinematic—but it showed little of the inner life of its characters. Theatrical movies such as *The Strawberry Statement* and *Getting Straight* made much the same mistake. We were all far too preoccupied with the externals.

But the experience served a purpose—it caused us to realize that the television writer could respond to his times with other-than-trivial entertainments. It might even be possible to confront issue-oriented material head-on. The trick was to do it without polemicizing, without self-congratulatory grandstanding, and without putting the audience to sleep. There was also the matter of convincing the networks that such material didn't necessarily have to fail in the ratings.

We looked around us. Bill Sackheim was making *Deadlock,* a grimly realistic two-hour film about race riots in a small city. Others, with Universal's nervous blessing, were considering bringing Robert Anderson's play about marital infidelity, *Silent Night, Lonely Night,* to the nation's television screens.

It seemed to be the proper time.

In television, as in motion pictures, the adaptation has certain advantages over the original idea in terms of getting a commitment to proceed. A piece of existing material, particularly a book or play, can be seen, fondled, and sometimes even read—it gives decision-makers a sense of security. An original idea, on the other hand, is ephemeral; it has a life only in the mind of its creator. We decided that if we were to interest the studio and the networks in something other than a pilot, our best shot would be to present them with a novel.

Three books had appealed to us over the years as vehicles for adaptation: *The Child Buyer* by John Hersey, *I Never Promised You a Rose Garden* by Hannah Green, and Ken Kesey's *One Flew Over the Cuckoo's Nest.* Each of these novels told a compelling personal story, and each was set in a contained world that made it suitable (and practical) for a television movie.

We wrote to John Hersey, who was kind enough to respond.

Unfortunately, his book was committed elsewhere. So was the Hannah Green novel. After considerable prodding, the studio checked out *Cuckoo's Nest* for us. It was owned by Kirk Douglas, and he was holding on to it. Years later he gave the rights to his son Michael, who, coincidentally, called us to see if we were interested in writing the screenplay. We were not available, so we had to turn him down. He made the film and it was a worldwide success; the screenplay by Bo Goldman and Lawrence Hauben won the Academy Award. We bled a little on Oscar night and filed the experience under a growing collection of might-have-beens.

When *My Sweet Charlie* popped into our heads it was for no apparent reason. We had read the reviews when it opened on Broadway with Bonnie Bedelia and Louis Gossett, but neither of us had seen it. It was written by David Westheimer, based on his novel, and it had a brief run. It came to mind one day when we were discussing possible projects; we vaguely remembered something about a black lawyer and a white southern girl living as fugitives in a deserted summerhouse on the Gulf coast of Texas.

We found copies of book and play and read them both. The material excited us enormously. It spoke simply and powerfully of the common humanity of two individuals from alien cultures. Westheimer's heroine was Marlene Chambers, a scruffy and hard-luck teenager who managed to get herself pregnant out of wedlock. Forced from home by her angry father, she eventually finds an abandoned summerhouse, and she makes it into a sanctuary and a touchstone, a special and secret place of her own. There she lives while the child grows inside her, dreaming the days away—until Charles Roberts intervenes. He has travelled south from New York to visit his roots, and, during a civil rights march, he has killed a bigot in self-defense. Hunted by the police, needing a place to hide, he breaks into the summerhouse—and comes face to face with a terrified girl who takes one look at him and screams, "It's a nigger!"

They are compelled by self-interest to live together, and as they circle each other with ill-concealed hostility, Westheimer examines white-black and male-female stereotypes, frequently turning them inside out. The white seems stupid and the black intelligent, a reversal of the usual cliché. But even with his vastly superior education,

Roberts is as much of a racist as Marlene. And her traditional southern fears of black rape strike him as hilarious—he points out that he
finds her singularly unattractive.

Finally, after many confrontations (some of them quite funny) they
work their way through their negative preconceptions to at first an
unexpected sense of tenderness and affection, and then a kind of love.
He corrects her English and she initiates him into the rituals of a
southern black man's speech patterns and behavior. And when they
are almost discovered, it is Marlene who rescues them with her quick
native intelligence. The story ends tragically. When she goes into
labor Roberts leaves their sanctuary to find a doctor. He is shot and
killed by a deputy who mistakes him for a thief.

My Sweet Charlie was exactly what we had been looking for, but in
the commercial sense it had a number of problems. It was "soft," a
network code word meaning "without action." "People stories," as
they were called, did not get ratings. It was also, in the context of the
times, controversial. One did not bandy about words such as "nigger"
on the public airwaves. And there was still another problem: Universal did not own the material. Nor did David Westheimer, as we
discovered when we made inquiries. The book and the play were
controlled by Bob Banner, a well-known independent television pack-
ager and producer who had mounted the Broadway production. Apparently Mr. Banner was not interested in selling.

One way to deal with reality is to ignore it. Convincing ourselves
that the rights would somehow become available, we looked around
for help. Universal, like any other large company, was a bureaucracy,
and we needed someone to run interference for us. The obvious
choice was Adrian Scott, and though he was busy he agreed to serve
as the producer. A meeting with Sheinberg was arranged. After reading the material, he shared our enthusiasm and said he would take it
to NBC for approval.

The entertainment field is notorious as the home of the "slow no."
But NBC surprised us. They gave us a fast no, turning down *Charlie*
immediately.

Their reasons, relayed to us from various sources, were pretty much
to be expected. The story had no action. It had no pilot potential.
And two comments in particular were passed along that gave us

further insight into network doublethink. The first was: "We can't have a black man and a white girl living under the same roof at nine o'clock at night." (Nine o'clock was the air time for *World Premieres,* and also, apparently, a time when children could watch the show and suffer permanent damage to their sense of moral values.) The second comment was terse and to the point: "We are not in the business of offending our southern affiliates."

For those who work in television it's almost obligatory to make fun of network people. It's a good way to let off steam, and many of the barbs are accurate. Contrary to popular opinion, however, the men and women of the network programming departments are not hired on the basis of congenital deficiencies of mind and character; they are bright, pleasant, and sometimes even dedicated human beings—much as, no doubt, the writers and readers of this book. Why, then, are they the object of so much animus from the creative community?

One reason, of course, is that they are the bosses. The buck stops with them, and legitimate questions can be raised about their qualifications. Although rarely from creative backgrounds, they make the ultimate decisions, esthetic or otherwise. More significantly, their job is to deliver an audience to an advertiser, and the size of this audience, endlessly monitored by the ratings, is the primary measure of their success or failure.

Capturing an audience, however, is an infuriatingly inexact science, and since the network people neither write nor produce the shows they broadcast, they are reduced to giving "input," which is usually nothing more than backseat driving. Therefore, and not always by choice, they often find themselves in an adversary position. An obvious alternative would be for them to leave the creative personnel to their own devices, since most decisions are simply matters of opinion, but then they would have no function and presumably no livelihood.

A workman on an assembly line in Detroit presses a button and effect follows cause: He knows precisely what will happen as a result of his efforts. But network people are constantly off-balance. The buttons they press seldom produce the expected, and thus they operate in a state of perpetual surprise and anxiety. A good show is not always a popular show. A series that violates all of the rules can become a hit. Success may strike for no other reason than that the competition is weak during a given time period. An unexpected blizzard keeps people at home and ratings soar. Flukes abound over which no one seems to have any control.

Dealing with this instability, especially when millions of dollars are at stake, leads to a conservative way of doing business. Instincts and gut reactions give way to research. Decisions are deferred, and when they are made they are often arrived at collectively, so that no one individual can be blamed. Risk is minimized as much as possible, and the reason television constantly imitates itself is the desperate hope that what worked before will work again.

This entire tradition mitigated against the acceptance of *My Sweet Charlie*. Experience dictated that a television film based on this material would fail as a commercial enterprise. Even worse, it would not be a quiet failure. The subject matter would almost guarantee irate phone calls, letters, and repercussions from affiliate stations in some parts of the country. There was nothing to be gained by programming it, and much to lose.

Fortunately, the networks are in a constant state of flux. Job turnover is high, the powers of internal blocs and factions wax and wane, and, to be fair, those in charge can sometimes be persuaded by sheer doggedness. We pressed Sheinberg and he pressed NBC. A resubmission was made, and once again the project was rejected. But then, for whatever reason (and by making whatever trade-offs were necessary), Sheinberg managed on his third submission to get development money for a script.

We quickly started to write. Our usual philosophy of adaptation is to be faithful to the source material, assuming it appeals to us in the first place. Some writers choose to make the work their own, but we tend to stay away from something that requires radical alterations. There is no right or wrong approach—it's a matter of preference—and in any case David Westheimer had made our job easy for us. His characters, especially the girl, were sharply defined, the story situation was strong, and our task was the relatively simple one of blending the book and the play into a film script, adding a minimum of new material.

We were finished within weeks. After reading the script, NBC no longer seemed to think that a television version of *My Sweet Charlie* would mean the end of the free enterprise system. They even began to make small noises of enthusiasm, although they expressed concern over the "old-fashioned" nature of some of the character attitudes. Their point was well taken. This was the era of black America's growing awareness of itself. Westheimer's book was already dated by the rapid thrust of social change, and modernizing the character of Charles Roberts, making him a more accurate reflection of the new black consciousness, became one of our continuing problems.

We also had a problem with Adrian Scott. He was troubled by the ending of the script. Charlie's death, he felt, was too negative and depressing. He wanted Marlene's baby to be born on screen so that there would be a balance: a life lost and a life begun. We argued that this was too neat, too sentimental. Not only would it violate the spirit of the Westheimer novel and play, but it would also be a standard Hollywood happy ending.

In spite of this disagreement, the three of us spent a great deal of time together discussing casting. We all realized that it would be difficult to find the right actor for the part of Charlie, especially since the network, then as now, was adamant about using "name" performers. And other than Sidney Poitier or Sammy Davis, there were few black actors whose names had, in network parlance, an "instant recognition factor."

We had seen Al Freeman, Jr., in Leroi Jones's savage off-Broadway play *Dutchman,* and we screened the film version to refresh our memories. His performance was electric, but there seemed little chance of convincing NBC to go with an unknown, however talented. For the same reason Lou Gosset, who had originated the role in New York, seemed an unrealistic choice.

For Marlene we talked about Bonnie Bedelia, Kim Darby, and Sally Field. When Patty Duke's name was mentioned there was a general feeling of unease. Bob Banner had set her to play the part in his Broadway production, but she had withdrawn for unspecified reasons to take a "rest." Hollywood, much like other one-industry towns, is a gossip mill, and Patty Duke was reputed to be "difficult." This was the last thing we needed, and we scratched her name from our list of possibilities.

Then three things happened in quick succession. NBC made a firm commitment to Universal for the film, Bob Banner agreed to sell the rights providing he would be the executive producer, and Adrian Scott begged off. His withdrawal was reluctant, but he was overextended with other projects and he simply didn't have the time. We now had our elusive "go." But there was no one to take charge.

We met with Sid Sheinberg and explained the situation. He asked us whom we wanted to replace Adrian, assuming we would name one of the other producers on the lot. Half-joking and half-serious–and with an arrogance born of total ignorance–we suggested ourselves. He mulled it over. Then he nodded. "All right," he said. "Who do you want to direct?"

In that brief moment, and with great casualness, he had suddenly placed us among the ranks of the producers. We had made our suggestion because we didn't want another and perhaps disruptive voice on the project, and now, without any argument, he had acquiesced and dumped it in our laps. We muttered something about Lamont Johnson, a director whose work we admired, and got out of his office with all deliberate speed.

For days afterward we were paralyzed by the prospect of shouldering the responsibility for a million-dollar production. Bob Banner, when we met him, seemed unfazed by our inexperience. He asked that we keep him informed on casting, said he'd be in touch now and then, and that he might ask one of his associates to hang around during the filming. But that was all. No expression of doubt as to our abilities. No naked displays of power. What was wrong with these people? Didn't they realize that we had no idea about the process of making a movie?

Actually, Sheinberg's almost whimsical vote of confidence was not as reckless as it might seem. He may have perceived in us two towering talents who would instantly grasp the complexities of production–but it's more likely, though less flattering, that he had faith in his own organization. Assuming the existence of a viable script, the studio could arguably make films without any producer at all. The casting department could choose the actors, the production department could lay out the schedule, the art department could take care of the sets, and various other fiefdoms could nurse things along to the final print. Then, too, we had mentioned Lamont Johnson, a man with all of the experience we lacked. Sheinberg knew that if we foundered, Johnson could move into the vacuum quite comfortably.

As a further means of protecting us—and the studio—we were turned over to George Santoro and Earl Bellamy for advice and counsel. George was the executive in charge of TV production. An amiable man with a lifetime knowledge of the nuts and bolts of movie-making, he would see to it that we didn't stray from the path of fiscal rectitude. And if there was something he overlooked, Earl, as his assistant, would spot it.

The process of fashioning a film, for television or theatrical release, is roughly broken down into three sequential steps: preproduction, production, and postproduction. The terms are almost self-explanatory. Preproduction involves script, casting, gathering a staff and crew, and selecting locations and/or building sets. It is a period of preparation and logistics. Barring unforeseen accidents, the decisions made in this phase are the most important. If the script is not good, the best director, cameraman, and crew, and the most realistic schedule and comfortable budget will only, in a harsh but accurate phrase, be adding cosmetics to a corpse.

The second step is production, which is the filming itself. Here the pressure, particularly on the directors and the actors, is intense. Still, many feel this is the most exciting part of filmmaking, as all of the elements coalesce and exhaustion, inspiration, and compromise—not to mention temperament—vie for prominence on a day-to-day and sometimes even on a minute-to-minute basis.

Postproduction is embroidery. It's a time to enhance the film, embellish it, and correct mistakes. In a relatively tranquil atmosphere (unless an air date is looming) the picture is edited, scored, and the soundtrack mixed, or "dubbed." The color balance of the print is adjusted and the entire package shipped off to the network. "Like delivering your child," as one producer put it, "to a sex maniac."

We were already deep into the preproduction phase of *My Sweet Charlie.* We screened *Deadlock* for Bob Banner and he seconded our choice of Lamont Johnson to direct. Our only problem was a Universal executive whom we shall call "Simon," who asked Sheinberg for permission to oversee the film. We were hip-deep in overseers already, and Simon's Johnny-come-lately appointment as "liaison" did not particularly delight us. We were in instant disagreement with some of his creative suggestions—he thought we should cast Tina Sinatra and Harry Belafonte in the leading roles—but there was also another factor involved: Having finally gained control over a project, we were perhaps too unwilling to share any part of it.

Since this was our first production we kept a log—more or less an occasional diary, dictated in haste whenever we had the chance. It was slapdash and scattergun, and we include sections of it here (along with addenda where necessary) to give some sense of the ongoing progress of a single television movie at a single point in time:

March 31, 1969

Lamont Johnson signed to direct.

April 1

Met with Lamont. Personable, articulate, an air of being very much in charge. Deep and resonant voice from his early days as a radio actor. Background in theater, as actor and director, and a long career in live and filmed TV . . . He likes script. Worried, as are we, that the many scenes in the summerhouse may become confining, static. Suggests moving some of them outside, and that much of the picture be filmed on location to give it a realistic look and texture. Hates shooting on sets as a matter of general principle. Acknowledges problems: location filming much more expensive than filming at studio. Transportation charges for cast and crew, cost of hotel accommodations, etc.

Later in day we go to screening room to see scene from a TV series submitted on behalf of Lou Gossett. It's an unfortunate choice – the selected scene doesn't show Gossett at his best. We'd like to meet with him, but he's in New York. His agent says he'll pay his own fare to fly out, but we feel it's not right to have him go to considerable expense and then perhaps not get role.*

April 4

Breakfast meeting at Beverly Wilshire Hotel with David Westheimer. Also attending: Bob Banner, Lamont, and Tom Eagan, Banner's associate. We are nervous – Westheimer rumored to have hated the film version of his book *Von Ryan's Express.* Suppose he's unhappy with our *Charlie* adaptation? What is the protocol? Do we argue with him? Stalk away from the table? Our fears prove groundless. Charming man, very pleasant and complimentary. Only minor comments. Suggests that we correct a few regionalisms.

April 9

Casting Marlene still a thorn in everyone's side. Finally, we arrange a meeting with Patty Duke. She doesn't want to get together – knows we intend to put her under a microscope – but she wants the part and we insist. The place is an Italian restaurant on Sunset Boulevard just before the cocktail hour. Empty except for Patty and her agent. We, Lamont, and Banner arrive. Patty awaits us in a big furry coat, obviously to hide the fact that she's overweight. At first everyone awkward. Lots of smalltalk. But she puts us at ease. Waves away a drink and orders coffee. Granted it's a performance, but the circumstances are stressful and she pulls it off.

    Later we huddle with Banner in nearby parking garage. He's impressed. So are we. So, we discover, is Lamont.

---

* Gossett was to make his mark on television in later years, winning an Emmy for his extraordinary performance as a slave in *Roots.*

April 10

Kim Darby's agent informs us she would only consider the part if *Charlie* is a theatrical film. Network executive's ridiculous comment about Patty reported to us: "Okay, her name means something, but can she act?"

April 11

Budget meeting with Simon and Earl Bellamy. Simon insisting that picture be filmed in L.A., on the beach. Unhappy that Lamont, with our blessing, left for a location scouting trip to Texas.

Sheinberg thinks we should all bite the bullet and make an offer to Patty.

Lamont calls long-distance at dinnertime. Rain and more rain in Texas. "I'm outrunning a hurricane." Nevertheless, he's been zipping around in a helicopter. Has found a house that he loves. As an added bonus, it has an abandoned lighthouse in its backyard.

April 14

Monday. Lamont drops by our office. Enthusiastic. He now wants to do *everything* in Texas. Not a single foot of film at the studio.

April 15

Al Freeman comes up again. NBC resisting–no "name" value. Simon pushes Harry Belafonte. We feel he's wrong for the part. Much too attractive and charismatic. Far from hating him, the little girl would swoon. Sheinberg suggests we at least check his availability. If not free, or unwilling to do a television film, then NBC may change its mind about Al Freeman.

Meeting with Herb Schlosser about psychiatrist pilot. NBC receptive to our idea of using the story we found in

Life as a point of departure. [*The Psychiatrist* was a teleplay we were writing for the network, and we were intrigued by an article we had read about an epidemic of drug use by most of the teenage population of Ft. Bragg, California. Eventually *The Psychiatrist* became a short-lived television series. We had nothing to do with its production, but those who did shaped it into one of the better series of its time, though it made little impact on the public or the press. Steven Spielberg, the director of *Jaws* and *Close Encounters of the Third Kind* directed two of the episodes.]

April 16

Met with Ken Grossman. [Grossman was the production's unit manager. His job was to deliver a budget, lay out a shooting schedule, and stay with the picture, supervising all of the so-called "below-the-line" details, until completion.] He wants to base the company in Galveston, Texas. The summerhouse is located in a small town called Bolivar, about an hour away by car and ferry boat. Meaning our actual shooting time is reduced by the travel time to and from the location.

Worked on rewrites of the script. . . . Then, at ten, over to NBC in Burbank to meet with Stan Robertson and Dwayne Ratliff. Spent an hour trading "niggers" for "damns." [Dwayne represented the network's broadcast standards department—i.e., the censors. Stanley Robertson, the highest-ranked black man in network television, had been assigned to monitor the production for NBC. The "censorship meeting," whether it be in person or by phone, is a ritual of the business. Grown men sit pleasantly over coffee and argue about the potentially offensive nature of words. Producers alternate between rage and cajolery; they often insert profane expressions into a script, with no intention of using them, so they have bargaining chips for trading. All of this because the networks ostensibly program "in the public interest," and must therefore launder the air so as not to offend any members of their national constituency.]

April 17

Knocked $100,000 from the budget. Still high . . . Belafonte no longer a consideration because his current film overlaps our schedule. . . . Bumped into Scheinberg in elevator: "NBC will approve Al Freeman."

Patty Duke signed. She goes to New York first to be a presenter at Tony Awards. . . . Now pressure from NBC over ending of script. Grumblings about Charlie being killed. George Santoro calls, obviously at behest of network: "Why does he have to die?" Our response: Why does Willy Loman die? Besides, America kills its blacks—if not literally, then symbolically and psychologically. We refuse to change ending.

April 18

Offer made to Freeman via casting dept. Everyone making suggestions for part of Treadwell. [Treadwell was an important character in the script. He was the proprietor of a small grocery store on the Gulf coast, and he reflected, to a degree, some of the negative racial attitudes of southern whites. The problem was to keep him from becoming, in writing and performance, a one-dimensional cliché.]

April 21

Al Freeman set. Telephone call from Patty Duke: "Can I eat lunch with Al in Galveston and not be lynched?"

April 22

Production meeting. [This is a gathering of the director and producers, the crew, and the heads of various studio departments. The script is examined page by page and all of the technical elements discussed.]

Coffee, doughnuts, cakes. Lots of suntans. Lamont presides. Should we bring dog from L.A. with a trainer, or find untrained dog in Texas? Network doesn't want any brand names shown on merchandise in Treadwell's store. Wardrobe man says Al Freeman's clothes can be bought in Houston. Set designer Bob Luthardt passes around scrapbook of color and black and white stills of the location. Prop man's comment: "All everybody does in this show is eat. You don't need me, you need a short-order cook."

After meeting, we call Al Freeman, tell him we're delighted to have him. But he doesn't sound very happy: "Hey, man, I've got script changes. I want this guy to be up to date." Nice way to start a relationship–we say hello and the actor says he wants rewrites. . . . Sheinberg calls about same subject: "Schlosser is still concerned that your script isn't contemporary enough." We get irritated, demand to know what everybody means by "contemporary"–black militant contemporary or whitewash-of-the-South contemporary? Sheinberg tells us to just think it over. "Don't let your liberal sensibilities run away with you."

April 23

Sirhan Sirhan gets the death penalty.

Al Freeman will meet us in Galveston; visiting relatives in Beaumont, Texas, first. . . . Lunch with Lamont and Simon in commissary–hominy grits on menu. . . . Patty arrives at office, claims she took off twenty pounds. Doesn't look it. We go with her to wardrobe where she tries on various contraptions for her stages of pregnancy. Ludicrous: All the fakes are too large. Check wardrobe for other actors. We say to rumple the stuff up, make it look real.

April 24

More script changes. Feel we are emasculating material. A line about the South that includes the words "down here" becomes "around here." . . . Discuss Treadwell choices. Hal Holbrook? Dean Jagger? E. G. Marshall?

Lunch with Lamont. Thinks Patty, based on yesterday's meeting, is "a very tense young lady." He wants Ed Abroms to edit the picture. Worked with him on *Deadlock* and likes him. Wants Gene Polito for the cinematographer. Hasn't worked with him for several years, but thinks he's right for job. This in spite of Polito's comment: "How can you shoot this thing on such a short schedule? Impossible."

Ralph Ferrin, the assistant director, brings us our plane tickets.

April 26

Dinner at Sheinberg's house with Sid and his wife, Lorraine. He comes in late, carrying a stack of scripts: "I'm a reading machine." They wish us a good trip.

April 29

We leave L.A. International Airport on eight o'clock morning jet to Houston. Patty arrives late with Tara, a dachshund, in her purse. She has a large fever blister on upper lip. "I always get this when I start a picture." Everyone discussing De Gaulle's defeat. We settle in on plane—us, Patty, Lamont, Pete [the wardrobe man] and Patty's dog. . . . Pleasant flight. Met at airport by Ken Grossman and introduced to Les, our driver. Levinson's suitcase missing.

Go to airport motel to read teenage boys for several parts. Some from Alley Theatre. Bearded boy, from Ardmore, Pa., scornful of script. Everybody's a critic. We make our selections. Patty made mistake of taking off shoes on plane and now can't get them on—her feet are swollen.

Off to Galveston and the Hotel Galvez. Looks like something out of a Mexican revolution movie. We're taken to the Glenn Campbell Suite (!) and have session with local press.

Al Freeman arrives. Very intense, edgy. Goes off with Pete to shop for wardrobe.

We take the ferry with Lamont to Port Bolivar and see our summerhouse. It reminds us of the one described in Westheimer's book, but it's far too large. Lamont says he will photograph it in such a way that it will seem smaller. . . . We all troop up to the top of rusted lighthouse, but can't get in because angry owl screeches at us. Intimidated, we get the hell out of there and go to store location for Treadwell's. Store owned by R. C. Roberts, Mrs. R. C., and daughter Cora. Mr. R. known as "Buster," and store called "Buster's Bait Shop." Mrs. Roberts informs us: "When Buster dies, he wants to come back as a fish. I want to come back as a rich lady's poodle." She tells us Buster has a bad heart: "He takes twenty-one hard pills a day." She complains because a tidal wave washed away her garden.

Back on ferry to Galveston. Look over automobiles for film and select one. A car is as much a part of a character as wardrobe.

Out to dinner at Golden Greek Restaurant. Lamont and Al not hitting it off. Al: "I want this show to reflect ideas." Lamont: "How do you film an idea?" Al: "Come on, man." Levinson, fuming: "If you didn't like the script, why did you take the job?" Al: "Because I'm going to fix it."

At this point portly gentleman drops by table. Introduces himself, says he's local representative of the Pearl Beer company. Will arrange for free beer. Then smiles benignly at Al: "Will you look at that boy eat! Always nice to see you boys eat. Real nice having y'all here." Al freezes. Then: "Yeah–because we like to eat." Everyone uncomfortable.

Go back to hotel suite, under a pall, and start to read script. Patty tries to be helpful but Al and Lamont argue. Al tells us emphatically what a black man in Charlie's situation would or wouldn't do. We blow up. Say we don't accept him as the sole spokesman for America's black population. Do we have to call our black friends in L.A. and take a vote on every line of dialogue? . . . Everything focused on Al–Patty just sits there. She finally says to him: "Is there anything I can do for you?" "Yeah," says Al. "Grow another fever blister." Furious, Patty slams out of the room. "The hell with this! I don't have to take this crap!" We all look pointedly at Al. He shrugs, gets up, goes to her by elevators and puts his arm around her. "Sorry I went through all this. It was just a matter of . . . form."

Terrible day. Rocky beginning. Nobody sleeps.

April 30

Rehearsal at beach house. Al concentrating on his part. Lamont realizes Patty is getting short shrift. Will rectify tomorrow. Disagreeable weather. Both Al and Patty are cold and wrap themselves in blankets.

Lunch at nearby café. Jokes about gumbo soup: "What's taking it so long?" "Relax. They're individually unfrozen."

More rehearsals in afternoon. Teenage boys ask for Patty's autograph while their girl friends sit nearby glowering. One boy: "I'm not gonna wash this pencil." No question that Patty is famous. Everyone seems familiar with her entire career, from *Miracle Worker* to *The Patty Duke Show.*

Late in day drive into Houston to interview actors at Shamrock Hotel. Noble Willingham—marvelous name!—perfect for role of man who picks up Marlene at ferry.

We take Al to dinner. Long, long meal as we try to get to know him better. . . . His studied economics in college, but acted, did radio shows. Little film work. Most recent movie was *Finian's Rainbow,* where he did Uncle Tom routine required by script. Maybe we're getting backlash of that. Real hangup seems to be working for Universal. Doesn't like studio's reputation as computer-operated assembly line. Talks about black revolution as it relates to show business: "Five years ago some of these militants were complaining that Negroes were never shown as doctors and lawyers on TV and in movies. Now Poitier plays these roles and they're putting him down." Atmosphere beginning to thaw among us. Man and wife at nearby table stare with sizzling disapproval at two whites and a black dining together.

Back to hotel and Al goes to bed. We invite our driver, Les, for a drink. He reveals: "Y'know, I hesitated about takin' this job. Thought all you Hollywood people would have me standin' at attention salutin'. They asked me: How are those people? I tole 'em you was just plain folks. That Al's a bright guy. Do actors always talk to producers that way?"

May 1

Script changes. . . . Patty in dress with hair pulled back. Al: "Today you look like a girl." They are growing friendlier, seem to like each other. . . . Our cameraman, Gene Polito, arrives with wife. Bob Banner's man, Tom Eagan, coming down in a day or two . . . Universal made offer to Hal Holbrook for part of Treadwell. No rush; we won't be shooting his scenes for a week or so. . . . Talk with Al in his room about jazz. He's less intense, more at ease.

May 2

Work on script, then ferry to Bolivar at noon. Rehearsals have been going on without us. Polito on scene, arranging for camera platforms. Lamont says he has blocked out first thirty pages. He has some excellent visual ideas, but we begin to sense he may go over schedule. Word comes in that we've lost Hal Holbrook. Carroll O'Connor also turned down part. [This was before O'Connor was selected to play the role of Archie Bunker.]

We meet in Lamont's hotel room with Ken Grossman, Polito, and Ralph Ferrin. The union requires us to hire a camera operator [the man who actually runs the camera under the instructions of the director and the cinematographer] from Chicago jurisdiction. We're getting someone sight unseen.

That night Al, laden with camera equipment, goes to his nephew's graduation, where he will be official photographer. Very proud—his nephew headed for Yale.

May 3

Tried to work on *Psychiatrist* script in morning. Then over to Bolivar on ferry with our art director, Bob Luthardt. Tells us he worked with Hitchcock on *Marnie* and *The Birds*.

Rehearsal at the house. Running out of Treadwell choices. Someone says: "We can cast whoever we want. We have NBC by the balls." To which Patty replied: "That's impossible."

Al and Patty throw us all a dinner party in the Glenn Cambell Suite. They have bought food, pots and pans and Al does the cooking. Bob Banner's representative, Tom Eagan, has arrived, and we invite him to join us. Also Mike Rosenfeld, a William Morris agent and old friend who has flown to Texas to see if he can sign Al for representation.

Al has whipped up a gourmet feast, and Patty orders bottles of wine from hotel store. We all drink too much. Al seems always to be on; his energy is wearying. Tells us he knows how to con Lamont: "He's a sucker for improvising. If I want changes in the script I finesse him into an improv and he falls in love with it." Then he relates what happened when he and wardrobe man went to local shop to buy clothes for picture: "I was introduced as Mr. Freeman, a distinguished Hollywood and New York actor. The salesman nodded and led me right over to the coon rack. 'Here, boy,' he says, 'you'll like this stuff over here.' "

We talk for a while about acting. Patty tries to understand the author's intention and creates the character within those parameters. Al rejects this approach. Both of them laugh about their shopping expedition to a Galveston grocery store. A woman came up to Patty. Indicated Al. "Are you two married?" Patty: "No." Woman: "Is he your manager?"

May 4

Talk with Tom Eagan, who has read our rewrites and also miraculously found time to go to Mass. He thinks script is much improved; the black man is becoming more contemporary. . . . Word comes that the truck with camera equipment is overdue.

We drive to Houston for brunch at Brennan's with Tom and Patty. He gives us background on *My Sweet Charlie*. Apparently Poitier and Mia Farrow wanted to do a film version. Banner took this package to Paramount, Columbia, Fox. They all turned it down.

Patty in good spirits. We grow to like her more and more. She's had a difficult life—working professionally since she was a child, with many hangers-on dividing up the spoils—but she seems to be coping.

That afternoon we have a production meeting in the hotel's Palm Room. Somewhat inappropriate name, considering not a palm in sight. The crew has arrived and we see there isn't a single black face among them. Doing a film about amelioration of the races with a nonintegrated crew. . . . Rain predicted for our first shooting day. Good, we need it. Lamont: "This is a very special, very intimate picture, most of it between the two principals. Therefore I want absolute quiet on the set—don't worry about lighting or equipment until after I've worked with the actors."

May 5

Day one of our schedule. Crew leaves for location on school bus. We go later on ferry with Tom Eagan. Scores of gulls. Water and sky silver, monochromatic. First shot is being lined up on road near summerhouse: scene with Marlene and boys in psychedelic van. We ask Luthardt to age the paint on the van: It looks too new. Patty's fever blister almost gone.

My Sweet Charlie, scene #46, is shot at 9:15. Mobs of tourists have arrived. "Is that Patty Duke?" "Yep." "Sure looks pregnant."

Sky now resembles a Wyeth painting. We drive to Buster's Bait Shop because we have heard, to our amazement, that Mrs. Roberts actually has a copy of the book. Universal, with all of its resources, had trouble coming up with one, but sure enough there it is in her hand. We ask where the hell she got it. "The wife of Buster can get anything in this world," she replies. "It's a real nice book. Folks around here thought the little girl got pregnant by the black man. I told 'em it ain't so."

On the set, Lamont is waiting for rain. He needs it for the scene where Marlene first discovers the house—she's driven inside by a storm. If the real thing doesn't come along, we've arranged to have the Bolivar fire company water truck standing by. But a few drops begin to fall and Patty is filmed running toward the house.

After lunch, more rain. Plastic raincoats are passed out to the crew. Patty is filmed running down the road again. Rain stops and we simulate it with the water truck for other angles.

Les drives us back at end of day. "I work Mondays and go home, have dinner, fall into bed and watch *Gunsmoke*. On Sundays I see *Bonanza*. I work for the police on Saturdays, go to work at 11 and get off at 7 in the mornings. I like to have a few drinks and watch TV. But I also visit my horses on weekends. I'd like to come to California. I'm a good house painter."

Crew goes into overtime, back late. We gather in Lamont's room and agree the Chicago operator must be replaced. Call the studio and Polito gets on phone to Earl Bellamy: "We did a close-up of Patty and he *lost* her. Lost her in a *close-up!*"

May 6

More rain. Postcards we bought rolled themselves into cylinders due to the humidity. Drive over with Les, who regales us with stories: "You know, my daddy in South Carolina once shot this guy in the ass. Dr. Webb fixed him up and my daddy asked him for the shotgun pellets. I'll never forget it, the doctor put them in a medicine bottle. Then my daddy gives the bottle to the guy he shot and he says: 'This time I'm puttin' these pellets in your hand, the last time they were in your ass, and the next time you steal my chickens I'm gonna put 'em in your head.' There's four things a man'll kill about in South Carolina—a huntin' dog, a wife, a still, and chickens."

Things moving slowly on the set. What else is new? Tom Eagan is an island of calm and objectivity: "You get this way after you've dealt with Sinatra, Allen Funt, etc. Also, you're spending someone else's money. That takes the pressure off."

Lunch with Al and his stand-in, a black man who looks like Lou Rawls. The makeup man is applying a bruise to Al's forehead. "Very difficult to create a bruise on a black actor. When it dries it tends to look phony."

Lamont's promise of six and three-eighths pages a day goes up in smoke. The camera operator is causing the delay along with other factors: antiquated equipment and the intolerable humidity. Then there are the sound problems: birds, planes, and cars from the ferry on the nearby highway. Ralph Ferrins with walkie-talkie on porch communicates with sheriff a mile away on highway to stop traffic. Tries to get sheriff: "Come in, Sheriff. Ralph Ferrins calling Sheriff." Then the beer-bellied individual himself taps him on the shoulder. He's standing two feet away drinking a glass of water.

Patty grows angry as she realizes the camera operator is missing shots. She is forced to repeat a difficult crying scene three times. Polito remarks to us that she has the same camera sensitivity as Loretta Young, with whom he worked.

Another conclave in Lamont's room and another call to the studio. *Charlie*'s dailies were sent to San Diego by mistake. ["Dailies" or "rushes" are terms used to describe the footage shot the day before. They are screened to give an idea of performance, lighting, and an indication of where readjustments, if any, should be made. When a company is on distant location, the film must be shipped to the laboratory, processed, returned to the company for screening, and then sent back to the editor so he can begin cutting the picture.] Ed Abroms has seen the dailies at the studio. Likes them. Tells us startling piece of information: Real rain doesn't show at all, fake rain looks terrific. [Rain is extremely difficult to photograph. It must be back-lit for it to "read."] Agrees that camera operator is making mistakes.

May 7

Dailies arrive and we finally see them. Operator has missed many of Lamont's effects—even cuts off top of lighthouse. Lamont upset. Patty running through rain, but no rain. Al distressed when he sees himself on film: he blends right into brown closet door in bedroom. "Look at me. Nothing but eyes and teeth." [At that time, since blacks rarely starred in television shows, many cameramen did not know how to photograph them properly.]

We realize we must reshoot several sequences, but where will we get the time in our already overcrowded schedule? Patty threatens to walk off the picture if reshooting is not done, then admits: "I'm just giving you something to bargain with."

May 8

Everyone depressed. We call studio and learn they are unhappy with the footage they've seen today. We decide not to tell Lamont. Why undercut his enthusiasm while he's working? Al's performance reportedly off, dull and undefined. Yet, Dan Petrie calls long distance [Petrie is a stage, film, and television director, the winner of several Emmys] and says he hears the film is remarkable. Whom to believe?

May 9

Alan Cahan gets the trade papers [*The Hollywood Reporter* and *Daily Variety*] in the mail. Cahan is our unit publicist, and he settles down happily to read them. "Ahhh. Like a letter from home."

Out to location. It's our first sunny day. Slow. Slow. Inching along . . . Simon calls from studio. "You're spending too much money."

May 10

More sun. And now hot. Bugs fill the air. They link up and fly around in pairs. "Like teams of writers," someone says. Called "double-bugs" or "fuck bugs."

Important scene in kitchen going badly. Patty fluffs a line. Angry with herself, she kicks her bare foot into a kitchen cabinet. . . . Antediluvian lighting pole crashes down. Could've killed somebody. Forty minutes lost resetting lights. Lamont only gets three and a half pages, admits he's two days behind schedule. We go over script and eliminate a scene so he'll have some time to reshoot earlier sequences.

Dailies good today. Al charged up watching them, obviously pleased. Likes sexual element he feels he's injected in scenes where he wrestles with the little girl.

That night we make rounds saying good-bye to everyone. Tomorrow we return to L.A.

May 12

We deliver Lamont's editing notes, on tape, to Ed Abroms. Abroms tall, thin, cocky. "Don't call me a cutter. I'm an editor."

Dailies quite good. Al is better, but still somewhat intimidated by the film process. He's more comfortable on stage, not used to performing in bits and pieces. When he and Patty play a scene together he's off and she's perfect, emotionally full. Finally, after many takes, he warms up, improves—but now she's tired and begins to wilt.

Check with casting department. Will Geer's schedule is tight; probably won't be able to play Treadwell. Six actors have now turned down part. Why? Answer: Who wants to spend a week in Galveston at short money playing a bigot? Next, Arthur O'Connell.

May 13

NBC and Universal throw a gigantic party on soundstage 28 for the owners and managers of NBC's affiliate stations across the country. We, along with some of the studio's actors, writers, and producers, are invited. Each of us assigned a table with the affiliates and their wives. At entrance, the leading man of a well-known series sweeps up with his date. An attendant in a straw hat says, "Welcome to Universal's *Sweet Charity* Ball, sir." The leading man gives him a wide grin. "Screw you, baby." Flashbulbs go off and we head inside to be seated at separate tables.

One hundred tables, one thousand people. Soundstage—known as *Phantom of the Opera* stage because picture was filmed there—is decorated to promote U's new release *Sweet Charity.* Flowers. Bars. Buffet tables laden with iced bowls of shrimp. Herb Schlosser comes over: "I really feel badly that we gave you so much trouble over *Charlie.*"

Levinson seated at table with group from the South. One of the station owners, spotting an actor dressed as the Phantom, asks: "Who's that? Senator Pastore?" Then he asks Levinson what his problems are. L mentions censorship. Man says his station is in Bible belt, so they have to be careful. L asks why *Laugh In* is so popular in the hinterlands, considering its risqué nature. Man's wife laughs, says: "I think it goes over their heads."

Link talks with Doug Benton, the producer of *Ironside,* who was seated at a table with an oil millionaire from Waco. Man asked, "How much is this studio worth?" Benton told him he thinks it was purchased for 11 or 12 million, but now worth many times more. Man, thoughtfully: "I can afford that." Then asks how much NBC worth. Benton guesses maybe a billion. Man: "With a loan, I might swing that." Says he and Lyndon Johnson got into the TV station business at the same time.

Sid Sheinberg gets up on stage and makes welcoming

speech: "NBC stands for Newness, Boldness, Creativity."
Followed by NBC executive who drily remarks: "There
was a time I was told NBC stood for *Ninety Bristol Court*.
[This was a Universal series that quickly flopped in a pre-
vious season.] Band strikes up and everyone dances. . . .
George Santoro finds us in the mob, says he tried to talk
Leslie Nielsen into playing Treadwell, but Nielsen turned
it down. We look around the party, see Dean Jagger and
Carroll O'Connor. A roomful of Treadwells.

May 14

We decide to cast Ford Rainey as Treadwell. We've
wasted too much time on this "name actor" nonsense.
Rainey has the right quality and is highly skilled. The
studio has obligations to another actor, asks that we reconsider. We refuse. Surprisingly, they go along with us
and Rainey is set.

We talk to Lamont long-distance. He's officially two
days behind schedule, but we tell him that dailies are
excellent. We have a feeling that the studio, for all its
reputation as a hard-nosed money machine, has fallen a
little bit in love with this project and is supporting it.
Good dailies help. The word gets around.

May 15

A day calculated to make us want to get out of the business. Or at least return to the nontraumatic pleasures of
writing in a quiet room. Santoro sends for us, and when
we arrive at his office he is on the phone to the head of
the production department. A grave conversation, George
sucking on his cigarette, shifting the papers on his desk,
saying things like: "Can we build the interior of the summerhouse here at the studio?" He hangs up and fills us in.
Ken Grossman got a call at five in the morning from a
"friend" in the Galveston Sheriff's Office. Their narco

squad has reason to believe Patty Duke is taking drugs. A friendly tip; he doesn't want to get involved. She's being watched and may be arrested and jailed.

We're all in a state of shock. Marijuana possession in Texas can carry a heavy sentence. We telephone Lamont, tell him to talk to Patty and if she's on something warn her to get rid of it. He doesn't think she is. Seems a few members of the local police brought some millionaires to the set and asked her to have lunch with them. She wasn't in the mood and turned them down. This may be their way of getting even. We tell him we'll call him back.

We all stand around George's office. Somber. One week left on the shooting schedule. George tells us a story: "I'm the production manager for a feature shooting in Utah. I get a call at three in the morning from the local sheriff. 'We got your star here in the pokey. The charge is rape.' 'And the girl? How old?' 'Fourteen.'" Studio lawyers were flown in to bail out the actor and a private investigator finds star innocent—girl lied. Somehow this story is not particularly comforting.

Sheinberg filled in on the problem. Also Tom Eagan. And then—together—we all realize we have no choice. If we blow the picture, we blow the picture. In human terms, Patty must be protected. A call is placed to Lamont, then we suddenly remember that Bob Banner is in Texas visiting the set. Banner is a southerner and very low-key. He knows Patty better than any of us. We talk to him and he agrees to take her aside and casually mention the problem.

May 16

Banner reports in. Everything fine. Patty denies any hard drug or pot use and he believes her. [She later told us that in fact she did turn down overtures from several members of the Galveston police force. Once or twice she thought her hotel room had been searched, and her greatest fear was that something would be planted.]

May 18

Attend a screening of *Me, Natalie* at UCLA. Patty the star, Fred Coe the director. We have reservations about the picture, but Patty is superb. She's outfitted with buck teeth and she's a completely different human being from the little ragamuffin in our film. That's what acting's all about: becoming someone else in a believable way.

May 19

Dailies of scene where Al confesses he killed a man. Lamont filmed with two cameras, a close-up and a medium shot. Al underplays. Lots of pauses—too many. We can delete them in editing by cutting away to Patty listening to him, and then returning to Al a beat before he starts to speak again.

Lamont calls. The atmosphere on the set is tense. Everyone is tired. Constant heat and humidity.

May 20

Ed Abroms says rough cut won't be ready for five weeks. [A "rough cut" is the first assemblage of a film without any refinements.] Lamont will be in Ireland by then, working on his new picture.

Again, dailies good, a very affecting scene between Al and Patty. We talk to Lamont at the end of the day. He and Al had an angry blowup. They are barely communicating. Lamont gives him directions and Al says, "Yes, sir." The crew is working above and beyond the call of duty.

We show a sequence to a sound technician for his advice about some problem areas regarding audibility of dialogue. As he leaves the room he says, "Christ, the talk in this thing. Nothing but talk, talk, talk."

May 21

Dailies surprisingly good. Potato-peeling scene. Al delightful. Is Lamont losing his objectivity? Are we?

May 22

Lamont wants to shoot the climax of the picture at night. [A faster and less costly way of shooting night sequences is to film them during the day, with filters on the lens. The film is then printed down in the lab. This is called shooting "day-for-night." Filming after dark requires complicated lighting, but the look is far more realistic and does not, in James Agee's phrase, "smell of the studio."] We vacillate. Universal wants to wrap the picture and bring it home. Still, part of our job is to protect the director from studio pressure. Finally we meet with Simon. It's a confrontation, we're all yelling at one another. Then he says, "Stop asking people what to do. Make up your minds and then tell them. If you're going to produce, be decisive." He's absolutely right—we've been too often guilty of waffling. Leave his office with new respect for him. Call Lamont and tell him to do it the way he thinks best.

May 23

Lamont tells us working with Al is now like pulling teeth. Nothing to be done, simply bad chemistry. Patty is unhappy with script and her performance. Al and Patty so upset by dailies they refuse to see any more of them. Lamont: "This picture is not my best work." We disagree. The film we are seeing is just fine. But then we're not in Galveston. It's easier to make judgments away from the firing line.

May 24

Finished all scenes in house. Climax coming up.

May 25

Meeting at NBC with Schlosser on *Psychiatrist* project. Sheinberg drives us over. Network makes firm commitment for a two-hour pilot film. Drive back to Universal with Sheinberg. He's desperately in need of driving lessons. Weaves all over the road as he talks. Tells us network policies are now influencing the feature business. "Motion pictures have to keep television in mind at all times—it's a very important market."

May 27

Last day of *My Sweet Charlie*. Filmed all night and into the morning. Last shot: sun coming up through car window as Marlene is driven away from house. Only time for two takes. In one of them, at Banner's request, she mutters, "My poor Charlie." We hate the idea. Corny as hell.

May 28

Lamont back from Galveston. He and Al parted without saying good-bye. We look at dailies. Disappointing. One of the two takes of Patty driving away is overexposed, can't be used. The other, naturally, has her line of dialogue, which makes us wince. We get the idea of running the end credits from the bottom of the screen to the top over the shot of her face. Perhaps we can time them so that they cover her lips when she says, "My poor Charlie," and then wipe her words from the soundtrack.

Another problem: When Charlie is shot, he flops down behind a bush. It's the obliteration of a character the audience has been involved with for two hours, but there's no moment, no dramatic emphasis. It's thrown away in a few seconds. We're depressed.

We arrange lunch for Lamont and Gil Mellé, the composer we have chosen. Discussing music difficult exercise in semantics. How loud is loud? How soft is soft? One man's dissonance is another's pleasure. Lamont says he wants a clear musical line, forlorn but strong: "Marlene is lonely but strong." He hears a chamber music sound. Gil inclined toward a "mini-symphony." [We misled the composer in this conversation, and the imprecise nature of language when discussing music came back to haunt us.]

Banner and others have suggested a title song, but we are opposed. Feel it's unnecessary.

Lamont tells us that the Roberts gave him and Bob Luthardt thirty-seven pounds of shrimp. The two of them carted the load to L.A. in a big ice brick on the plane.

June 24

Today we see the first rough cut of *My Sweet Charlie*. Lamont is long gone, in Ireland, but Ed Abroms has followed his taped editing instructions. Present at the screening: us, Banner, Eagan, Abroms. Group reaction: loose, long, an early montage sequence much too "busy" with optical effects. Amazingly, Al comes off not only well, but extremely likable. The hostility on the set is not apparent. . . . Simon sees cut later in the day. He wants the montage out. Complains that it is eighteen minutes before Marlene and Charlie meet. Wants deep cuts to bring them together earlier. We're irritated. Too many cooks.

July 2

Lamont calls Sheinberg from Ireland. Has heard that Simon wants to eliminate the montage and he's furious. We tell him that we want to keep it in, but that it has to be simplified. Lamont will be unavailable to make his director's cut, so now the final choices are up to us.

Abroms suggests a way to make something powerful out of Charlie's truncated death scene: freeze the frame and hold for a long moment as he's shot. Allow audience to be saturated with the harshness of the event. We like the idea but think it would be even better if, after the frame is frozen, the camera moves in on him, closer and closer. [This move-in was accomplished optically. The frame was held and then gradually blown up larger and larger in the lab, thus creating the illusion of a camera move where none existed. The freeze frame, unfortunately, has been overused to the point of cliché. It was far from new when we put it into *Charlie* in 1969. Perhaps the most stunning use of the device was the ending of Truffaut's *The 400 Blows*.]

Simon tells us a lawyer friend of his watched the picture with him. He was moved by the experience and loved Al's performance.

July 14

Editing with Ed Abroms on the Moviola. Fine tuning.

July 19

Dinner in Burbank restaurant with Lorraine and Sid Sheinberg. Waiter, a refuge from Stage Deli in New York, intimidates us with Jewish mother bombast. We all meet Simon and his wife at studio and go into Screening Room 3. We bring along tape recorder for comments. . . . *My Sweet Charlie* rolls. Everyone quiet, no coughing or shifting in chairs. Laughter from women, from Sheinberg during potato-peeling sequence. Finally ends. Sheinberg: "That is a *good* movie." Lorraine: "It's a beautiful picture." Various criticisms. We listen carefully, since at the moment we are totally subjective and it's nice to have a fresh perspective.

July 20

Man walks on moon.

July 21

We are earthbound in the editing room. More fine cutting. Banner wants Patty's line put back in at end of
picture. We say no. Our feeling: play against sentiment in
sentimental scenes. He goes along with us. However, we
agree with him that montage still too busy. Further refinements needed.

July 25

Sound and music run. [This is an important part of
postproduction. The picture is screened for the composer
and technicians from the sound department. The placement and duration of the background music cues are discussed, along with the required sound effects. In addition,
the dialogue is analyzed to see whether any of it should be
redone in a process called "looping."] *Charlie* needs very
little music. And though some dialogue is hard to hear,
we decide to keep most of the original track for the sake
of performance. Loop lines, no matter how well done,
never sound quite like the real thing.

July 29

Al due in for looping. Arrives late. Refuses to add southern accent to help Treadwell scene. . . . We take him to
lunch in the commissary. Joined by Howard Rodman.
[Rodman is a highly regarded television writer; as the
story editor on *The Naked City,* he was largely responsible
for the distinctive flavor of that notable series.] Rodman
says he's bored with discussions of race. "Can't we talk
about something else?" Al next wants to do Leroi Jones'
The Slave as a feature film. Says he might not even watch

Charlie when it airs. Didn't enjoy making the picture. "We spent the first week of rehearsal blocking scenes. No damn work on performance at all." Complains about cinematographer. "He resented spending the extra time lighting me." We tell him he came off likably. Al: "Then I failed."

[This was the last time we saw him, although we spoke occasionally on the phone. For many years he starred in a soap opera in New York, and he gave a powerful performance as Malcolm X in *Roots II*.]

August 1

Patty arrives in a simple red dress with a head cold. Can't loop her until cold disappears and vocal quality returns to normal. We show her the film. Strange feeling—the girl sitting next to us in screening room is not the girl on the screen. She likes *Charlie* and likes her performance. Feels she overacts slightly to compensate for Al's underplaying. Talks about the "drug" incident. Nothing to it. A case of a few local cops attempting to get even with her for not dating their friend.

August 7

Screening for David Westheimer and his wife. David's opinion perhaps the most important to us, and he approves.

August 15

Patty comes in for looping, her cold gone. Does all of her loops quickly and perfectly. Not one mistake. We try to make her laugh so she'll blow a line or two. She finally cracks up when she has to sing "Little Town of Bethlehem" and sees us wincing and holding our ears.

August 20

The Gil Mellé music is recorded on the scoring stage. Lovely theme. But the opening music over the ferry boat is too lush, too symphonic. Not simple enough. Our fault—we told him we wanted something with the feeling of Elmer Bernstein's *To Kill a Mockingbird* and that's exactly what he gave us.

August 23–24

The picture is dubbed. Our first time doing this, so we place ourselves in the hands of the dubbing team. There are three of them, and they appreciate the fact that we gave them scripts to read a week ago. Seems this is unusual. Why? Should be standard procedure. . . . They do an excellent job, but opening music still too ponderous. We decide to remove it entirely and go with the natural sounds of water, gulls, and the ferry engine. It's a desperation measure, but it works. However good the music might have been, this is much more unusual—and interesting. Thanks to a series of mistakes, we have an arresting opening. But will an audience keep from changing channels for eighteen minutes before our two protagonists meet?

[Strangely, when the film went into syndication long after its first network run it had mysteriously acquired a folk song at the beginning.]

January 20

My Sweet Charlie aired on NBC. Almost a year since the day we first read the book. We attend a small party at the home of Patty's manager. Watch the show. Feeling of anticlimax. We've seen it so many times it seems stale and listless. No idea whether it will have any impact.

January 21

Sheinberg calls Levinson at 7:30 in the morning. Jubilant. "We broke the bank." The ratings are enormous. Reviews coming in from all over the country—all good. At the office, phone never stops ringing. Still more reviews, dozens. Telegrams. One of those rare days spent six feet off the ground.

Charlie gets a 31.7 rating and a 48 share in the Nielsens. Unheard of for a television movie. Top-rated television show in America that week, top-rated TV film ever.

May

We are in Europe on vacation. Tom Eagan cables us. *Charlie* nominated for eight Emmy Awards by the Television Academy. . . . Lamont Johnson has already won the Director's Guild Award as Best Television Director for the show. The NAACP has given it its Image Award as Best Program of the Year. It has won the Golden Gate Award for Best Television Film at the San Francisco Film Festival. And the Critics' Consensus, composed of television critics, picked it as one of the season's three distinguished TV accomplishments.

June

Emmy ceremonies in grand ballroom of Century Plaza Hotel. *Charlie* wins three: Patty for Best Actress, Ed Abroms for Best Editing, and us for Best Script.

Good reviews and golden statuettes are balm for the ego, but if *My Sweet Charlie* had any importance, it was largely due to the practical reality of the numbers. A "soft" TV film, a "people story," had delivered impressive ratings. Confronted by this aberration, the networks were forced to reexamine some of their hard and fast rules and inch their way, if only a fraction, in the direction of greater flexibility.

Suddenly, post-*Charlie,* the television film had a function other than as a vehicle for the showcasing of pilots. George Gent, under the headline "Movies Made for TV Are Gaining Importance at Networks," wrote the following for the *New York Times:* "As Hollywood dismantles its large production studios, movies made for television like 'My Sweet Charlie' are becoming the talk of the industry, and it is already apparent that they will play an increasingly important role in TV's immediate future. . . . Sparked by NBC's success with the format, ABC and CBS have entered the lists with feature series of their own."

Charlie also had an unexpectedly pleasant dividend. As the first large-scale hit of its kind, it encouraged many writers and producers to take some of their better projects to the networks instead of to the motion picture companies. It was hardly the millennium, but at least there was more receptivity to unusual–and even controversial–material. The word "nigger" had been uttered on the air and irate viewers had not stormed the battlements of NBC. A story with human relationships as its chief ingredient, without car chases and shoot-outs, had held a massive audience for two hours, thus invalidating certain basic network assumptions. Those in charge were momentarily bewildered enough to listen to ideas they would have previously rejected.

Looking back, it seems ludicrous that a drama pleading a rather standard liberal case for better understanding and communication between the races should have been even faintly controversial. But in 1970, before Norman Lear and *All in the Family* altered the public's perception of what television can say and do–and in spite of the pioneering ground broken by Reginald Rose and *The Defenders*–the networks were intimidated by the specter of Senate investigations, fearful of viewer backlash, and subject to the whims of conservative affiliates.

Still, numbers were numbers, and the profit motive is a wonderful antidote for timidity. If *Charlie* could deliver higher ratings than every other television show aired during a given week, then perhaps there was something to be said for TV movies in general and for serious subject matter relative to the usual run of escapist fare.

As the log of the production makes clear, the nature of the medium is collaborative. *My Sweet Charlie* was an ideal training experience for us, but it wouldn't have been possible without the support and resources of a huge, general-service studio with close ties to the network. Somehow the entire organization, from Sheinberg to the assistant editor, sensed that the film was an attempt at something different and made a commitment to it. This can be a danger—creation by committee has crippled numberless projects—but in this particular case we needed as much help as we could get. The balance between what advice to take and what to ignore is not always easy to recognize, but we had a clear idea of what we wanted, and we were lucky. The fact remains that *My Sweet Charlie* is an example of the Hollywood studio system at its occasional best.

4 / Columbo

The Series

There are significant differences between the television movie and the television series. Each requires its own set of muscles, as well as a different kind of commitment from those on the firing line. The TV film can be handcrafted; energies are geared to a one-time-only operation, a single piece of work, and the end is always in sight. But the series can seem like a runaway horse—no one quite knows when it will stop. A show that we created called *Mannix* had an eight-year run, and Ivan Goff and Ben Roberts, the producing-writing team most responsible for its success, stayed with it (no doubt much to their surprise) for seven of its eight seasons.

The series has its own peculiar characteristics. Unlike the novel, the play, or the film, it exists over time: at the minimum usually thirteen weeks, and at the maximum almost a decade. In some ways it is analogous to the soap opera, and it has been compared to the serial novel of the nineteenth century, when readers queued up to get the next installment of an ongoing work by Dickens or Conan Doyle. It has also been compared, less flatteringly, to the comic strip.

Since it is the most plastic of television's entertainment forms, it can change directions and even incorporate feedback from its audience. *Happy Days,* for example, included in its cast a minor character named Arthur Fonzarelli. Unexpectedly, the "Fonz" caught on with the public and became a national fad. Mail poured in and ratings escalated whenever he appeared. The show's producers responded by building up his part, and after a few seasons the tail was wagging the dog: Fonzie had replaced the original lead characters as the primary motivating force of the series.

Many critics, when a new show makes its debut, only sample the first few episodes; they then either embrace it or write it off. But shows change. The feedback principle comes into play, and there's often much tinkering because the production staff has the advantage of observing its mistakes on a week-to-week basis. Episode twenty may be entirely different from episode one. *The Mary Tyler Moore Show* and *All in the Family* received lukewarm reviews when they appeared. Now they are the objects of near-veneration. *The Rockford Files* was thought to be just another private-eye series when it started its well-deserved long run, but it gradually began to develop—unnoticed by those who too quickly dismissed it—an offbeat humor and a raffish sense of satire. Perhaps the most famous example is *Maverick,* a formula Western that metamorphosed (again, over time) into a beguiling send-up of the genre.

There are, of course, many disadvantages to the long-term aspects of the television series, not the least of which is creative fatigue. Those in charge grow bored, or tired, and diminishing returns set in. Norman Lear has said that a hit show should rest on its laurels and go off the air after a four-season run. Apparently this is not an idea whose time has come. The laws of economics—or, if you will, simple avarice—mitigate against the cancellation of a success, since it is far more profitable to have an existing series renewed than to put a new series on the air. The operative words are "amortization" and "long-term syndication potential."

There is also the matter of network involvement. In the case of a one-shot television movie that is over the moment it is aired, the network can only have influence before the fact. But if a marginal series manages to survive for a season or two there is plenty of time for "corrections," "readjustments," or whatever euphemism one may choose for network interference. The opposite side of the coin is that

nobody bothers a success. Unless, that is, someone in power antici-
pates a barely perceived "softening" somewhere in the future, and sets
about correcting a series out of existence. This is known as "curing a
hit."

The producer of a television series, though he is usually well paid,
has a difficult and frequently thankless job. He must serve many
masters: the production company that employs him, the network, his
star actor, the audience as reflected, rightly or wrongly, by the ratings—and, if he has any pride in his work, his own taste and his sense
of public responsibility.

The producer is the engine that drives a series. He must hire writers
and develop scripts, cast the actors for every episode, select the directors, worry about shooting schedules and budgets, keep his cast and
crew happy, edit, score, and dub each segment, and see to it that the
series receives its fair share of on-air and print promotion. It is a job
that requires strong organizational capabilities, as well as what Dale
Carnegie used to call, in a simpler time, "the ability to get along with
others."

The producer will usually have a small staff: an associate producer,
who serves as his assistant, and a story editor, who meets with writers,
separates the wheat from the chaff, and frequently rewrites the scripts
when they come in—as will the producer if he's a writer (or thinks
he's a writer). Peering over the producer's shoulder may well be a
creature named the executive producer. This worthy can either be an
absentee landlord (meaning he packaged and/or created the series,
takes a fee, and steers clear of any involvement); or else he may choose
to be in actual charge of the entire operation, in which case the
producer becomes a "line producer," primarily concerned with the
technical aspects of production and with little influence over the so-
called "creative choices."

Two factors dominate any producer's waking hours: the need for
material (not necessarily good material—just material) and time. The
nature of the medium forces him to preside over an assembly line that
runs on an ever-accelerating basis. Like a Lewis Carroll character, he
must run faster and faster just to stay in place.

This requires an explanation of such arcana as "lead time" and "air dates." Traditionally, a network would commit to a new television series in March, and the series would premiere in late September. This would give the producer approximately six months or so of "lead time," a period in which to hire a staff, prepare scripts, and begin shooting to meet his September deadline. A new episode would go on the air each week thereafter.

Reflect for a moment, however, and certain mathematical realities will become all too apparent. If it takes four weeks under optimum conditions to complete one segment of a TV series, and a new segment is needed for airing each week, then the producer will quickly run out of time. At best he may have four or five shows "in the can" by early September; within five weeks they will have been aired and now he will need shows six and seven—not to mention eight and nine—and all the way up to show twenty-two if his series is renewed at midseason. The calendar becomes his enemy as his backlog of available segments diminishes. Often, somewhere down the pike in early December, an episode in the final stages of editing and dubbing has to be finished and on the air in a matter of days—and the next segment must follow inexorably a week later. And the next. And the next.

To alleviate this situation, the network may throw in an occasional "preemption," usually some kind of special, so that the producer can buy himself a week of time here and there. And during nonpeak viewing periods such as the Christmas season one or two of the early episodes may be rerun. Nevertheless, the producer is on a constant treadmill, and matters of quality become the least of his concerns.

Clearly it would be in everyone's best interest for the networks to provide more lead time, but in recent years quite the opposite has been the case. For competitive reasons the networks have been taking much longer to evaluate the new pilots, and they have pushed back the announcements of their schedules until mid- and even late April. To compound the problem, they have moved up the start of the new season, premiering their shows in early September. The hapless producer now has even less time at his disposal and the viewing audience, as always, suffers most.

None of this applies to situation comedies. They are taped, or filmed with three cameras simultaneously, and they can be readied much more quickly than the dramatic series. But they do share one problem in common with the dramatic shows: the difficulty of finding scripts.

The Writers Guild of America is a trade union with a long and turbulent history; it has protected both screen and television writers from the abuses that arise in a company town where the writer has minimal power. Its membership is composed of five thousand or so men and women, and most of these are seldom, if ever, employed. Only a handful—at most a few hundred—work regularly, and these writers are responsible for almost all of what is seen on American television.

The reason for this is that the industry parcels out assignments on the basis of "track records" or "credits." If a writer is fortunate enough to get "hot" he is in constant demand, and as he continues to acquire better credits he becomes even more desirable. Breaking into this charmed circle is not easy. Credits beget credits, and if the answer to the perpetual question: "What's he done?" is "Nothing much," then those who do the buying send up immediate waves of resistance. The new writer is left to wonder how he can get his first assignment when his acceptance frequently depends upon his last one.

The "track record" syndrome results in many shows vying for the talents of very few writers. As soon as the new network schedule is announced there is an instant mating dance as television producers hurriedly attempt to "lock up" one of the favored writers. But the writer doesn't dare take only one assignment at a time. If he did—if he worked on his teleplay for a month or so—he would discover when he turned it in that all of his markets are closed. Knowing this, and recognizing that he cannot earn his yearly nut with just one script, the free-lance writer often takes as many assignments as he can get.

This results in a process known as "juggling." During any given day he may be working on an outline for one show, a first draft for another, and meeting with a producer to offer a "notion" or a "springboard" for a third. What's left of his time is spent in dodging phone calls when he has missed delivery dates and, presumably, thinking up new ideas and sleeping.

Both producer and writer are victims of a process over which they have no control: They are in the grip of economics and the seasonal nature of the medium. But they exacerbate the situation by acquiescing, along with the networks, to the track record philosophy. To some degree this is understandable—the veteran writer feels he has earned his position of stature by virtue of his previous work, and the producer, given his many pressures, wants someone he can depend upon. But this hardly leads to the infusion of new blood, and young writers can be forgiven for viewing the endless pleas for usable material with a somewhat jaundiced eye.

Generally speaking, the neophyte gets a chance because the writers who are in demand are not available and the producer has no other option. Or else a series may be coasting along comfortably in its second or third season and its producer, with most of the wars behind him, can relax and look around for budding talent. But risk-taking is a luxury that requires time, and the basic fact of life in the world of the television series is that time is in desperately short supply.

Edward Albee may write one play every few years. A decade can slip by between the books of a prominent author. But a successful television writer may turn out seven, eight, or even a dozen teleplays a year. Few writers are talented enough to maintain a level of quality with such an enormous output.

Why do they write so much? There are several answers, the most obvious being that producers ask them to. And pay them well for each script. Also, many writers enjoy the pace of TV, and some even take pleasure in the craft itself. Then too, once a certain standard of living is achieved, it must not only be maintained but improved upon. Or so it would seem from the prolificity that abounds.

Much of the foregoing also applies to the directors of television series. Those in demand are snapped up, their schedules booked months in advance. A director will prepare a show in six or seven days, shoot it in the same amount of time, and then move on to the next one. Many directors will go from episode to episode for an entire season. Talent aside, one stands in awe of the sheer animal energy required for such an existence.

Even the most conscientious producer cannot change the system, so he must work within it as best he can. At any given moment his choices will be limited and he must constantly seek the most acceptable alternative. If Writer A isn't available, he must move on to Writer B. If a script is hopeless, and there's no time for rewrites, he must attempt by imaginative casting and stylish editing to dress it up as much as possible, hoping that good performances and technical dazzle can compensate for flaws in logic and the odor of the familiar. He knows that most of the talents he has assembled would like to "move up" into television movies, pilots, or feature films, and he must somehow convince them of the worth of their work so that they are not simply putting in time.

If he succeeds he will consider himself lucky to come up with a handful of shows (out of the many that he makes) that will please him. But all of them will be mediocre unless he has a strong sense of what he wants his series to accomplish, and what it can be at its best. This does not mean inundating every segment with heavy doses of controversy and themes of cosmic importance. The series may only be intended as light entertainment. But there is good entertainment and bad entertainment, the well-crafted and the shoddy, and the producer should know the difference between them. He should also be prepared to be rewarded for his efforts by a quick cancellation while his opposite number across town, grinding out a slipshod product, achieves an unwarranted success. It helps to be philosophical and smoke a pipe.

The average viewer neither knows nor cares what a producer does—he can hardly be expected to concern himself with the tribulations of a well-paid Hollywood executive. But once a network has made a commitment to a given series it is the producer who is most responsible for its content, and hence for what goes into the homes of millions of Americans. Since many series are exported, he may also have something to do with the way this country is perceived by audiences around the world. So it is not inflating his importance to suggest that his problems may have some relevance to others outside the rather insular Hollywood TV community.

To better understand these problems, it might be instructive for the reader to step into the shoes of a television producer and live his life during a single business day.

You are in charge of a series called, with a stunning stroke of egalitarianism, *Mr. Smith*. It's an hour-long action-adventure drama that made its debut a month ago. Today is a Tuesday in October. What follows is a composite, though by no means atypical:

7:00 A.M.

You are awakened by a call from your set, where your company has just started shooting. The assistant director is on the phone, and he informs you of the day's first crisis: An actress with a small part has not appeared. Her husband has just called from a hospital near their home—she's had an attack of food poisoning and is presently in deep communication with a stomach pump. She will not be able to come to the studio. Unfortunately for you, she is in the first scene scheduled to be filmed. The AD wants to know what you want him to do and whom you want for a replacement. What you really want to do is go back to sleep, but you force yourself into a state of reasonable consciousness and tell him to shoot the second scene first to gain some time. This turns out to be impossible; the set for the second scene is on another soundstage, and another company is using it. They are running late and will not be able to vacate until nine o'clock. It will be available and redressed by ten, so a potential three-hour delay, which will cost thousands of dollars, is in the offing. Your stomach is now in a knot and you wonder if *you* have food poisoning. You tell the AD to ask the director to rehearse the scene anyway and you'll call right back. Then you search your house for your casting director's telephone number until you remember it's at the office. The Information operator can't help—you don't know his address and Los Angeles is a hodgepodge of many communities, each with its own telephone directory. You call your secretary, interrupting her while she is brushing her teeth. Luckily, she once worked for the casting director and knows where he lives. You call him and explain the problem: You need an actress, made-up and in wardrobe, immediately. He explains that agents are not in their offices until ten in the morning. You point out that you're fully aware of this fact, but this is an emergency. He suddenly remembers a girl who lives near the studio. He'll try to reach her. You call your set to relay the information, but the line is busy. You get dressed.

8:00 A.M.

You finally get through to the set. The replacement has just arrived, half-asleep, and is being fitted. She has requested cue cards for her dialogue and they are being prepared. The director is using the time to rehearse the next few scenes, but the show is already an hour behind schedule. You leave your house and fight the heavy freeway traffic to the studio.

8:40 A.M.

You stop by the soundstage before going to your office. The new actress is coming along nicely and you thank her for bailing you out. She says sweetly that you've never hired her before and she hopes in future you'll consider her for a better part. It's a zinger, charmingly delivered, but you're grateful she was available on such short notice and you promise to recommend her to other producers on the lot. You say good morning to various members of the crew and consult with your director about ways to make up the lost time. He says he will simplify a later action sequence, but he's not happy about it; he had some complicated and interesting visual ideas that will now have to be shelved. Your associate producer buttonholes you and leads you to the script girl. She has some bad news. The pace of this particular episode is quite rapid, and according to her time projection the show will come in three minutes short. Another consultation with the director. He says there's no possible way he can pad for three minutes. Another scene will be required. And if another scene is scheduled, how can he finish the picture without running into overtime? You ask your associate producer to come up with new scene ideas, but he reminds you that he will be on the dubbing stage all day, mixing the sound and music for one of the finished episodes, and he will be unavailable. Your leading lady stops you as you are about to leave the set. She wants a meeting. You say you'll try to see her after lunch. Is something wrong? She nods and her eyes brim with tears. You try to soothe her and promise to give her all the time she needs.

9:00 A.M.

You stop by your leading man's dressing room. He's in a sour mood, asks about the ratings of last Friday night's show. You say you'll have them this morning. He's read the rough pages of the next script and doesn't like them. You assure him, in the parlance of the trade, that you'll "run them through your typewriter." He asks for a meeting to go over his objections. He also tells you that the following Friday he wants the day off. He's been asked to host the opening of a department store in Chicago. It will be good exposure for him, it will help the series in a major market, and they're offering him a lot of money. You remember the schedule for the following Friday—he works in every scene. You tell him you'll try to shift things around.

9:15 A.M.

You arrive at your office, late for an appointment with a writer. The director of your next show is also waiting, and he complains that he hasn't received the last act. You look in on your story editor, who is rewriting it. You tell him about the three-minute scene required for the current show. Quickly, the two of you manufacture a scene that can be filmed on existing sets. The story editor clears his desk to write it, setting aside his work on the last act for the upcoming show, and your new director grumbles that no one has any time for him. He says he can't even find a decent parking space on the lot; in desperation he left his car in a red zone by a fire hydrant. You ask your secretary to help him out and the two of you agree to have lunch. Then you meet with the writer. He has an interesting idea and you both begin to develop it until you're interrupted by a call from the dubbing stage. Would you come over? Apologizing to the writer, you hurry from the office. On the dubbing stage you and the associate producer attempt to iron out a problem with a music cue. The composer is present and he thinks the sound effects are overwhelming his music. You find a compromise that satisfies no one and return to your office. Calls are backing up, particularly one from your network liaison man. The ratings are in. On the New York and Los Angeles overnights your show got a 30 share, up one point from last week, and the nationals are the same. Feeling almost chipper, you call the network man. He tells you two things: The network wants a major conceptual change in future scripts, and next Friday night's show must have five minutes deleted because of a public-affairs announcement. You explode. Next Friday's show is completed and ready for delivery. It will take endless time to edit out five minutes and redub. And the concept suits you fine. That's what the network bought and what you've been giving them. Isn't it a bit late in the day for changes, particularly since the ratings are up? He asks for a meeting at his office that afternoon. You refuse; you can't get away. After an argument, you both hang up with the problem unresolved. The writer, meanwhile, has been waiting patiently, discussing new res-taurants with your secretary. You tell him you'll make a story commitment for his idea and arrange for another meeting later in the week to hash over his ending; it needs work. You apologize for keeping him so long while you were on the dubbing stage. You begin to feel as if all you do is apologize. Then you call back the network man and apologize for shouting at him. He apologizes for shouting at you. Actually, you both rather like each other. He says he'll come to your office because he knows you're busy and you clear an hour tomorrow morning.

10:45 A.M.

There is a long list of calls. An actor you've hired for the next show has, unbeknownst to you, grown a beard. It doesn't fit the script and you must convince him to shave it off. A writer who is late with a first-draft teleplay will not be able to get it in for another week—there's been a death in his family. You offer condolences and then remind him that the last time he worked for you he had another convenient death when he was late with an assignment. You look over a Standards and Practices memo on a new script and your heart sinks. They have blue-penciled it to the point of total blandness. It's the one script so far you feel strongly about, so you have your secretary set up a meeting with the head of the department, hoping you can persuade him to be more flexible than his subordinates. There is a call from the set (such calls take precedence over everything else) and you deal with a disagreement between your director and leading man over a matter of interpretation. You tell the actor that the ratings are up and he becomes almost cheeful.

11:15 A.M.

The mail comes in. Three or four reviews of your last segment, one full of praise, the rest knocks. The knocks are correct. Two unsolicited scripts from unknown writers. You are not permitted to read material unless submitted by an agent—an edict of the studio legal department—so you return the scripts with an explanatory letter. You also write to the network complaining that your series is not receiving its fair share of on-air promotions. This is not completely true, but it is politic to keep the pressure on. The composer who is scoring your next episode calls to discuss the musical approach to a love scene. He's had second thoughts and now wants to use a synthesizer. Electronic music is becoming a cliché, but you're familiar with his work and admire him, so you tell him to use his own best judgment. A friend phones from another studio. Did you have trouble with a certain actor he is thinking of hiring? You did, but you equivocate, not wishing to cost the man a job. Your friend, unsatisfied, says he'll call someone else. More letters dictated. A telephone conversation with the head of the makeup department about wigs for an upcoming segment. Your story editor comes in and shows you the three-minute scene. The two of you polish it and send it off to be Xeroxed. You make arrangements for the five minutes to be excised from Friday's show.

11:45 A.M.

You have an appointment with the studio executive in charge of budgets. You go to his office and he complains about the money you are spending. You complain about studio inefficiency. It's a ritual. You tell him that a week ago you were filming a scene outdoors on the studio back lot, and that two other companies were filming nearby. One was doing a car chase, the other a gunfight. The noise was so deafening that your actors couldn't be heard. You had to wait for silence, and any delay, of course, results in a loss of time and money. You suggest that the production department get on the stick and schedule companies so that they don't interfere with each other. The executive tells you what you already know: eight television series and two features are being made at the same time and the lot is overcrowded. Every department is working beyond capacity. You remark that this is not your problem; your sole responsibility is your own show. He tells you that the next time you come up against noise, you should film the scene anyway and loop in the dialogue later. You say that looping is artificial, it's the enemy of good performances. He says he doesn't care—you're spending too much money. The meeting ends as it began: an impasse.

12:10 P.M.

You're late for your luncheon meeting with the director of the next show. You're always late, and you wonder if you'll ever get organized. You meet him at the commissary and the two of you grab a booth in the already crowded room. Your associate producer joins you; he's free for forty-five minutes while the sound mixers break for lunch. Your own lunch is a work session. The director has never done your show, but he will be on a soundstage filming it in a matter of days and it's your job to familiarize him with the terrain. You and he have not even met until that morning. You hired him because you had seen one or two things that he has done that you liked, and also because he had a two-week opening in his schedule. You tell him about the series, which he has never seen, and about the strengths and weaknesses of the actors. He wants to be filled in on the cameraman. Is he fast? Slow? Cooperative? He'd like to drop by the set and introduce himself. Will the current director mind? You explain that the company is going on location after lunch. He can catch up with them tomorrow. Everyone discusses casting for the new show. How many "name" actors does the network require? The director recommends several newcomers he's worked with in a local stage production. He wants to know if you can persuade the network to let two of them play lead roles. You say you'd like to meet them and then you'll see what you can do. He grumbles again about the missing last act. You apologize.

1:15 P.M.

You go to a projection room to watch the dailies of yesterday's film. With you is your editor. You work with three editors; each one is assigned a different segment of the series and they rotate on the shows. For the next half hour the two of you watch the isolated "takes" and discuss them. Your director will be long gone as soon as he completes the current episode, so you and the editor must make decisions about the cutting of the film. You point out a nice moment you'd like preserved. He suggests a staccato cutting style. Mindful of the fact that you're running short, you warn him about cutting too deeply or the show will be underlength and fail to meet its network time requirements. The editor says that if he doesn't pull it together it will just lie there. Other problems are in evidence: An actor is overplaying broadly. A brand-name cereal box is visible on a kitchen shelf and this is against network policy. The lighting is too dark in one scene. Your editor says he thinks it can be printed up; he'll run a test on it at the lab and let you know. Finally, the director's best shot of the day, involving a complicated camera move, seems to be ruined by a scratch on the film. Is it a scratch on the print or a scratch on the negative? If it's the latter it can't be used. Again, the editor says he'll check.

1:45 P.M.

Back at your office, another writer is waiting for a story conference. But your leading lady has chosen this moment to stop by. You ask the writer if he'd mind waiting. You settle the actress in your office, get her a cup of coffee, tell your secretary to hold your calls, and ask what the problem is. She says she wants to leave the show. There is really nothing for her to do. Every script is tilted toward the leading man, and she feels extraneous. She's worked only a day in each of the last three episodes. You sigh. This is not a matter of ego or temperament—she's a serious and thoroughly professional young woman, capable of fine work, but in the scramble to prepare scripts the character she plays has been slighted. You tell her that her point is well taken, but that quitting the show is far too drastic a solution. It may also cause contractual repercussions that may be harmful to her reputation. You promise to give top priority to her needs. You assure her that within a few weeks things will improve and that you will have at least two scripts prepared that will feature her. She seems mollified, asks if one of the scripts can be written by a woman. You say you'll try. She points out that you haven't hired a single woman writer. You wince; she's quite right. When she leaves she's feeling better—and she has talked you into making a cash pledge to a feminist organization she represents.

2:15 P.M.

You and the writer settle down with the first draft of his script. You give him your notes and the story editor's notes. With the memory of your previous meeting fresh in your mind, you suggest the leading lady be given more to do in one or two scenes. You also ask for a new opening; you saw something similar on another series. The writer says it's a convention of the genre, but you persuade him to try for something a bit different. He gets up to leave, promising the rewrites in a week or so. You urge him to work faster if he can, tell him his teleplay can be the basis of a good show, and try to keep his enthusiasm up.

3:15 P.M.

Your assistant director calls in from location. The company is shooting at an old railway depot in the inner city area, and things are moving at a snail's pace. The leading man doesn't know his lines and the crew is lethargic. You ask if the director is between shots. He is, and he comes to the phone. The two of you discuss the problem of lost time and he says he'll do the best he can. He complains about your crew. They seem to have broken up into factions and there is discord between the camera crew and the electrical crew. One man is apparently the ringleader. You compliment the director on his dailies and caution him about the actor who is hamming it up. The director says he'll try to hold him down, but reminds you that he didn't cast the actor—you did.

3:30 P.M.

You stop by the dubbing stage. Several reels have been sent out for new sound effects, so at the moment everyone is waiting around. Two of the mixers are playing Ping-Pong on a table in the middle of the room. You draw your associate producer aside and tell him about the reported dissension among members of the crew. You want him to spend the entire day on the set tomorrow to see if there's any evidence of friction. If so, changes will have to be made. You stop by the editing rooms and look at a trailer [a brief preview at the end of each segment] of an upcoming show. To your dismay, the editor has chosen footage that gives away several of your story surprises, including the identity of the murderer. He hasn't had time to read the script or see the show, so he doesn't know he is upsetting any applecarts. You ask him to remake the trailer, tell him what to leave out and what to add, and hurry back to your office.

4:10 P.M.

You are late for a meeting with your next director and your unit manager. A shooting schedule has been laid out and the two are already in a heated debate. Day Two is a nine-page day, with two moves, and the director feels that it is impossible. He thinks he'll be lucky to get six pages on film and suggests that the remaining three pages—a rather simple scene—should be shifted elsewhere. You suddenly remember your leading man's trip to Chicago and fill them in. They go pale. The schedule will have to be torn apart and remade. Now the art director bustles in with sketches and discusses available sets for the next show. He'd like the director to join him on a quick tour of the suggested soundstages so he can lock everything up. But the director is overscheduled—casting is coming up and he's making a day-long location scout tomorrow. The art director gets a little hysterical. Other companies want those sets. Unless a decision is made today, nothing will be available. The director cancels a business date and arranges to meet the art director on stage 12 in an hour.

5:00 P.M.

Casting. Actors line up outside the office, supplied with scripts by your secretary. You begin the process of cold readings with the director and the casting director. Each actor is allotted ten minutes, but it's an arbitrary amount of time and some of the readings take longer. By the end of the session you have interviewed and read seven actors. One or two of them are good possibilities for several of the smaller roles, but you ask for another casting session tomorrow.

6:15 P.M.

An emergency call from location. A generator has broken down and the camera and lights are inoperable. An hour has been wasted trying to phone the studio—the lines were busy—and now a replacement generator is on its way. But two hours have been lost today, and to finish tonight will require overtime. And everyone will be exhausted tomorrow. And tomorrow is only Wednesday. You commiserate, hang up, and place a call to the executive in charge of budgets. You intend to rake him over the coals because of faulty equipment and because the studio will not hire enough telephone operators to keep the lines open at peak calling hours. This is going to be the high point of your day, a good five minutes of malicious fun. But when you reach his office you find that he's left for home.

6:30 P.M.

You are making your last calls, to agents and to a reporter who wants to interview your leading man, when your story editor slouches in and collapses into a chair. You open a bottle and pour both of you a drink. He drops the new last act on your blotter for your evening reading entertainment, along with outlines for two upcoming shows that have been delivered by messenger. You both sip at your drinks and talk for a while. Your secretary buzzes; she'd like to go home. You send her off, the story editor lurches out, yawning, and you take a few moments to glance at the trade papers. Then you stuff scripts and outlines into your attaché case and greet the cleaning woman, who is waiting outside for you to depart.

6:50 P.M.

In the absence of any immediate crisis, you leave for home. There will, of course, be bumper-to-bumper traffic on the freeway.

10:15 P.M.

Your leading man calls you at home. The company has just wrapped for the day and he's blazing mad. Can't anything be done about these ridiculous hours? Can't you hire better directors? You set aside the script you were reading and begin to calm him down. . . .

None of the above is intended to generate a movement for the canonization of producers, nor is it the opening salvo in a campaign for higher salaries. But when the annual lamentations commence over the banality of much of television's output it helps to understand why those in charge—and in TV that means the producers—are so often unable to come up with anything worth watching, even though they may have the best of intentions.

The conditions described here are more or less the norm, and they are obviously inimical to good work. But they will not change as long as the industry continues to function as presently constituted. Art, if any art there be, is accidental. Everyone is too busy trying to meet deadlines to give much more than a passing thought to considerations of quality. Raising the level of the television dramatic series to the point where it would satisfy many of its critics (though possibly not the majority of its viewers) would require considerable restructuring of the system itself and, most important, the support of the audience. Neither is likely to happen until and unless the new technology changes the face of the medium as we know it.

Columbo was our baptism of fire in the world of the series. The success of *Prescription: Murder* prompted immediate network interest in furthering the adventures of the little man in the raincoat, but when Peter Falk was approached he declined. He was preoccupied with building a motion picture career and his one previous foray into series television, *The Trials of O'Brien*, had been a failure. The sheer drudgery of filming twenty-two segments, capped off by low ratings, was still fresh in his mind, so when NBC made their initial overtures he turned them down.

In terms of our own career, we had little interest in devoting a year or more of our professional lives to the good Lieutenant. We had given birth to him in a script we wrote called "Enough Rope" (which was aired on *The Chevy Mystery Show,* a summer replacement for Dinah Shore), we had shepherded the stage version into production, and we had written the two-hour television movie. By now his eccentricities had begun to pall for us and we wanted to forget him.

But the rotating mini-series, introduced by *Name of the Game,* gave NBC a new way to entice Peter Falk. Would he consider doing six episodes instead of twenty-two? He mulled it over and said that under those circumstances, a limited series that would only occupy a fraction of his time, he might be interested.

Meanwhile, we were in postproduction on *My Sweet Charlie* and were also at work on a new project: *McCloud.* A pilot script had been written by another writer, loosely based on the motion picture *Coogan's Bluff,* and Sid Sheinberg was unhappy with it. He asked us to salvage it if we could; its fate as a series depended on a major rewrite. He urged us to leave further work on the *Psychiatrist* to others and concentrate on *McCloud.* Prompted by the basest of motives, a vision of royalties from two series instead of just one, we agreed.

It was then that NBC asked us to write a new two-hour *Columbo.* Encouraged by their conversations with Falk, they now wanted a pilot. Their request struck us as absurd. They already *had* a pilot, *Prescription: Murder,* and since it had aroused all the interest in the first place, why make another? The logic of this escaped them. They had made up their minds that they wanted a second *Columbo* film and Universal was not in the business of turning down network commitments.

Mired in the world of *McCloud,* and unconvinced that *Columbo* was the stuff of series television, we suggested a compromise: We'd supply a story for the two-hour film if we didn't have to write the script. We recommended a contract writer-producer named Dean Hargrove. He was approved by the network and it was decided that once again Dick Irving would direct.

Our story involved an intricate kidnapping and murder plot, and we chose a brilliant lady lawyer for Columbo's antagonist. Hargrove wrote a charming script and Irving, with Ed Abroms as his editor, gave it a stylish production. Lee Grant was cast as the lawyer (her performance won her an Emmy nomination) and Billy Goldenberg supplied a lush and exciting music score. Aired under the title *Ransom for a Dead Man,* the show was a success, both critically and in terms of the all-important Nielsen numbers.

Each year in February or March, Manhattan is the setting for a rite of spring undreamt of by Stravinsky. Studio executives and independent producers descend on the city for what is known as "the selling season." Armed with pilot films and a backlog of "concepts," the invading horde sequesters itself in various hotel suites and begins to bombard the networks with high-powered salesmanship. The object of all of this is to get a new series on the schedule, or else keep an existing series on the air.

In recent years the nature of the selling season has changed, but in March of 1972, when Sheinberg and his associates deployed themselves at the Sherry Netherland Hotel, they had only a few weeks to hawk their wares and convince the three networks that theirs was the better mousetrap. If successful, their efforts would result in much of what America would see on its television sets in the fall.

Sheinberg, among his other offerings, had one surefire package: a ninety-minute series, aimed for a Sunday night time period, called *The NBC Mystery Movie.* It would include three rotating shows under its omnibus title: *McCloud,* which had already aired the previous season as part of a now-defunct series; *McMillan and Wife,* to star Rock Hudson in his TV debut, and *Columbo.*

What happens in New York chain-reacts—or self-destructs—in Los Angeles. When Sheinberg returned with his bag of sales, it became instantly necessary to staff all of the new shows, commission scripts, and race into production to meet September air dates. Producers immediately competed with one another for writers, cameramen, and crews. A period of tumultuous activity ensued, not only at Universal but at studios all over town.

The expected call came one morning in April and we met with Sheinberg. He asked us if we would produce *Columbo.* He also told us the ground rules: Peter Falk was due to begin rehearsals for Neil

Simon's new comedy, *The Prisoner of Seventh Avenue,* on September 12. Could we complete six ninety-minute *Columbo* films by then?

For reasons that still mystify us, we accepted the assignment. Within a few days we acquired an energetic and knowledgeable associate producer, Bob O'Neill, and Dick Irving recommended a young writer named Steven Bochco for the position of story editor. We moved to a larger suite of offices, shut the door, and began work on a ninety-minute script. Half a dozen months and several lifetimes later, not six but seven *Columbo* films were finished and ready for the verdict of the viewing public.

There was, as always, no time for reflection; we literally began making conceptual decisions on the walk from Sheinberg's office to our own. Fortunately, we had *Prescription: Murder* as a prototype. The first order of business for many series is to make radical changes as soon as the pilot is sold. But we had an instinctive feeling that there was strength in the *Prescription: Murder* format, and we decided not to vary it. Each and every *Columbo* would make use of the so-called "inverted" mystery form, a method of storytelling invented by an English writer named R. Austin Freeman in the early part of the century.

According to Ellery Queen in his study of detective fiction, *Queen's Quorum,* Freeman posed himself the following question: "Would it be possible to write a detective story in which from the outset the reader was taken entirely into the author's confidence, was made an actual witness of the crime and furnished with every fact that could possibly be used in its detection?" Freeman answered his own question by employing the device in his book, *The Singing Bone,* and based on our experience with the two Columbo movies we had a hunch that it would work on television. We had no idea that it would become an eventual trap for us and for all of the other writers who banged their heads against the wall of the inviolate *Columbo* format.

We made other decisions those first weeks, the most basic of which was that the series would not be what is known as a "cop show." We had no intention of dealing with the realities of actual police procedures. Instead, we wanted to pay our respects to the classic mystery fiction of our youth, the works of the Carrs, the Queens, and the

Christies. We knew that no police officer on earth would be permitted to dress as shabbily as Columbo, or drive a car as desperately in need of burial, but in the interest of flavorful characterization we deliberately chose not to be realistic. Our show would be a fantasy, and as such it would avoid the harsher aspects of a true policeman's life: the drug busts, the street murders, the prostitutes, and the back-alley shoot-outs.

We would create a mythical Los Angeles and populate it with affluent men and women living in the stately homes of the British mystery novel; our stories would be much closer in spirit to Dorothy L. Sayers than to Joseph Wambaugh. Besides, our rumpled cop would be much more amusing if he were always out of his element, playing his games of cat-and-mouse in the mansions and watering holes of the rich. We even decided never to show him at police headquarters or at home; it seemed to us much more effective if he drifted into our stories from limbo.

When the series went on the air many critics found it an ever-so-slightly subversive attack on the American class system in which a proletarian hero triumphed over the effete and monied members of the Establishment. But the reason for this was dramatic rather than political. Given the persona of Falk as an actor, it would have been foolish to play him against a similar type, a Jack Klugman, for example, or a Martin Balsam. Much more fun could be had if he were confronted by someone like Noel Coward.

It was a matter of contrast and juxtaposition. In the country, the country mouse is just another mouse. But in the city, where he's likely to become the object of amused condescension on the part of his urban brothers, he's far more interesting. And since much of Columbo's character is reactive, the opulent settings and smooth-as-silk antagonists gave him something to respond to.

Our final decision was to keep the series nonviolent. There would be a murder, of course, but it would be sanitized and barely seen. Columbo would never carry a gun. He would never be involved in a shooting or a car chase (he'd be lucky, in fact, if his car even started when he turned the key), nor would he ever have a fight. The show would be the American equivalent of the English drawing room murder mystery, dependent almost entirely on dialogue and ingenuity to keep it afloat.

Because of these elements—and constraints—*Columbo* was a difficult show to write for. The format was reasonably new, and many of the writers we approached either didn't understand it or else understood all too well and felt it wasn't worth the effort. They could hardly be blamed. Most of the detective series of the time were relatively easy to construct. Story lines followed predictable patterns and if things got dull an action sequence could always be inserted to provide momentum. But we didn't want action. In its place we were asking for a cerebral battle of wits between only two characters. Each episode had to contain an elaborate perfect crime, as well as a satisfying and surprising solution to that crime. We needed complicated plots, clues, and an endless variety of purely verbal confrontation scenes.

We arranged a screening of *Ransom for a Dead Man* for sixty-odd free-lance writers. Such screenings are common; they are a way of introducing writers to a new show. In theory they will whet the appetites of those assembled who will then hurry home, explode with ideas, and contact the producer with requests for meetings. In our case, only two out of the sixty expressed any interest. One of these was Jackson Gillis, a veteran of the long-running *Perry Mason* series and an expert at mystery plotting. Gillis wrote two scripts for our first season and thereafter became *Columbo*'s story editor for several years.

Because of the difficulty in finding writers, most of our scripts were put together "in house." We would plot them, Bochco would rough out a first draft, and then everyone would do a final polish. We'd often sit in the office having daylong story sessions that would end in near-migraines for everyone in the room. Friends were pulled out of the halls for reactions. A writer-director named Larry Cohen dropped by to say hello and was immediately put to work on an idea that had resisted all of our efforts. He quickly solved it, and because he was that rara avis, a writer who understood the show, Universal employed him in future seasons just to come up with *Columbo* story premises.

Our first scripts made their way to the network and the response was not effusive: NBC had major "conceptual concerns" with our approach. How could we have made the terrible blunder of keeping our leading man offstage until twenty minutes into the show? Didn't we realize that Peter Falk was our star? The audience would expect to see him at once, and here we were perversely delaying his appearance. One of the executives called it, with considerable heat, "the longest stage wait in television history."

There were other complaints. What was this business about an unseen wife? * And why a wife at all? Columbo should be free of any marital encumbrances so that he could have romantic interludes on occasion. Why hadn't we given him the traditional "family" of regulars? At the very least he should have a young and appealing cop as his assistant and confidant. And worst of all, the scripts were talky. They should be enlivened by frequent doses of adrenalin in the form of our old friends "tempo" and "jeopardy."

There are only four responses a writer-producer can make to network suggestions: He can ignore them, he can cave in, he can argue, or he can threaten to quit. We opted for the last of these multiple choices. We also pretended to a confidence we didn't feel in the hope that conviction, or at least the illusion of conviction, would be persuasive in an industry plagued by uncertainty. And we were lucky; we

---

* Mrs. Columbo became all too visible several seasons later when she was yanked in from the wings to star in a series of her own. Her emergence into the limelight was the brainstorm of Fred Silverman, who had just left ABC to become the president of a foundering NBC.

We were asked to participate, but the venture was such a flagrant ripoff, and seemed so ill-conceived, that we declined. Universal owned all television rights to the Columbo name, and they cheerfully proceeded without us. We did, however, make one recommendation: that Maureen Stapleton be offered the leading role. But NBC insisted on Kate Mulgrew, an actress from the daytime soaps. Although a capable performer, Miss Mulgrew was hopelessly miscast; everything about her was almost guaranteed to violate viewer expectations. Still, she had the advantage of being young, and youthful set-owners – the most desirable audience in the eyes of the advertiser – are presumed by the networks to run screaming from their homes if a wrinkled face appears on screen.

Mrs. Columbo went on the air and fared poorly, but to the surprise of the industry Silverman renewed it. There was the obligatory salvaging operation – a divorce was decreed for the poor woman and the series was christened with a new title, *Kate Loves a Mystery* – but the ratings continued to dwindle and Kate was finally given the *coup de grace* in the ritual bloodletting of mid-season.

had time on our side. If *Columbo* was to meet its air dates the scripts had to be filmed as written. Any delay, caused either by conceptual changes or a walkout by the creative personnel, would throw the series hopelessly off schedule. NBC backed away and grudgingly left us to our own devices.

And then there was Peter Falk. Stars of television series are not a particularly homogeneous group. Some of them, a Robert Young or an Arthur Hill, are agreeable types who learn their lines, say them well, and go home. Others are temperamental and thrive on chaos. Falk was a breed apart. He returned to television reluctantly after a happy filmmaking experience (*Husbands*) with his friends John Cassavetes and Ben Gazzara, and we suspected that he had a deep psychological resistance to the idea of doing a series. Then too, he was mistrustful. He barely knew us and he resented putting himself and his career in our hands. It soon became evident that his method of protecting himself was to try to exercise control over the elements of the show. A clash was inevitable.

Clash we did. But it was a strange kind of jockeying for power, since Falk was as intelligent an actor as we had ever worked with, and he was almost as familiar with the Columbo character as we were. He was also extremely likable; even in the midst of an argument we couldn't help feeling a genuine affection for him. But in matters of metabolism and methods of operation, we and Falk were very far apart. Under the gun of the ever-present deadlines of series television, we were inclined to make rapid decisions and move on to the next crisis. Falk, on the other hand, tended to mull and ponder; he didn't like to be rushed and wanted to keep his options open. In an uncanny way he was very much like Columbo: clever, reflective, and oblique. And so a Pirandello-esque game of cat-and-mouse was played out in our office as well as in our scripts.

By early May we were all involved in intrigues worthy of John Le Carre. Falk insisted that someone he trusted be placed on our staff to look out for his interests. As soon as this was done we noticed that he somehow mysteriously managed to acquire advance copies of our scripts in outline and rough first drafts. These were not nearly ready to be seen; quite naturally he was dissatisfied with them and tended to view with suspicion our promises that they would be improved by rewriting. We countered his ploy by keeping all material under lock and key. He made it a habit to drop by the editing rooms to monitor the progress of various segments. We instructed our editors to close their doors or to actually leave the building if Falk approached. When he insisted that he wanted to watch dailies, we wrote scenes that had to be filmed away from the studio, scheduling them so that he would be on location when dailies were shown.

All of this was a foolish waste of energy, but given the siege mentality of series television, a sense of proportion is difficult to maintain. Falk was insecure and trying to make a contribution. Actors are usually powerless to control their fates in television, and he was seeking any leverage he could find. But we were equally insecure, and we resented his intrusion into areas that were primarily our responsibility.

In a strange way his intransigence was useful. The studio insisted that each of our segments had to be filmed in ten days, a woefully inadequate schedule. But Falk refused to be hurried. In the middle of shooting he would engage the directors in lengthy discussions of story and character and we would invariably drift into overtime. Each episode took longer and longer to make–twelve days, thirteen days, even fourteen days–until word got around that we were a "problem" show with a "difficult" star. When studio executives tried to pressure Falk he would explode into diatribes about the Universal assembly line. He had not played killers and gangsters for nothing; a Falk eruption was chilling to behold. The executives would retreat to the safety of their Tower offices; they were up against a shrewd street fighter and they didn't know how to deal with him. All of which left us with more time to make a better show. Falk knew exactly what he was doing, and for once his interests and ours coincided.

Whatever our complaints about him, there was no denying that he seemed born to play the role. When we created Columbo we were influenced by the bureaucratic Petrovitch in *Crime and Punishment* and by G. K. Chesterton's marvelous little cleric, Father Brown. But Falk added a childlike wonder all his own. He also added the raincoat and

wore the same suit, shirt, tie, and shoes for the entire six-year run of
the series, giving *Columbo* the somewhat dubious distinction of having
the lowest budget for male wardrobe in the history of the medium,
with the possible exception of Big Bird.

Falk cared deeply about the series, and our conflicts with him were
never personal. But there were some epic fireworks. In our first script,
for example, we had written a scene where Columbo, driving to the
site of a crime, was pulled over by a motorcycle cop because one of his
headlights was broken. Falk felt the sequence was unbelievable; no
one could have a shattered headlight without knowing it. For hours
on end the three of us debated this idiotic point in voices loud
enough to prompt others in the building to complain. Finally we
took our unresolved argument to lunch. But as we crossed the lot
toward the commissary we happened to notice Falk's Jaguar parked
nearby. One of its headlights was broken. Confronted by this, Falk
thought it over, Columbo-like, and gave in on the story point. He
even picked up our lunch checks.

Some of the turmoil stemmed from the fact that Falk had nothing
to do during the long weeks of preproduction. Once the series began
filming, however, his energies were fully engaged and there was quiet
on the battlefield—until he got it into his head that he wanted to
direct.

It is not unusual for the lead actor of a series to direct an occasional
segment. But it rarely happens in the first season. And few television
characters have as much to do in each show as Columbo. Nevertheless, Falk was adamant. The studio took the position that he had been
employed to act, not direct, and we were suddenly confronted with
the irresistible force and the immovable object—with us in between.

Falk let it be known that he was not feeling well. He was ignored.
Then his illness apparently overpowered him and he took to his bed.
We had one more day to film on our third episode and no leading
man. Desperately, we dressed another actor in the raincoat and filmed
him from behind, hoping that Falk would dub in the voice at a later
date.

Our schedule rapidly fell apart. Falk returned, he was briefly suspended, then he was reinstated. Agents and lawyers descended on the

Black Tower with notes from his doctor. Threats of litigation filled the already sulfurous air. Our offices took on the aspect of the Berlin bunker during the last days of World War II. NBC was in a corporate frenzy; they liked the footage they were seeing and they had even put in an order for an additional segment. Now, suddenly, it was possible there wouldn't be any *Columbo* at all.

When in doubt, capitulate. At least that seemed to be Universal's view. After weeks of resolute firmness the studio, pressured by the network, gave in to Falk's demands. We were instructed to find a suitable script for him to direct. Falk was an instant hero to every actor on every television series. He had, to coin a misshapen metaphor, brought the Black Tower to its knees.

We had been expecting a collapse in the studio's position and we were in a vengeful mood, so when we presented Falk with his script it was fashioned, by design, to drive even the most experienced director out of his mind. The villain was an architect, and much of the picture would have to be filmed at a construction site. We had already picked the location: Century City, a massive new development of steel and glass. Scenes would be shot in a gigantic hole in the ground, swimming with dust, while an actual office building was being erected. The excavation had the look of a crater on the moon.

To Falk's credit, he prepared diligently. He consulted with other directors and even spent his weekends at the construction site lining up shots. But the filming of the picture was a nightmare for him. He picked up a cold and almost lost his voice. Concentration was impossible because of the perpetual din of pneumatic drills and rivet guns. And work on the building never stopped; nothing as insignificant as a television crew was going to halt the march of progress. Every time Falk would change his mind about a shot and try to reshoot it he would discover his set was no longer there—a girder had gone up where his actors had stood moments before. We took to visiting the location and smiling down at him from the rim of the hole. He'd shake his fist at us and plow on with the filming.

Interestingly, the picture that emerged was well-directed. But Falk's performance was off. The adrenalin he needed to direct tended to interfere with his acting; he couldn't calm himself sufficiently as he ran from one side of the camera to the other, and so the usually low-key character of Columbo became, in this one instance, almost manic. But the construction site gave us fascinating production values and we were pleased with the film. It was the most expensive of all the *Columbos*, but the studio was too sheepish to complain about costs. As of this writing, Falk has never directed again.

For a seemingly simple show composed mainly of conversation, *Columbo* was a potential minefield for directors. Given its essentially static nature it needed visual variety, and to that end we played as many of our scenes as possible against arresting backgrounds. Falk's hole in the ground was but one example. Our other directors had to contend with chemical plants, yachts, and even an actual cable car suspended halfway up a mountainside.

We asked Ed Abroms if he would supervise our editing, and his contribution was invaluable. He inserted optical effects that amused the eye, his pacing energized any number of sluggish scenes, and whenever any of our actors—including Falk—got an advanced case of the cutes, Abroms would snip out the offending footage and leave it on the cutting room floor. In gratitude we assigned him the last episode of the season to direct, and he was the only director to bring us in on schedule.

Another of our directors was a young man who had been at Universal for a while and whose short subject, *Amblin'*, had impressed us. Almost casually we asked him if he'd like to do a *Columbo*, and just as casually he agreed. We were completely unprepared for the technical skill and visual imagination of his work, and when he showed us his first cut we told him to freeze it; it certainly needed no help from us. His name was Steven Spielberg, and he rapidly moved into motion pictures where he directed *Jaws* and *Close Encounters of the Third Kind*.

The look of a series is the province of the cinematographer. Many shows have a flat and one-dimensional appearance; light is pumped in with no regard for artistic effect. This approach saves time, but in our view it's unsatisfying. We agree with those who scornfully refer to it as "color by jellybean." But on *Columbo* we had the opposite problem: our cameraman, Russ Metty, insisted on a dark and murky look for the series, while we thought it should have a brighter feeling.

"It's a cop show," he would mutter. "You want it to look like a goddamn musical?" Metty was a member of the old school and not easily budged. He had photographed *Touch of Evil* for Orson Welles (he told us Welles was a "nice kid") and our explanations about *Columbo* being a *different* kind of cop show fell on deaf ears. We finally learned that his secret vice was a taste for fine cigars, and after we presented him with a box of Monte Cristos the lighting miraculously improved.

September 12 approached, and Falk prepared to leave for New York and the Neil Simon play. Ironically, during the final weeks the three of us found ourselves in frequent agreement on most of the decisions affecting the show. We had developed a grudging respect for his instincts. And Falk, after attempting to write a script for the series (he came up with a promising first act and then ran headlong into trouble), began to see why good material was not in plentiful supply. It had been an education for all of us—stormy, but not without value.

Seven *Columbo*s were now scattered about the Universal lot in various stages of completion, some in editing, some in scoring, some in dubbing. The members of our crew were absorbed by other shows. We had not even been on the air and our work was almost finished. It was an odd feeling: there would be no out-of-town tinkering and our mistakes could never be corrected. Ten and a half hours of film had been assembled in five months, and now there was little for us to do but wait for our national opening night.

The impact of a successful television series is a peculiar phenomenon of popular culture. Best-selling novels, hit plays, and even highly acclaimed motion pictures take many months to filter into the consciousness of the public. But the fallout from a series, or a mini-series such as *Shōgun,* can be instantaneous.

Columbo was an immediate popular and critical success, quickly establishing itself as the hit of the new season, and within weeks the character, the raincoat, and even some of the show's catch-phrases were popping up in newspapers and magazines across the country. Peter Falk imitations were impossible to avoid on variety programs and nightclubs, and stoop-shouldered and squinty-eyed ten year olds drove their parents close to the brink with dialogue from the various episodes. More recently, a *Jaws* or a *Star Wars* would have the same effect, but this was in the early seventies, long before media hype became the art form of the decade.

The series began its run among the ten-most-watched television programs of the week and it stayed in that position for years, frequently moving into the number-one slot. The inevitable *Columbo* game was marketed and *Columbo* books, in one of the first of the now-prevalent publishing tie-ins, made their appearance on the nation's paperback racks. Falk, backstage in *The Prisoner of Seventh Avenue,* complained that no one visited his dressing room to discuss the play; all they wanted to talk about was Lieutenant Columbo.

We were, of course, delighted. We gave interviews praising Falk. He gave interviews praising us. He was on the cover of *Time* magazine, which proclaimed "The Year of the TV Cop" and called *Columbo* "the most influential, probably the best, and certainly the most endearing cop series on TV." The critical community took notice not only of the show, but of the scripts. Cecil Smith, the television columnist, spoke of "the brightest dialogue and most intricate plots around." And when the Television Academy released its nominations for the Emmy, every single writer in the Best Writing Achievement in Drama category was the author of a *Columbo* script. On the night of the awards ceremony Falk won an Emmy, as did we, and as did Ed Abroms for Best Editing.

The NBC Mystery Movie, including *Columbo,* received a quick renewal, but we decided not to stay with it for a second season. We wanted to do another motion picture for television and we needed a respite from the demands of the series form. The studio wasn't happy with our decision, but we pointed out that the style of the show was now well known and scripts wouldn't be quite as hard to come by. We also promised to contribute some stories for the second batch of six or seven episodes.

As the summer before the second season approached, NBC ruminated and gave birth to two ideas. The first was that *Columbo,* in spite of its success, needed another continuing character. With malice aforethought, we decided to give them one. Steven Bochco was writing a script and we asked him to introduce a new member of the Columbo family—a dog. He gleefully complied, inserting a nameless mongrel into his teleplay. Somehow the most incredibly ugly beast in Los Angeles was found to play the part. It was an inspired choice. The dog looked like a blob of Silly-Putty, and in scene after scene it remained so totally inert that it almost seemed to be stuffed. The film was screened for NBC executives and there were no further requests for another continuing character. Unfortunately, the original dog died—an event that almost went unnoticed given the poor creature's monumental passivity—and its replacement, though capable, lacked star quality.

The network's second suggestion was more damaging. They reasoned that if *Columbo* was a hit at ninety minutes, it would be even more successful if the episodes were inflated to two hours. Universal, mindful of the excessive cost of the series, quickly agreed. Another thirty minutes would bring more money from NBC and some of the overages could be absorbed. Economically, it was a good idea. Creatively, it was a disaster. Scripts were padded. Scenes were filmed and inserted to bring the program up to length. Over the next few seasons there were more and more two-hour *Columbo*s. This was also true of the other shows on *The NBC Mystery Movie,* but *McCloud* and *McMillan and Wife* had looser formats and could more easily incorporate the added time. *Columbo* remained a hit, but we came to feel that very few of the segments could justify the additional thirty minutes.

Novelty and style are valuable aspects to any creative enterprise, but it's almost axiomatic that they will wear out their welcome over time. One cannot read successive doses of Hemingway without the eventual feeling that enough is enough. Conversely, the works of less stylistic writers will not be as irritating because they are not as distinctive; in the McLuhanesque sense they are "cool" as opposed to "hot."

In television terms, *Dragnet* is an example of this effect. What was originally a fresh and inventive style of storytelling became, through endless repetition, virtual self-parody. *Columbo* had the same problem. The very qualities that made it interesting eventually gave it a feeling of predictability. And the two-hour shows only emphasized this weakness. In a way it had no business being a series; it wasn't conceived for longevity.

There are theories, however, that television audiences like repetition. They certainly liked *Columbo,* and they stayed with it long after it had passed the point of diminishing returns. Fortunately, in Peter Falk the show had a star of great staying power. In our absence he gradually took over full control. Producers came and went—six more followed us over the years—but Falk was the constant, and in many ways this was beneficial. He fought for better scripts, publicized the series as often as he could, and enriched and deepened his performance. In our opinion he wasn't ruthless enough in the editing room—he allowed Columbo to linger far too long and far too cloyingly on the screen—but the continuing success of the series was largely due to his efforts.

Columbo was distributed around the world. It even managed to supplant televised baseball as a national obsession of the Japanese. And its popularity in Rumania was such that the State Department asked Falk to make a brief film explaining to the Rumanians—who were apparently on the verge of riot—that more *Columbo*s would be forthcoming.

It also spawned a host of imitations, so-called "character cops." The first was Barnaby Jones, and then Cannon. A year or so later Kojak made his debut, sucking on a lollipop instead of a cigar. If Columbo was a shabby cop in elegant surroundings, Kojak was just the opposite: an elegant cop in shabby surroundings, with macho Greek bravado in place of Columbo's rumpled humanity. Finally there was Baretta, and Robert Blake began to out-Falk Falk, replacing him as the new nemesis of the Black Tower.

Younger writers gave the series needed infusions of talent. One of them, Steven J. Cannell, went on to co-create *The Rockford Files.* Another, Peter Fischer, became *Columbo*'s story editor before joining us on the *Ellery Queen* series and then creating *The Eddie Capra Mysteries,* a series of his own.

Columbo survived for six seasons, outlasting the other programs on the *Mystery Movie.* It won many more Emmys, including another to Falk, and it continued to enjoy a vast following. Our only connection with the series was to read the scripts and send notes to the revolving-door producers. We'd usually have a post-mortem lunch with Falk after each segment aired, and once in a while he'd call us for advice on scripts, but that was the extent of our participation.

Richard Alan Simmons became *Columbo*'s producer during its final season. He knew Falk well–he had produced *The Trials of O'Brien*–and the series finished on a high note. When we complimented him on his efforts he shook his head somberly and complained about the around-the-clock rewriting, the struggle for material, and the fact that he was working so many nights and weekends he barely had time to see his wife. It sounded very familiar.

Falk moved on to a motion picture career. *Columbo* had been both a help and a hindrance to him. It gave him wide recognition, but it also threatened to permanently identify him with just one role. The last time we saw him he had remarried and was uncharacteristically mellow. We told him that we missed working with him. He may have been a monster, but he was *our* monster, and we had a certain masochistic nostalgia for the *Sturm und Drang* of that first season.

We recalled a meeting with him soon after the series had established itself as a hit. He had just returned from New York and we informed him that we were leaving the show. He was genuinely distressed and urged us to stay. Surprised, we reminded him that the three of us were in constant conflict. We had kept him away from dailies, we had hidden scripts, we had even ordered the editors to lock their doors to him. Why on earth would he want us to continue for a second season? Falk smiled. "Because now," he said, "I trust you."

5 / That Certain Summer

Controversy on Television

Kenneth Tynan, the British critic, once complained that the New York play going audience looks upon the theater as an after-dinner mint, and much the same is often said of the television audience. The phrase, "When I get home from a hard day's work I want to be entertained," is reputedly the cry of the Common Man, and the networks have all but embroidered it into flags to be waved in the faces of those who have the audacity to suggest there might be a national appetite for thought-provoking and unsettling material. Even intellectuals are rumored to go slumming when they turn on their sets—though Shakespeare, Pinter, and Robert Graves may be available on PBS, many of them succumb to *Charlie's Angels* and *Mork and Mindy.*

"Entertainment" is taken to mean "light diversion." The possibility of capturing and holding a mass audience with serious fare (or what passes for serious fare relative to the general run of prime-time TV) is rarely acknowledged. But the audience is a contrary beast. *Holocaust,* for example, violated every rule of sound programming: it was unrelentingly grim and it dealt with some of the most tragic events in all human experience. Yet it was watched in near-record numbers, presumably by the same viewers who made *Three's Company* into a national hit. Since it lacked star power in the form of recognizable "name actors," one can assume (time period and the nature of the competition aside) that the audience chose to watch it on the basis of its subject matter. And since the systematic extermination of European Jewry hardly fits the "after-dinner mint" philosophy, it follows that the definition of "entertainment" may not be quite so narrow after all.

More often than not the Common Man watches pap, as expected—but then he perversely tunes into *Holocaust* or *Roots,* or even worse, he makes *60 Minutes* into a hit show, when everybody knows that documentaries are supposed to be the least popular form of programming. His occasional tendency to fly in the face of the predictable provides a loophole through which some of the better television films are able to maneuver.

Another reason why the networks will risk quality drama is that these shows often get a flurry of publicity before they are aired. And publicity is essential because of a little-noted difference between the television movie on the one hand, and series, books, plays, and motion pictures on the other: word of mouth does not exist for the individual telefilm until *after it is over.* The electronic theater opens for business and then closes on the same night. There can be no ground swell, no recommendation passed along from friend to friend, no "sleeper" that catches fire and gains momentum.

All of the talk, therefore, must be generated "up front." The audience did not know that *The Autobiography of Miss Jane Pittman* was a fine drama until *after* they had seen it. But the *reason* they watched (like *Holocaust* it had no star names to attract them) was because the critical press, in rare unanimity, told them it was worth their time.*

Because post-show word of mouth is useless, the networks seek to create pre-show excitement, and one way of doing this (buttressed by heavy on-air promotion) is to lean in the direction of exploitable material. Sex is exploitable. The human animal's triumph over crippling disease is exploitable. Major stars (though rarely major writers and directors) are exploitable. And controversy is exploitable. But

---

* Even Pauline Kael reviewed *Pittman.* This was an unusual departure for her, and quotes from her notice in the *New Yorker* were used as part of the promotion for the film.

controversy is a double-edged sword. It may attract an audience, but it is also risky because of potential backlash from sponsors, the government, affiliates, or pressure groups.

As already noted, Reginald Rose's *The Defenders* was the first television series that made a specialty of controversial subject matter. Week in and week out it examined such issues as abortion, euthanasia, and blacklisting. Toward the end of its run it grew a little desperate and was reduced to doing a story about cannibalism, but for the most part it was a responsible series and received awards and respectful critical attention. The only complaints were that it sometimes sidestepped the very issues that it raised, and that all too often it stacked the deck—the abortionist, for example, was almost Christ-like in his decency, and a far cry from the more typical back-room abortion-mill practitioner of the time. But the series was an attempt at something new, and as such was entitled to its mistakes.

East Side, West Side also confronted social problems (including the death by rat bites of a black ghetto child). Starring George C. Scott as a social worker, it was more realistic than *The Defenders*—there were seldom neat solutions or happy endings—and perhaps as a consequence it quickly went off the air.

Other series, including *Dr. Kildare, Ben Casey, Judd for the Defense,* and *Sam Benedict* occasionally ventured into controversial waters, and in the seventies there was a brief vogue for "relevancy" dramas about storefront lawyers and the drug culture. But it was the situation comedy, not the dramatic series, that made controversy a way of life on television, most notably on the shows produced under the wing of Norman Lear. *All in the Family* was audacious from the start, and once it was firmly established Lear used it as a vehicle to explore everything from racial prejudice to sexual dysfunctions. Some grumbled that he and his writers merely skimmed along the surface of complex issues, but others felt that the very raising of these issues over the public airwaves, particularly on a series of such wide popular appeal, had a salutory effect.

Maude followed in the tradition of *All in the Family,* trailing in its wake still more controversial themes: alcoholism, male menopause, and a reprise of the abortion issue. But in this case the abortion was not handled with kid gloves—Maude was pregnant, she decided she didn't want a child, and after considerable soul-searching she had it aborted. There was a vast hue and cry when the program was aired (the network received 24,000 letters of protest), but aired it was, and Lear pressed on.

Inevitably, controversy became an end in itself, almost a gimmick. It was injected arbitrarily into one show after another for the sole purpose of attracting attention. Writers took to congratulating themselves for their courage in violating taboos. As one of them remarked to us proudly, "I did the Vietnam war on a Western a few weeks ago. Sort of an allegory." A *Maude* writer of our acquaintance seemed annoyed that *The Mary Tyler Moore Show* wasn't controversial enough. "I heard they finally got some guts," he told us wryly. "They're doing a show that takes a stand against mayonnaise."

He missed the point, of course, that controversy in and of itself has nothing to do with whether or not a show is esthetically (as opposed to socially) worthwhile. One of the best, and arguably the most famous single television drama was Paddy Chayevsky's *Marty,* and it was hardly controversial. Its theme was human loneliness, and it made its mark without shock value or heavily underlined social significance.

Still, its understandable why television writers are fascinated to the point of excess by subject matter that was previously forbidden. After years of being muzzled by sponsor and network restrictions, they have at long last been permitted to deal with contemporary experience on a less than superficial level. The time is not far gone when a gas company sponsor of *Playhouse 90* blipped out the word "gas" when it was used to describe concentration camp ovens on *Judgement at Nuremberg.* In the recent past blacks were transformed into whites, ethnic backgrounds were replaced by vague and inoffensive Mittel-European antecedents, homosexuals didn't exist except in the limp-wristed routines of stand-up comics, and men and women never talked about sexual activities, much less indulged in them. Even in 1969, when *My Sweet Charlie* was made, there was strong resistance, although it was beginning to be reflexive.

Mild as they may seem today, *Charlie* and *Silent Night, Lonely Night* were the first controversial motion pictures made for television. Since then the audience has been confronted by rape, child abuse, wife beating, and even incest—and one waits with teeth on edge for the first teleplay about necrophilia. Many of these dramas are seriously intended. Others are "safe controversy," in which a writer may take a militant stand against, say, prejudice (an act of courage comparable to throwing one's support behind the condemnation of bacteriological warfare) and yet have the advantage of being able to throw all those emotion-charged racial epithets around. *Hardcore,* a theatrical film of a few years back, is a perfect example of the have-your-cake-and-eat-it school. The writer-director took the audience on a seamy tour of the underbelly of the pornography industry, but his moral posture was one of contempt. While he was exploiting his subject matter he was also excoriating it, thus having it both ways.

Hollywood is a relatively liberal community, and as Ben Stein pointed out in his curious book, *The View from Sunset Boulevard,* many of television's writer-producers are anti–big business, pro-poor, and anti-military. Stein can be faulted for his narrow choice of interview subjects, as well as for the broadness of his generalizations, but he came up with some interesting hypotheses. And it's a fact that no television movie has taken a position in favor of the Ku Klux Klan or against welfare. TV advocacy usually reflects liberal attitudes. This is not to suggest that an organized conspiracy is afoot, or that Spiro Agnew was right when he chastised an in-group affinity for some left-of-center party line. But it should be noted that many controversial television films—including ours—are manifestations of a liberal (one might more accurately say "humanistic") philosophy.

In the final analysis no one, neither the creators of a drama, nor the audience, nor the critics, should be seduced by subject matter alone. The important thing to consider is the quality of the work. Some years ago an impressive series called *The Senator* did a two-parter that was loosely based on the National Guard shootings at Kent State. It was ponderous propaganda, discursive and doctrinaire, and virtually reeking with self-importance. Yet on the same series there was a simple story (written by Joel Oliansky, who also wrote *The Law)* about a man assigned to serve as a bodyguard for the senator. It was impeccably done, well written, well acted, and well directed. Really nothing more than a character sketch, an anecdote, but in realizing its intentions it was head and shoulders above the more bloated Kent State story, although the latter was far more "controversial."

We have received more than our share of praise for exploring so-called forbidden territory, but our chief satisfaction comes when someone tells us that he or she was moved by something we wrote. It's easy to pick a controversial subject out of a hat. The difficult part is to make it come alive.

When we finished our work on *Columbo* we were certainly not searching for anything controversial. All we wanted was an idea for a television film that we could noodle along at a leisurely pace. We needed an antidote to the near-hysteria of series production, and the last thing on our minds was to become involved in a confrontation over one of television's major taboos.

One day in late 1971, after a morning of much coffee and little creative output, we stopped by the office of a director friend who had recently come to the studio. During the conversation we invited him to lunch, but he declined. One of his two sons was visiting him that afternoon and he wanted to be available.

It was only after we had left his office that we remembered he was a homosexual. It was not a dark secret; he had introduced us to his male lover, and though he was not blatant about his proclivities, neither did he make any great effort, in the comparatively tolerant atmosphere of the entertainment industry, to hide them. We knew he had been divorced, and yet the fact that he had children caught us by surprise. Did his family know about his sexual preferences? What happened to the lover when the sons came to town? Was he sent packing for the duration or was he on casual display? How did a man make the transition from a heterosexual to a homosexual way of life— and, most interesting, what were the effects of such a profound metamorphosis on his children?

At first we asked ourselves these questions out of simple curiosity. We had a number of homosexual acquaintances, but none had been married, and the combination of the so-called "alternate life-style" with the act of parenting was new to our experience. Curiosity quickly gave way to professional interest, and we found that we were thinking of the situation in terms of its story potential. What would happen if a divorced father, a homosexual who looks forward to annual summer visits from his son, were to take a male lover and set up housekeeping in a kind of marriage, conventional except for its lack of legal sanction and, of course, the gender of the "spouse"? How would he deal with his son's next visit, especially if the boy, who is on the threshold of his own sexual awareness, has never been told the truth?

The idea fascinated us, but given the realities of television we assumed it would have to be written as a short story, or play, or a book. Homosexuality, not quite yet a political cause and anathema to many Americans, was simply too threatening to be the stuff of TV drama. Those who didn't consider it an aberration would rather not discuss it at all, and it seemed doubtful that they would welcome a film on the subject, however carefully rendered, into their homes.

At one time on Broadway the plays of Williams, Inge, and Albee had been forced to resort to evasions and euphemisms. But the theater had finally loosened up–the word "shit" had been uttered in a Lillian Hellman play without the shade of Anthony Comstock charging up the aisle–and *The Boys in the Band,* dealing openly with homosexual relationships, had been a success. Mainstream fiction, as Gore Vidal discovered to his dismay when he published *The City and The Pillar,* was loath to traffic in homosexual themes, but John Retchy's *City of Night* had become a best-seller and Publishers Row had suddenly (and pragmatically) entered into a new age of enlightened open-mindedness. Even motion pictures, always a step or two behind the stage and the novel, had given audiences Penelope Gilliatt's fine study of an aging homosexual *in extremis, Sunday, Bloody Sunday.* But television? Not likely.

This fact was borne home when we casually mentioned the idea to an NBC executive. He looked at us with genuine alarm and said, "We wouldn't touch something like that with a ten-foot pole." It was perfectly acceptable for Bob Hope or Johnny Carson to mince about the screen doing broad parodies of homosexual behavior, but anything else, anything not derisive or played for laughs, was out of the question.

Our own attitudes about homosexuality were moderately liberal and not especially complex. When we thought about it at all we felt that what consenting adults did in private was pretty much their own business. And in our minds the piece we were contemplating was not a "homosexual" drama—rather, it was the story of a father and son.

Early in January we had lunch with Alan Epstein, a young executive at ABC. His network was now fully in the business of making television movies, although, unlike NBC's two-hour productions, ABC's films were ninety minutes in length and they were called *Movies of the Week* instead of *World Premieres.* Alan asked if we had any ideas for telefilms and we said yes, we had one, but his network wouldn't go near it. As expected he insisted that we tell him the premise ("premise" being a favorite television word that is used interchangeably with "story" or "notion"—i.e., "What's the premise of *Finegans Wake?"*) We told him and he surprised us; instead of backing away he seemed interested. "Would you do me a favor and tell this to Barry?" he asked.

By "Barry" he meant Barry Diller, the executive in charge of ABC's TV film division. We had never met Diller, but in the small world of network television he was a controversial figure. In only a few years he had moved from the mailroom of the William Morris Agency to his present position, and he was reputed to be difficult, opinionated, and in absolute control of his projects. We agreed to a meeting with great reluctance. NBC, by dint of our long relationship with them, had begun to trust our judgment. But ABC was a new ball park. Why did we have to prove ourselves all over again? The answer, of course, was that NBC had a ten-foot pole that wouldn't touch our story, and if we wanted it on the air we had only two other markets. Since CBS was not clamoring at our door, we had little choice but to enter the lion's den.

The lion's den was white and contemporary, an airy inner sanctum with windows overlooking Sunset Boulevard and a silver pop art shopping bag in a glass case. Diller was brisk, intense, and professional, not at all the arbitrary martinet we had been led to expect. He listened as we described our idea in a few sentences and then, without preamble, he said, "I like it. You have a deal."

We were somewhat at a loss. Decisiveness is not a hallmark of network executives. Diller seemed ready to close the meeting; as far as he was concerned our business was at an end. We quickly came up with two conditions. One was that we would write a script rather than an outline. And the other was that after we completed thirty or so pages we would turn them in. If we and Diller liked them we would finish the teleplay. But if we were dissatisfied–or he was–we would all agree to forget the whole thing. Our reason for this second condition was our concern that we wouldn't be able to pull it off. With a script on a less delicate subject we could afford to fail, but with this material a failure would not only be a public embarrassment, it might also reinforce unfortunate stereotypes.

Again, Diller gave his assent. He told us there would be corporate problems because of the nature of the project, but he assured us he was fully behind it and would fight to have it made. So much for prejudging on the basis of reputation.

Writing what eventually came to be called *That Certain Summer* (a title we dislike to this day) was not as troublesome as we expected. Once we realized, after conversations with homosexuals and psychiatrists, and after considerable reading in the field, that absolutely no one agreed on the causes or even the exact nature of homosexuality, we were freed from our somewhat clinical frame of mind and began to ponder what our characters would do in a given situation as individuals, not as prototypical representations of a certain way of life.

Strangely, our most difficult creative problem was to find an occupation for our protagonist, Doug Salter. Clichés instantly suggested themselves: design-related fields, interior decorating, the theater, antiques. Eventually we came to see that we had been brainwashed by our own conditioning into seeking occupational pigeonholes for America's gay community. Conversely, if we moved in the other direction–warehouse foreman, truck driver, security guard–we would be dealing with a mirror-image of the same cliché, and compounding the problem by gingerly avoiding even the slightest whiff of an artistic sensibility.

We felt it was essential that Salter and his lover should be members of the upper middle class. Most plays and works of fiction dealing with the subject tended to view homosexuals as exotic and frequently pathetic denizens of an underground subculture. But since our film would be seen in the homes of twenty-odd million people, we wanted our two men to reflect the values and living standards of the middle-income American. In this way we hoped to minimize any protective distancing on the part of the viewer. It would be easy for an audience to reject or feel superior to Midnight Cowboys, the world of chic East Side gay bars, or bizarre queens who seek sexual encounters in gas station restrooms or all-male steambaths. But the nice men next door, or down the block, with "respectable" occupations and traditional life-styles, could not be so casually dismissed.

Both of us, by coincidence, were having work done on our homes, so we decided to put Salter in the construction business. And since Gary, his lover, was intended to be a more modern homosexual, reflecting the growing awareness of the younger generation of gays, we made him a sound engineer.

The script had an intentionally simple story line. Nick Salter lives with his divorced mother in Los Angeles, and each summer he flies to San Francisco to spend a week or two with his father. This particular summer Doug is living with a lover, and though Gary obligingly moves out before Nick's arrival, the boy begins to sense, though not quite understand, that his father's relationship with this good-looking and personable "friend" is strange and somehow threatening. Gary tries to win his approval, but Nick grows increasingly hostile.

Doug is not yet willing to share the truth with his son—he feels he's still too young and unsophisticated to be told—and when Nick finally realizes that his father is a homosexual he runs away from home.

Janet Salter flies to San Francisco, where she confronts her former husband and his lover. Nick eventually returns and Doug at long last is honest with him, telling him that he's always been a homosexual, and that now he has chosen to live openly according to his preferences. Nick rejects his father and returns to Los Angeles with his mother.

Reduced to its bare bones, the plot comes perilously close to soap opera. We attempted to counter this by understatement and by avoiding, to the best of our ability, the clichés and the tone of High Seriousness that all too often creep into material of this nature. Not at all confident that we had succeeded, we finished the first thirty pages and sent them off to Diller. He was strongly supportive. Other than suggesting that Nick Salter's age be reduced from thirteen to twelve (a mysterious request having something to do with puberty) he reiterated his firm commitment to the project. We finished the script and Universal received the all-important work order: *That Certain Summer* was now officially on the list of ABC's *Movie of the Week* schedule. All we had to do was make the picture.

We sent the script to Lamont Johnson and he agreed to direct. Casting, however, was not quite so simple. Even before we made any offers, word got back to us that very few actors would be willing to play the part of Doug Salter. At a party one leading man told us he would never portray a homosexual. "My fans wouldn't accept it," he said with a straight face. We asked him if he would consider playing Hitler. "Of course."

We finally decided on Hal Holbrook, but when we approached his agent we were told, "I can't recommend it to him. I think it would be dangerous, professionally, for an actor to play this role." We pointed out that Peter Finch had not damaged his career when he appeared as the homosexual doctor in *Sunday, Bloody Sunday,* but Holbrook's agent was unmoved. "Who saw that picture?" he asked. "Six people in New York, five people in Chicago, and ten people in Los Angeles. It was an art film. You're asking Hal to play a homosexual in front of twenty million people."

Fortunately, Holbrook ignored his agent's advice and agreed to undertake the part. We then selected Martin Sheen for Gary. Both of us had been impressed by Sheen's performance on Broadway in Frank Gilroy's *The Subject Was Roses,* and we had seen him recently in the television version of *The Andersonville Trial.* We felt he was a fine and flexible actor who had yet to achieve the recognition he deserved.

ABC, in common with the other two networks, insisted on "star casting." Holbrook was a television star, but at that point Sheen was not, so the rules of the game dictated that we had to find a well-known actress to play Janet Salter. The part was small, secondary to the roles of the two men and the boy, and all of our submissions were met with polite but emphatic turndowns. One actress said, through her agent, "When they write something with a lesbian in the lead, I'll do it. But it's the man's show."

Diller relented as our start date approached and told us to cast any good actress, regardless of the name value. Ironically, one of us bumped into Hope Lange in a supermarket. We had assumed she was in Arizona doing a series with Dick Van Dyke, but here she was in Los Angeles buying groceries. We sent her a script and she accepted. In spite of ourselves we had a "name" actress after all.

Casting the part of Nick was difficult. The role called for considerable skill and experience, but most child actors have all the reality of processed cheese. Since Hal and Hope were to be the mother and father, we had the additional complication of finding a boy who could conceivably be the issue of such a union. Our casting director paraded one freckle-faced youngster after another through the office. Each was well qualified to romp with a shaggy dog in a Disney film, but none had even the barest comprehension of the role.

When Scott Jacoby read for the part he dazzled us. But he was wrong in the physical sense; he was a street-wise kid from New York and it would require an enormous suspension of disbelief for the audience to accept him as the offspring of the patrician-looking Hal and Hope. We vacillated and finally offered him the role on the theory that he was so good he would be able to transcend his physical inappropriateness by the sheer force of his performance.

Alice in Wonderland has always been a handy frame of reference for the television business. It and Joseph Heller's *Catch 22* are required reading when one tries to understand the inverted logic and frequent absurdities that are encountered on the journey from idea to final answer print. A grounding in Kafka and Machiavelli is also useful.

While we worked on the preproduction of *That Certain Summer* there were, as Diller had predicted, internal rumblings at ABC. No one spoke to us openly, but rumors abounded that we would not be permitted to make the film. Our script was far too pro-homosexual. It was much too antihomosexual. Washington and the FCC were concerned over the propriety of our subject matter. Militant gays were preparing to picket the studio. All of this was grist for our never-dormant paranoia. One of our problems was quite specific and hardly a product of our feverish imaginations–no one would let us film in any of the houses we selected. We had gone with Lamont and our production manager to Sausalito, a charming hillside community across the Golden Gate Bridge from San Francisco, and we had chosen a half-dozen locations that seemed right for Doug Salter's home. But when the owners of these houses read the script they turned us down. Some of them were homosexuals and they told us they simply didn't wish to "make waves."

Meanwhile, we suddenly began hearing about two gentlemen whom we began to think of (following our continuing fixation on Lewis Carroll) as Tweedle-dum and Tweedle-dee. They were on retainer to ABC and they served as hired guns to run interference with Congress, the media, and the medical establishment. If there were questions about violence, sex, or the suitability of material from a legal or psychiatric standpoint, T & T were produced to make appropriate statements. One of them, Melvin S. Heller, M.D., was a clinical professor of psychiatry, and the other, Samuel Polsky, Ph.D., was a professor of law. Both men were co-directors of the Unit in Law and Psychiatry at Temple University's Health Science Center in Philadelphia. And both of them had been sent our script.

Their response was contained in a letter sent to Alfred R. Schneider, a vice-president of ABC and the man charged with the responsibility for program content. It read, in part:

> It is our feeling that you have tremendous potential in this script, which appears to be a pioneering effort to portray a hitherto unspeakable subject as far as television goes. On the other hand, it is realistic to anticipate an enormous amount of flack, criticism and controversy should this program be aired by the American Broadcasting Company. . . .
>
> We think that criticism must be anticipated from three sources. To many individuals, any public treatment of the matter of homosexuality is condemned as the airing of an "abomination, an unnatural act, an immoral act carrying with it all the sins of sodomy."
>
> There would also be opposition expressed in legal

terms, but here we would point out that the recent preoc-
cupations of citizens with the rights of individuals to practice adult, consensual acts, and the concept of crimes
without victims, have led to a different application of the
law with reference to adult homosexuality.

A great deal of vigorous criticism may be expected
from those individuals with the least ability to tolerate any
manifestation of their own unconscious tendencies in that
direction—namely the overly compensated latent homosexual, whose impulse toward homosexuals is to stomp
them into the ground, or banish them to long terms in
prison.

The responsible answer, for the Am Broad Comp, in
our opinion, consists in presenting a fair and balanced
view of the problem. . . .

First, we feel that perhaps some character could be introduced in the drama who is struggling with his own
latent homosexuality and whose very anger and outward
over-reaction would be effectively indicated. This might
serve to de-fuse some of the more vigorous over-reactors
in the male audience, by giving them someone in the play
with whom to identify. . . .

Second, and less important, the script should be shown
to appropriate groups (physicians, clergy, lawyers, educators, or others) to secure their endorsement of a serious
attempt to present a heated social issue in dignified and
sensitive dramatic form. . . .

A caveat should be noted here. We believe that this
program needs to be differentiated from the militant pros-
elytizing of the so-called Gay Liberation Movement,
which is apparently not above doing a certain amount of
recruiting on selective college campuses.

Third, the imaginative use of leader material and advertising could also act to balance the presentation. . . .

The important elements to be emphasized in our opinion are the following: The representation of the problem
contained in this script demonstrated dramatically the

tragic proportions of an all too common family conflict that no one dares mention. If it allows one forlorn youngster or parent to speak the unspeakable and communicate across the gulf of interpersonal despair, then the film brings with it a significant social value. . . .

The policy problem facing ABC is much clearer than the answer. There is no question that the safest course of action would be to duck this challenge and perhaps the wisest counsel would be to do so. Even with the suggestions we have made for achieving a more balanced presentation, this subject is sufficiently controversial so that ABC would have surfaced an issue that will reverberate, very likely, for months after the presentation. There is no doubt in our minds, however, that the job is worth doing, needs doing, and can be done with sensitivity, restraint, and fairness.

We knew nothing of this letter, but had we been aware of it we would have been annoyed but not unduly concerned. Heller and Polsky seemed to be engaged in a typical corporate dance, covering their flanks by coming down firmly on both sides of the issue. Their flattering remarks about "sensitivity" and "pioneering efforts" are adroitly balanced by caveats and "on the other hands." In one paragraph they counsel that the safest course of action would be to "duck the challenge," while at the same time they say that the "job is worth doing."

The truly disturbing parts of the letter, the suggestion that the script be submitted to a panel of doctors and educators for some kind of Establishment sanctification, as well as the idea of inserting a character for the sole purpose of defusing latent homosexuals, would have caused us to bridle (as would the snide and hostile remark about militant gays recruiting on campuses), but we would have assumed the network would ignore such nonsense and allow us to proceed without interference. As it turned out, we would have been wrong.

Our immediate problem was of the nuts-and-bolts variety—we needed a house. Luckily—and very close to the eleventh hour—our staff got permission to film in the home of a married couple. Husband

and wife were both attorneys who were active in the protection of homosexual and women's rights, and though the house was in a suburb of Los Angeles instead of San Francisco, Lamont devised a method of connecting it with our Sausalito locations so it would appear to be just across the Golden Gate Bridge.

In early May we received what is known as a "shooting script review" from ABC's Department of Standards and Practices. Every single television script at each of the three networks is subjected to this process—it is read by an "editor" (i.e., censor), and his or her notes are relayed to the producer of the program. The ABC memos commonly state, in red letters:

> Kindly forward such revisions as are necessary to effect the modifications requested below. If revisions are acceptable . . . no supplementary review will be forthcoming. . . . This review does not constitute a Broadcast Standards approval of subsequent script changes or changes in method of treatment in production. A separate screening report will be issued upon viewing the Rough Cut film.

The last sentence is a clear indication of where the power lies. The network controls the film up to and including its rough cut, and it can still order changes well after the actual production.

The notes on *That Certain Summer,* with several significant exceptions, were relatively mild, and some were obviously negotiable. We were unaware that the major decisions over content were being discussed at a higher level between Schneider and Heller and Polsky.

Some of the comments were as follows:

> Page 8, sc 23—I don't think your story needs any visual subtleties, such as "the unmade king-size bed" to make its point.
>
> Page 9, sc 25—Avoid unnecessary commercial identification of prop jet in its landing sequence.
>
> Page 31, sc 73—To avoid commercial conflict, dummy up label on aerosol shaving can.
>
> Page 32, sc 73—Please substitute "tail" for "butt."

Page 43, sc 87 – The two young men passing by will not even be holding hands. Their dress, their walk, mannerisms, etc., will identify.*

Page 51, sc 108 – Gary puts his arm on Doug's shoulder. This must be nothing more than "casual" as described.

Page 57, sc 134 – Delete "Where the *hell* is he?"

Page 59 – Delete ". . . too *damn* busy . . ." and "Who the *hell* . . ."

Page 64, sc 152 – Delete or substitute for the line "But neither one of them keeps my bed warm."

Page 72, sc 166 – It will be preferable that the line "But to me it's just . . . another way of loving" be deleted or in some manner modified. Perhaps ". . . another way of living." And the line "We love each other" will need to be said in some other way, less explicit.

We digested these notes, decided where we would refuse to compromise as well as where we could make the requested changes without doing any harm, and prepared for the usual session of trading off a "hell" here for a "damn" there. But something much more crucial was in the wind. We were suddenly notified that we were to meet with the Messrs. Heller and Polsky in Barry Diller's office. Friends at the network had given us a copy of H and P's letter to Schneider, and we were warned through the grapevine that if we did not pass muster the entire project would be scuttled.

The Mad Tea Party took place on a morning in June. It was a landmark day in the life of one of us (Levinson), because a few hours earlier his wife had given birth to a baby girl. He arrived at the ABC reception area in a state of euphoria and exhaustion, not having slept at all the previous night. Link, fortunately, was well rested and girded for battle, and Charles Engel, Universal's liaison with the network, had come along as a corporate Praetorian Guard.

---

* In the world of Standards and Practices, heterosexual lovers can hold hands on America's television screens; homosexual lovers cannot.

Everyone in the entertainment industry "takes meetings." Woody Allen made proper fun of the phrase, as well as the process, in his film *Annie Hall.* One meets to "spitball a premise." Or to "get a reaction." Or to "throw names around." Some of these meetings are useful, but all of them, particularly at the network level, can be dangerous. Enthusiasm has a way of evaporating. Suggestions can be made that radically alter something worthwhile. Entire projects can crumble under the weight of too many negative vibrations. This particular meeting was a problem because we were interested in making the best possible film and Heller and Polsky were interested in protecting ABC, goals that were not necessarily compatible.

Diller ushered us into his office and introduced us to the two professors. They were affable and relatively benign. Pleasantries were exchanged. Much sport was made of Philadelphia, home of Heller and Polsky and former home of Link and Levinson. It was agreed that it was a fine city in spite of the jokes, ours included, made at its expense.

Decks having been cleared, the Subject was at hand. Heller and Polsky told us that they felt—others felt as well—that our script would be perceived as prohomosexual by the viewing audience, and thus stood in opposition to "the prevailing climate of public opinion." Questions of the Fairness Doctrine and Equal Time would be raised. ABC would be vulnerable to criticism unless we rewrote with an eye to "balance."

We countered that the script was neither pro- nor anti-gay and we suggested that a much larger issue was involved: the question of the writer's rights to use the public air for the expression of opinions, popular or otherwise. Was controversy to be denied anyone who wrote for television because of equal-time considerations? If a writer dared to take a position, must the countervailing view always be incorporated in the script? What if "balance" was in conflict with good drama? And by giving equal weight to opposing opinions, didn't the writer risk eviscerating his material to the point of all-things-to-all-men blandness?

Heller and Polsky did not want to be trapped into a philosophical and, from their point of view, unproductive debate. They urged us to add a police officer to the script, or, as they put it, "an Archie Bunker character" to serve as a lightning rod for the "latent homosexual viewer," someone who would condemn homosexuality from a position of quasi-authority and who could be pointed to as an example of "balance."

We resisted. The conversation drifted to homosexuality itself, and we suggested that its causes—and whether or not it was in fact a "sickness"—were very much in dispute. To our astonishment, Heller exploded. "Don't give me your show-biz, cocktail-party analysis!" he thundered. "I've treated these guys and I know them. They hate women, they can't get it up, they're hostile as hell." He continued in this fashion for a while and then fixed us with a probing look. "Why did you two write this script in the first place? I know you did it for the money, but what were your other reasons?"

On the defensive—and apparently on the couch—we explained that we were under contract and were therefore paid regardless of our writing services. We summarized the background of the idea and mentioned some of our research, pointedly singling out those authorities whose assessment of homosexual behavior was at variance with Heller's. He hastily assured us that he liked the script and acknowledged its accuracy from the psychoanalytic standpoint. "Particularly in the oral sex symbolism between father and son and the clitoral implications."

Dazed, we exchanged glances with Diller, who gave us a helpless shrug. Heller, noting our confusion, was eager to explain. In an early scene, Nick and his father are visiting an attractive young woman. She sends Nick off to look for her hidden wine cellar so she can be alone with Doug. When he returns he says, "I found your hidden panel. It's pretty easy to open. You just press that raised thing near the top." This was Heller's clitoral reference. The fact that we had written the line with no such intention delighted him; obviously our unconscious was more accessible to him than to us. As for the oral sex between father and son ("A healthy working out," as Heller put it), it came down to a home movie sequence where Doug and Nick lie side by side in a meadow, blowing at a dandelion.

While we were still reeling from this Byzantine interpretation, Polsky moved in with a stern lecture about the law. If our show were to be aired, and someone were to take ABC to court, network attorneys would have to show, via the script, that all sides had been considered, all bases touched. "You have to give them something to defend themselves with."

The meeting grew heated. Heller—or perhaps Polsky—began borrowing cigarettes from us, claiming that he had given up smoking and didn't have his own pack. Polsky—or perhaps Heller—suddenly had a camera in his hands and was taking pictures "for my kids." We half-expected the Dormouse to pop up from a teakettle under Diller's desk.

We finally agreed to two changes. There was a scene in the script between Gary and his brother-in-law, Phil. Rather than inject a cop or an Archie Bunker, we suggested that we use Phil as the lightning rod for Heller and Polsky's "latent homosexual." But we refused to have him openly condemn the gay life-style. Instead, we'd make him solicitous and ponderously broad-minded, an ersatz liberal whose attempts to be reasonable about his brother-in-law's sexual preferences are patronizing and ultimately a greater condemnation than naked disapproval.

The second change was the insertion of several lines of dialogue in the final scene where Doug speaks to his son. After the phrase, "A lot of people—most people I guess—think it's wrong . . . they say it's a sickness . . . they say it's something that has to be cured. . . ." we added the following: "Maybe they're right. I don't know . . . I *do* know that it isn't easy. If I had a choice it's not something I'd pick for myself."

We justified (rationalized?) the addition by reasoning that it's easier in American society to be rich, white, and straight than to be poor, black, and gay, and since Doug was not a masochist he would probably rather be in the mainstream than a member of a minority all too often reviled and subjected to harassment.

Later, we were to deeply regret adding these lines. They came back to haunt us time and time again, but for the moment, in Diller's office, they seemed a reasonable compromise. Heller and Polsky, however, were by no means satisfied; they wanted more changes. The atmosphere in the room grew contentious—the Mad Tea Party had turned into a Teamster's bargaining session. After two hours, and in spite of the air-conditioning, we were all sweating. But we had finally reached the point where we refused to budge.

Calls were backing up and Diller brought the meeting to an end. We departed in a grim mood, unhappy with the changes we had agreed to make and not at all sure we would be allowed to continue with the film. We took some satisfaction in the fact that a great deal of money had already been spent; actors had been committed and a crew was being assembled, so at the very least ABC had a financial inducement to proceed.

As we were waiting in the underground garage for our cars the final Alice in Wonderland touch occurred. Heller and Polsky ambled up and, incredibly, they engaged us in an amiable conversation. It was as if the meeting had never taken place. One of them said they'd like to visit the studio for lunch and he wondered if we could arrange it. The other commented on the pleasantness of the climate—as opposed, we assumed, to the climate of public opinion that had so preoccupied him earlier.

We were less than gracious and they seemed surprised by our manner. Why were we so upset? Didn't we know that the meeting was just *pro forma?* Hell, they were being paid to be consultants, and now they had consulted, and that was that. Nothing to worry about. Just a ritual that had to be observed.

Assuming our anxiety had now been put to rest, they chatted on in a friendly fashion about L.A. vs. Philadelphia, about the freeways, about everything except the morning's rancorous face-off. They were genuinely disappointed when our cars arrived and the conversation had to end.

In a subsequent letter to Schneider, they finally climbed halfway down off the fence. Acknowledging "fairly sharp differences" at our meeting and the fact that we regarded some of their suggestions as "banal clichés," they nevertheless wrote the following:

> The point is not whether heat will be engendered, but whether a heated subject is presented with fairness. . . . On balance, enough of the opposing viewpoint has been sug-

gested to meet the requirements on fairness in dramatic presentation, albeit minimally rather than generously. . . . Pioneering is seldom the safest course to take. This is, however, an area worth pioneering, and this is a script worth defending, and capable of being defended, as a fair and reasonably balanced effort, if the balance includes artistic merit as well as an exploration of certain feelings and attitudes pro and contra homosexuality.

Making the film was something of an anticlimax, and events progressed with reasonable smoothness. Holbrook was annoyed early on because of an interview he gave to a San Francisco paper (he explained what we were doing with great care, stressing the desire of all of us not to exploit or sensationalize the material, and then was greeted on the first day of filming with the appearance of his printed remarks under the headline: "HOLBROOK PLAYS HOMO"), but otherwise there were few glitches.

On the set we all alternated between a grim feeling of responsibility and, curiously, an antic and almost scatological sense of the absurd. The jokes were lewd, many of them surprisingly antihomosexual. Under the guise of humor everyone seemed to be purging resentments, fears, and hostilities that had been stored up for years. Then the filming would resume and cast and crew would return with seriousness and great care to the work at hand. This odd duality—the surfacing of unconscious anger directed at an alien life-style while at the same time exploring that life-style with compassion—continued until we all became aware of it and attempted to resolve it with some setside group therapy. The joking diminished but the anxiety remained; we were all afraid of creating something that would either ring false or be an embarrassment.

Given a script that was essentially talk, Lamont concentrated on the performances. It was a pleasure to watch him serve the material rather than call attention to himself by the employment of intrusive camera techniques. Flashy angles, shock cuts, and zoom lenses have their place, but some subjects call for a paring away, a simplification, and when we complimented Lamont on his restraint he smiled. "I did all that tricky stuff a long time ago," he said. "Now it's pretty much out of my system. In fact, today I'm planning something that's staggering in its audacity—instead of going from one scene to another with a straight cut, or racking in and out of focus, or making a sound bridge, I've just about decided to use . . . a dissolve!"

One sign of a good film director is his sense of staging, his ability to move actors and camera in arresting and satisfying patterns. Comprehending the dynamics of spatial relationships is a rare gift; it enables the director to tell a story not only through his actors, but also by the way he allows a given mass, whether animate or inanimate, to occupy a given space.

Many directors break up scenes into master shots and close-ups. They station the actors against a background, have them perform with the camera at a comfortable distance, then move closer and replay the same dialogue, taking endless close-ups and over-the-shoulder shots. The results are frequently mechanical. A good director, even with the usual time pressures, will take risks; he will move the actors within the frame, have them cross and recross, creating long shots, medium shots, and close-ups without cutting.

Lamont, for example, decided to film the last scene of *That Certain Summer* in one long master, requiring a variety of subtle but complex camera moves. In the scene, Doug Salter watches, through an open door, as his wife and son drive away in a cab; when they are gone he crosses to sit on one of the steps of his staircase and looks blankly into space. Gary descends from the living room above, tries to comfort him, and then leaves. The camera moves in on Salter until his stricken face dominates the screen.

Most directors would have broken up the sequence, thereby protecting themselves and putting less stress on the actors. But Lamont *wanted* the actors under stress, and he felt the fluidity of an uninterrupted take would enrich the performances. It was a matter of technique serving content.

Holbrook responded perfectly to the challenge, even to the point of allowing himself to cry. Crying is an easy trick for some actors, and the ability to turn tears on and off is frequently mistaken for depth of characterization. But Holbrook's tears were almost too painful to watch—there was nothing superficial about them. In our concern over possible overstatement we had deliberately kept Doug Salter dry-eyed at the climax, and we asked Lamont to reshoot the scene without the tears, but the power of Holbrook's expression, with his eyes wet and streaming, created such a haunting image that we all agreed to use the first take. It's probable that had Lamont fragmented the scene into a series of cuts, Holbrook would not have reacted as he did and a moment of strong emotional catharsis would have been lost.

Ed Abroms had been launched as a director on *Columbo,* but he agreed to edit *That Certain Summer* for us. He and Lamont worked on the picture for weeks, and though we were intensely curious we stayed away to preserve what little was left of our objectivity. When we asked how the film was coming along we were told, "Not bad." Or: "It's okay." Both Lamont and Abroms seemed so casual—almost to the point of indifference—that we began to think they felt the picture was a failure and were mercifully letting us down as easily as they could.

We had only one disagreement with Diller. He had become enamored of a rock star named Cat Stevens, and he decided that we should have a song over the titles. He told us he could get Stevens to write one for us, which would be something of a coup, and he was startled when we resisted the idea. We had gradually come to believe that the less music in a film the better. All too often "wall-to-wall" music has been used to carry a weak picture. Network executives and producers seem to be afraid of silence. They want themes, songs, and in the event the dialogue is in any way oblique, they want the music to make the point. Good composers recognize that leaving out is sometimes more important than putting in, but they are often pressured into providing underscoring where sound effects, or no sound at all, would be more effective.

Diller thought we were making a mistake by rejecting his suggestion, but he didn't force the issue. We hired Gil Mellé to write the music and we asked for a sparse score that would not be overly emotional. In all, there were only thirteen minutes of music in *That Certain Summer,* and none whatsoever during the last part of the film.

Lamont and Abroms finally invited us to see the director's cut. We sat with the two of them in one of Universal's barnlike screening rooms, paper and pencils at the ready for note taking. We never used them. The film worked, at least for us, on almost every level. Holbrook was remarkable; Sheen brought subtle values to what was at best an underwritten part; and Scott Jacoby was that rarity, a child actor without affectation. When the lights came up we saw Lamont and Abroms grinning at us. They had deliberately downgraded the picture so as not to raise our expectations.

A screening was arranged for Diller and other ABC executives, including members of Standards and Practices. Diller was deeply moved and requested only a minor trim or two because he felt that one scene was too painful. (He even authorized us to come in a few minutes shorter than standard format so that we wouldn't have to add any padding.) The rest of the picture remained untouched. It was one of the few cases in our experience where there were almost no changes between the first and the final cut.

As everyone filed out of the screening room we noticed that the West Coast head of Standards and Practices seemed to be in a state of shock. He looked at us as if we had defiled the flag, shook his head, muttered an unfelt "Good luck," and made a hasty exit.

Most television films are promoted by rote—a network department cuts a "trailer" (thirty- and sixty-second preview spots), a press kit is sent out, a few interviews are arranged between the actors and the press, and an ad is designed for selected newspapers in key viewing areas. In the case of certain films, prescreenings are arranged for the television critics, particularly Judith Crist, whose post as resident critic for *TV Guide* gives her enormous influence.

Diller wanted considerably more. He felt that *Summer* required special treatment, not only to attract an audience but also to deal with the homosexuality issue. He made two decisions. One was to "run the sprockets off the film," as he put it, by holding screenings on both coasts for opinion-makers. The other was to let the public know, through news stories and advertising, exactly what the picture was about. We objected to this latter approach because we thought it could be misconstrued as a reverse come-on, a way of attracting people by telling them that perhaps the material was a bit too "adult" for average tastes. We also felt that too much emphasis on the plot and subject matter would rob the film of some of its suspense and surprise.

Diller, however, did not want anyone to watch without knowing in advance exactly what he or she was in for. In a real sense he was forewarning the audience, so that viewers wouldn't blunder upon the program and be taken by surprise. If they chose to turn on their sets, and if they had been previously informed as to content, then they'd have less grounds for complaint. *Caveat emptor.* We had a different name for the procedure. Privately, we called it "de-fanging the opposition."

An interoffice memorandum was circulated at Universal a month before the air date, stating that the film would be screened for fifteen press and "word-of-mouth groups" (wonderful phrase), including college students, lawyers, members of the American Civil Liberties Union, California government officials, foreign reporters, clergymen, and, no doubt in an attempt to cover all bases, disc jockeys. Similar screenings were to be set up in New York, and *Summer* would be close-circuited to all local stations in advance.

Someone, either at ABC or Universal, suggested an unusual idea. Since theatrical motion pictures often have sneak previews and pass out preview cards to the audience, why not do the same, and for the first time, for a television film? We were intrigued by the notion. Some motion pictures have been recut and occasionally ruined after a thumbs-down response from a sneak preview audience, but our film was forever frozen because an air date, scheduled and publicized, waited just around the corner. We had absolutely nothing to lose. And what we had to gain was that most precious of commodities, an honest reaction from an unbiased audience. Those who filled out the cards could choose to remain anonymous; we could safely assume that their comments would be truthful, with little or no concern for the network, the studio, or our egos.

The cards cascaded into our office over the next few weeks. It was an unusual experience—never had we received such immediate feedback. And all of it even before our film went on the air. What was extraordinary was that almost everyone who responded signed his or her name. Some even included their telephone numbers. Most of the comments were favorable–some were not–but almost all of them were thoughtful and articulate. What follows is a random sampling:

"Excellent treatment of the subject."

"Congratulations. A magnificently touching drama, the effect of which will unfortunately be negated by commercial breaks. The acting is excellent and the seriousness of the situation clearly expressed. I would heartily recommend it."

"Glad this will have a television release."

"Who cast boy as son of Hope and Holbrook? Jessel and Germaine Greer, yes. Hope and Holbrook, no."

"Well done, tasteful, but slightly pedantic."

"Sensitive handling of a controversial subject. You are all to be commended for making it as tasteful as it is without succumbing to the more sensational aspects that films like *The Boys in the Band* and *Fortune and Men's Eyes* have stressed."

"Best film ever about homosexual relationships. Don't be discouraged if Nielsens are bad."

"Congratulations on presenting in a *film made for TV* a misunderstood and little discussed but usually tabooed subject. However, the subject was simply not explained enough in the critical father-son talk."

"Please don't show this movie on TV first. There are not enough good movies like this for theatrical distribution."

"Excellent. One of the most tender films I've seen in a long time. Too good for just TV."

"I was surprised to see that a made-for-TV film could concern itself with the subject of homosexuality in a manner as to not embarrass itself with naiveté nor lower itself with sensationalism."

"I enjoyed it up to a point. However, it is my feeling that the writers were not being completely honest. I don't feel a wife, woman, mother, would have accepted the situation as complacently. Maybe it had to be toned down for TV."

"I appreciated the movie for its honesty, lack of sensationalism and simplicity. The acting was obviously deeply felt and the sincerity of intention, to educate without caricature—so prevalent to homosexuality as a rule—was much appreciated."

"*Très grand film. Très sobre and très discret. Interpréte avec un talent. Superbe par tous les interprètes. Félicitations sincéres aux auteurs.*"

"Not for TV. Otherwise, good."

"Too bad such talent is wasted on such sickness."

"The kind of movie after which you sit stunned in your seat wondering why you came to watch it. After working a twelve-hour day in this business I don't need to be depressed by the product."

"Created an involvement I've never before experienced."

"Too tame and dull."

"I rate a picture according to the times I squirm in my seat, wishing the damn thing would end. *That Certain Summer* was definitely a NO squirmer."

"Well directed, beautifully shot, rich in characters. Heavy for TV, but it's about time."

"A delicate, sensitive film. My only cut would be just prior to the tears on Doug's face as he sits on the stair. A face in turmoil reflects a sorrow too deep for superfluous tears. Congratulations on a TV first."

"Good production values. Sensitive handling of a touchy subject. But why wait until the last ten minutes before mentioning 'the word' homosexuality? Also, why didn't the wife feel any of the blame? After all, she never talked to the boy either."

"I am tired of seeing gay people portrayed as sick or guilt-ridden. While this movie dispells a lot of the former, I feel it portrays gay people as still too much of the latter."

"There are certain things that should remain anonymous—this picture should and the homosexuals that produced it."

"Perhaps it should be used in universities in a number of fields to study."

"Thought the whole film was handled very well. Hal Holbrook's performance was beautiful. I would certainly recommend it to my friends and even to my ten-year-old son as a beautiful answer to his questions on the subject."

"Why does TV wait so long before opening the door on taboo subjects? After all, it is basically the same public that goes to motion picture theaters. As for children—well, they need a serious treatment and interpretation of what they are already learning on the streets in a usually distorted fashion."

"Such delicacy and truth it hurt to watch, but it's a good hurt."

"I see no point in making a picture on such a subject."

"Excellent and in good taste. Makes one think TV has finally come of age."

"It's a beginning."

That Certain Summer aired on November 1, 1972. ABC switchboard operators stood by in major cities to deal with an expected avalanche of calls from outraged viewers, but the reaction was mild. With the exception of a phoned-in bomb threat to a station in Sacramento and a precautionary announcement about "parental guidance" tacked on by a station in Miami, the show ran without incident. Either Diller had done his work well, or else the public took the program in stride.

We were stunned and delighted as calls, letters, and reviews streamed into our office. The notices were the best we had ever received. For the most part, however, *Summer* was seen not so much as a drama but rather as a ground-breaking effort in dealing with a controversial subject on television. Some of the critics approached it as a play, and all praised the acting, but most fixated on the homosexual aspects and the suitability of such material for home consumption. As the TV critic of the *Boston Evening Globe* remarked, "I guess the major accomplishment of *That Certain Summer* was just being on the air."

It was all but inevitable that the film's subject matter would overshadow its execution. We had tried to tell a story about a father-son relationship, but the element of homosexuality so dominated media attention that the merits and defects of the piece as theater were largely ignored. Still, we had little to complain about. Many of the critics called the film a "milestone" and a "landmark." Merle Miller, the author of one of the best books about American television, *Only You, Dick Daring,* commented in the *New York Times:* "It's a simply marvelous film—beautifully written, superbly acted, and directed and produced with tender care." Charles Champlin, the motion picture critic for the *Los Angeles Times,* took one of his rare glimpses at the small screen and decided that *Summer* "represents a landmark in the emergence of television as a dramatic medium."

Not everyone agreed with him. The critic for the *Baltimore Sun* was blunt: "Let's just say that *That Certain Summer* fell victim to television, as television is presently conceived and directed . . . it moved laboriously from scene to scene without rewarding the viewer for his steadfast loyalty to the set." The West Palm Beach, Florida, reviewer gave us a glowing notice, but pointed out: "What is more pertinent here is Channel 12's decision to substitute two other presentations in place of the network broadcast. Eleanor Larsen, program director for WEAT-TV has said *That Certain Summer* was viewed by the station staff prior to the broadcast date and that 'we do not feel that at the present time it is in the best interest of the community to show a dramatic fictional program dealing with that subject.' " And Rona Barrett informed us, over the air, that "many congressmen and senators are screaming that bold films like *That Certain Summer* aren't the kind of breakthrough TV sorely needs."

Happily, many critics understood what we were trying to do. Writing in the *Chicago Sun-Times,* Ron Powers said, "Perhaps most startling about a drama written for television, with its audience massively conditioned to pat endings, is this: There is no happy resolution to the conflict." Referring to *Summer, Time* acknowledged that "commercial TV can, when it wants to, handle sensitive, controversial subjects with intelligence and maturity," and *Newsweek* noted that "considering the delicacy of its theme, it strikes nary a bogus note—no mincing mannerisms, no saccharine confrontations, no easy answers." Frank Judge, in the *Detroit News,* commented, "I received some 40 letters attacking the whole idea of presenting such a theme on television. . . . I hope that the . . . protesting letter-writers were among those who saw the picture, because I am sure they would have to agree that there was nothing offensive in it. By television standards—no, strike that, by any standards—this was drama at its best." He did, however, add a warning: "I pray that the success of this film doesn't set off a trend where every cheap producer in Hollywood gets into the act."

Not surprisingly, there was an eruption of negative reaction from the militant gay community. In a series of letters to the *New York Times* they catalogued their grievances. Why did the two male lovers never touch or kiss? Why did Doug Salter cry at the end of the film—his tears were a repudiation of the life he had chosen for himself. Why did his son reject rather than accept him? Finally—and here our capitulation to Heller and Polsky's demands was brought home—why did Salter say that if he had a choice he wouldn't be a homosexual?

The gay sensibility, much like the new black self-awareness that came into being while we were making *My Sweet Charlie,* had altered during the time span between the conception of our film and its airing. When *That Certain Summer* was shown on television the militants had arrived at a point where they did not wish to be reminded that there were still many among their number who were troubled, unsure, and not quite ready to face society with a strong sense of self-identity. The character of Doug Salter was a homosexual in transit, and therefore not as liberated as the militants may have wished. They wanted propaganda, not drama. As for the "if I had a choice" speech, their criticism was valid. The fact that we inserted it under pressure was hardly an acceptable excuse. We should have resisted its inclusion, or else deleted it from the final cut.

One of the most thoughtful reviews addressed itself to the reaction of the militants. It was by Ralph Sepulveda, Jr., and it appeared in the *Village Voice*. It read, in part:

> . . . having been involved to some extent in the gay movement for over a year now and being rather familiar with the more-radical-than-thou attitudes one frequently encounters in these circles, it's hardly surprising to me to find that the majority of gay militants . . . are among the movie's most vociferous detractors. Some may ask just what *would* satisfy them and others might reply, in turn, that perhaps some sort of gay Doris Day movie in which everything was peachy and rosy and everyone concerned lived perfectly marvelous lives would be the thing. . . . For of course the gay militants . . . want everything all at once.
>
> They want to he held up as long-suffering victims of a hostile, bigoted society, so that any work attempting to deal with homosexuality must lash out bitterly at the society that is to blame. And they want to see themselves up on the screen as good and beautiful, as an oppressed minority that is finally rising up in anger to fight back, and any note of negativism . . . is not to be tolerated.
>
> A view of a homosexual like Doug Salter who isn't totally liberated, who hasn't achieved the highest level of consciousness that many of us claim to have attained, just won't do for our gay liberationists, I'm afraid (although surely they must know better than anybody else that thou-

sands of men are very like Doug and probably just as many are still fighting their homosexuality, still denying it even to themselves, still settling into marriage, as Doug did, in the hope that they will somehow be "cured"). *That Certain Summer* does not make a pitch for gay liberation nor does it intend to, though that is exactly what the gay militants will complain is wrong with it. In a sense, this movie is beyond the revolution.

Political fashions change with the seasons. Years later, *Summer* was shown at the Museum of Modern Art. We were present for a question and answer session after the screening, and one member of the audience, a feminist, stood up to confront us with what she felt was the film's major failing. The house where Doug and Gary lived was beautifully furnished—the paintings, the accoutrements, all indicated a refined and tasteful intelligence. Yet the few glimpses provided of the wife's house showed tacky furniture and motel art on the walls. Were we not making a chauvinistic statement? Why did we find it necessary to idealize the surroundings of the two men and denigrate the wife by placing her in a vulgar environment?

We patiently explained that for reasons of tight scheduling we had to film the wife-at-home sequences as close to the studio as possible, and the house we used was the only residence available. There wasn't time to re-dress the set, and we photographed it as we found it. As for the art and furnishings of the Salter home, they were a reflection of the couple who lived there. The feminist was not mollified by this, and quite obviously continued to believe that we, albeit unconsciously, had taken a deliberate slap at women in general.

Physical proximity to the audience, which is one of the rewards of working in the theater, is denied to those who earn a living in filmed television. Perhaps that is why many TV folk read the reviews so voraciously, and it's certainly the reason why letters from viewers take on a special importance. *That Certain Summer* triggered stacks of mail. Many letters were from homosexuals, expressing gratitude. An example of one of them, unfortunately all too typical, concluded with the sentence: ". . . I must leave this letter unsigned in order to keep my job, my child, and the house I live in. Only more films such as yours, presenting us in a human light, will end this malignment."

Some letters, particularly gratifying, came from television writers, producers, and directors, who said that the acceptance of *Summer* would motivate them to take more chances on TV. And, of course, there were protests. One, addressed to the station manager of the ABC affiliate in a town in North Carolina, was signed by nineteen people, and it began: "I viewed a portion of the homosexual movie, 'That Certain Summer,' last Tuesday night. I was very, very disappointed in the station showing such an ungodly, indecent movie, and especially on prime time when most of our children are still up. As a mother I'm very frightened to know what's being shown on TV for our children and teenagers to see." After various quotes from the Bible, the letter stated that we, the makers of "that filthy movie," would have to stand before God and account for our work.

One simply doesn't know how to respond to a letter of this nature. The culture gap is too wide. Ultimately one tends to dismiss it, and others like it, and go on with business as usual. But the lady from North Carolina speaks for a constituency that is by no means limited to the Bible belt—similar protests came from more cosmopolitan urban centers—and in the aftermath of many controversial programs the networks and local stations, as well as the writers and producers, are often bombarded with mail that reflects a deep-seated distress on the part of a segment of the American viewing public that does not want to confront issues on the cutting edge of social change. For them, the purpose of television is to reinforce values that make them comfortable. Advertisers are fully aware of this fact, and it's a source of occasional wonder to us that we and some of our colleagues (particularly Lear in the early days of *All in the Family*) are still able to write about subjects that, to many in the audience, seem inappropriate, threatening, and even dangerous.

The most moving single piece of correspondence came from the chief of the department of psychiatry at a Michigan hospital. He told us that the program had saved a life.

That Certain Summer was viewed by a young man on the eve of his contemplated suicide. Your show so boosted his understanding and courage regarding his secret homosexuality that he changed his mind regarding death as an answer. . . . For the first time in his life he dared talk of his secret to another person, a fellow worker. She too had seen *That Certain Summer.* To his surprise his problem was met with pleasant understanding; she suggested that he seek professional counsel from me. He did so immediately.

"Now he is safe and all goes well. This valuable hard-working young man now seeks a full life. Not death . . . The death would have been charted up as another needless and unsolved auto accident. . . . You of ABC have assisted many to a better understanding. Perhaps some will cope with their fellow man more appropriately. . . .

We were left somewhat breathless in the wake of the show. The awards season was soon upon us, and *Summer* began collecting plaques, scrolls, and statuettes. When viewed from the detached perspective of the nonparticipant, awards may not be of cosmic importance in the general scheme of things. Yet there's no denying that we enjoyed renting tuxedos, congregating in various ballrooms, and having the chance to appear on television where we might be seen by old flames and former English teachers.

Holbrook, Hope Lange, Sheen, and Scott Jacoby were all nominated for Emmys, as was Lamont, Ed Abroms, and the picture itself. We were nominated for best script. Sheen, opposed to awards on principle, asked that his nomination be withdrawn. Holbrook lost and won an Emmy the following year for his portrayal of the commander of the *Pueblo*–a strong and masculine role. He–and we–laughingly met at the ceremonies and speculated that perhaps, just perhaps, the voters remembered his performance in *Summer* and were now honoring him for the safer role. To our delight, Scott Jacoby won.

The Writers Guild selected us for the Best Television Script award and we had the pleasure of receiving the Silver Nymph for writing at the Monte Carlo Film Festival, which was presented to us by another ex-Philadelphian, Princess Grace of Monaco. We won, we were told, after much debate. The Russian and Rumanian delegates on the jury felt that homosexuality was a purely American phenomenon, and therefore had no relevance to other countries.

6 / The Execution of Private Slovik

The Docu-drama

In an age when cemeteries are called "memorial parks," and janitors have been transformed into "custodial engineers," it is not surprising that certain forms of television programs should be labeled like so many soup cans. Of these many and varied catch-phrases, the most troublesome is the term "docu-drama." Clearly, these are two words that do not belong together—they are mutually exclusive, the product of a semantic shotgun wedding. In the public mind a "documentary" exists as a form of truth, of history. From *The March of Time* to Edward R. Murrow's *See It Now*, to *60 Minutes* and *20/20*, there is the expectation, however unrealistic, that we are observing that which is actual, as opposed to that which is imaginary.

"Drama," on the other hand, is created from whole cloth. A writer populates his story with fictitious characters who move about under his arbitrary guidance and who, if he is a television dramatist, will be portrayed by actors who perform in front of a camera and are captured on celluloid or tape. In short, make-believe.

Blending these two seemingly antithetical forms is at best a hazardous business. There are those who insist it shouldn't be attempted at all, that no matter how sincere and conscientious the dramatist may be, and no matter how diligently he honors his sources, he will nevertheless present the audience with a hybrid that is neither fish nor fowl, misleading them as to history and failing to fulfill the requirements of drama.

Even the pure documentary has its detractors. Frederick Wiseman, an able and respected practitioner of *cinema verité,* is constantly under critical fire because he shapes and gives order to the film he exposes, making choices by the simple acts of selecting his subjects and deciding which moments to photograph. *60 Minutes* is frequently condemned for slanting its stories and for manufacturing egregious confrontations. Little wonder then that drama, which by its very nature involves selectivity, compression, and point of view, is considered by many to be an improper way to explore real people and events.

Shakespeare put words in the mouth of Julius Caesar, as did Shaw and Thornton Wilder. Playwrights and novelists have pillaged history for centuries, turning the quick and the dead into spokesmen for their own philosophies. This is common practice, and the objections to these liberties have been minimal. But television brings with it a strong element of credibility that historians and other critics of the medium feel changes the perception of the audience in a significant way. Shakespeare did not practice his art in the context of the Six O'clock News, and there are those who are convinced that the TV viewer cannot easily distinguish between reality and dramatic truth, especially when they cohabit the same piece of furniture.

Accordingly, it is all very well for Shaw to give us the Shavian version of a conversation between Antony and Cleopatra. But let television writer Ernest Kinoy create dialogue for President Truman and General MacArthur during their private meeting on Wake Island (as he did for the docu-drama *Collision Course),* and he becomes an immediate candidate for tar and feathering. Kinoy points out that he knew what Truman said he said, and he knew what MacArthur said *he* said, and he also knew the results of the meeting. But historians are not appeased by this, and charges of distortion, simplification, and misinformation seem to surround many television projects that attempt to deal with nonfictional material. One wonders why academicians are silent on the issue of authenticity when works by Shaw and Shakespeare are presented on television. Or is it only permissible to play hob with the truth when a suitable number of centuries has intervened and none of the actors wears business suits?

There have been docu-dramas on television almost since its inception. One carry-over from radio was the CBS program *You Are There,* in which the ubiquitous Walter Cronkite and his associates were seen, bristling with cameras and microphones, covering the death of Socrates or (the mind boggles) the crucifixion of Christ. *Armstrong Circle Theatre* made a specialty of the form, and *Kraft Theatre* had a technically remarkable live version of Walter Lord's book *A Night to Remember,* which dramatized the sinking of the Titanic.

The category is more or less a loose one, and if biographies are included then the famous series of films on Abraham Lincoln, presented on *Omnibus,* can be said to fall within its scope. More recently, there have been biographical teleplays about the lives of Lou Gehrig, John Kennedy, Howard Hughes, Scott and Zelda Fitzgerald, and Eleanor and Franklin Roosevelt.

The new wave of docu-drama began in 1973 with a taped presentation of *Pueblo,* Stanley Greenberg's adaptation of his off-Broadway play. Greenberg also wrote *The Missiles of October* and *Blind Ambition,* and he has become perhaps the most sought-after practitioner of the form. The first television movie that could be called a docu-drama was *The Execution of Private Slovik,* and after that there were literally dozens of reality-based TV movies and mini-series, from *Roots I* and *II, Helter Skelter* and *Ike,* to one-shots such as *Kill Me If You Can* (the Caryl Chessman story), *The Ordeal of Patty Hearst, Tail Gunner Joe, Fear on Trial, Ruby and Oswald, The Defection of Simas Kudirka, A Man Called Intrepid, Friendly Fire, Attica,* and *The Ordeal of Dr. Mudd.*

Almost as soon as docu-dramas became a prevalent form of programming, the reaction set in. The *Saturday Review*'s Karl Meyer called them "crooked as a camel's back," and in the *Los Angeles Herald Examiner* Miles Beller, summing up for the opposition, complained: ". . . where does 'docu' end and 'drama' begin? . . . today's docu-dramas fail to illuminate eternal truths about man's underlying condition. Instead, they tease us with their half-truths, tantalizing but rarely enlightening . . . they offer platitudes in the place of profundities, speak in clichés rather than in powerful language." Beller also worried that TV authenticates images, and therefore gives the stamp of truth to dramatic condensations and rearrangements of history.

For the defense, Fay Kanin, the adapter of *Friendly Fire,* remarked: "Only in television today can a writer find a platform to deal with contemporary events and ideas. I cannot do it in the theater . . . I cannot do it in the movies, which seem to be occupied with juvenilia and comic strips . . . I have found a place in television. I think it's the one place where I can do serious, responsible work."

David Rintels, a former president of the Writers Guild of America, wrote a thoughtful piece for the *New York Times* in which he, too, gave spirited support to the writer's inalienable rights to utilize history. A part of it is worth quoting:

> Writers and producers, or some of them, are accused of distorting history, of advancing their own prejudices and conceptions in reckless disregard of the facts . . . Anybody may disagree with a writer's judgement, but I believe that most writers who dramatize real people and events have a moral code that tells them: Make no change that is not absolutely necessary to tell the story better, more understandably. Make no change in the facts when the facts are not in dispute or subject to misinterpretation. Never change the essence of the story or the event or the character. Make no change that will make a difference as to how history is perceived. Make no change where a participant in the event will be unfairly damaged. Never invent unless it is necessary to fill a gap, or for reasons of completeness or clarity.

The debate continues. Several years ago a group of television people met with historians and media critics to see if they could resolve some of their differences, or at least come to a clearer understanding of each other's positions. In seminars and group discussions they attempted to find some common ground. A random sampling of their remarks may give some idea as to the complexity of the issues.

David Wolper (Television Producer): "I have believed that the docu-drama is a creative interpretation of reality. It is not reality itself. . . ."

David Susskind (Television and Film Producer): "I'm tired of being lectured by men of good intention that we don't go deeply enough, or we're not aware of human context, or we haven't researched sufficiently. . . . I don't think we need this patronization. We're professionals. . . ."

Eric Foner (Professor of History at City College, City University of New York): "I was interested that in the three categories of problems—ethical, dramatic, and legal—no one included a category of historical. Whether or not everybody is aware of it, you are, in fact, teaching history. . . . I think the first thing that ought to be done by people who are involved in docu-dramas is to realize that your selection of the facts is an interpretation. The very subject you choose to present is itself a political decision. . . ."

Frank Rich (Critic): "I'm willing to accept the premise that every fact in *Backstairs at the White House* was accurate, but what was that show telling us? What did they do with those facts? It was telling us that all the presidents in this century were a bunch of cuddly guys . . . and they had no particular strong political positions. It wasn't clear how they got us in the wars and took us out of the wars and so on. That show was a complete disservice to history even though it was factually accurate."

Gary Deeb (TV Critic): "George Schaefer mentioned last night that he was blasted by some critics for his *Sandburg's Lincoln* series and he said, 'Well, we were very true to Carl Sandburg.' I agree that he was. But I think most of the criticism was that Carl Sandburg was a starry-eyed romantic when it came to Lincoln. And I think if you are going to use Carl Sandburg as the end-all, be-all for Abraham Lincoln, then you get the praise from those who go along with Sandburg's interpretation of Lincoln and you get harsh criticism from those who think you were a fool for going along with it."

Richard Reeves (Journalist): ". . . Alan Landsburg gave one of the most extraordinary statements I've ever heard anyone give in a public or semi-public forum. What he said was that he had toiled in the vineyards of documentaries and he got terribly frustrated by photographing the outside of the White House and not being allowed in the Oval Office to find out what happened. Then he said, 'Thank God docu-drama came along . . . and allowed me to guess what was happening in the Oval Office.' He then continued to say what a marvelous opportunity this was and ended up by saying, 'And now I can tell the truth. I can tell what's really going on in the Oval Office.' That to me is a political story–that many Americans are going to be told one man's guess. . . . I mean, that statement, made in public before one of his shows, would have Congress in session for hearings within an hour."

Paul Selvin (Attorney): "I get two very strong impressions from the historians and the press that I find very, very troubling as an attorney that represents writers . . . The first is . . . the implication that the form of docu-drama itself should not be utilized . . . that you would impose a restriction on the creator that goes so far as to prevent him from even using the form, which I find utter anathema, as someone who pays attention to the First Amendment. . . . The second thing that I find very troubling is that . . . when the form is utilized I find that the press and historians want to impose a significant amount of what I would call restrictions–which is just a nice word for censorship . . ."

Stanley Greenberg (TV Writer): "I'm writing historical drama, which is a very old and honorable form of drama. Now, Schiller said that the only way to write history is to lie. And it occurred to me some time ago, and to other playwrights about the same time, that it would also be very interesting to try to write history by telling the truth. . . . As I study the facts, a point of view begins to shape itself . . . an informed point of view. . . . I think what I have written is true and that my point of view is correct. And I'm prepared to defend it."

Frank Swertlow (TV Critic): "I think there is an important need for docu-drama in our society, because I think there is a great failure of TV news to understand our society and our past."

All of this was years in the future when we decided to make a film of *The Execution of Private Slovik.* The term "docu-drama" had yet to be coined, and the acrimony over the form itself did not exist. We were, as always, looking for stories to tell, and the saga of Eddie Slovik had fascinated us ever since we read about it in William Bradford Huie's book when we were in college.

Shortly after ten o'clock on the morning of January 31, 1945, in the town of St. Marie aux Mines in eastern France, Private Edward Donald Slovik was shot to death by a military firing squad. He was executed in the snow-covered garden of a residence on the outskirts of town, and according to all accounts he conducted himself with considerable bravery.

What makes Slovik special—in the historical sense—are the following series of facts: During the Second World War there were roughly 40,000 American soldiers who deserted. Of these, 2,864 were tried by general court-martial. Forty-nine were sentenced to death. Only one—Eddie Slovik—was executed.

As Huie puts it:

> . . . such death sentences—since the Civil War—have not actually been executed. Not in the Indian wars; not in the Spanish-American War; not in the First War; not in the Second War; not in the Korean War. Despite all the heavy sentences, nobody was shot to death. . . . And this is because it was widely held that the people of the United States no longer demanded—indeed, would no longer tolerate—the extreme penalty for a citizen who refused to fight. So the military representatives of the United States followed a practice of commuting the death sentences, reducing the prison sentences systematically, and releasing the deserters shortly after the wars were over. This was the practice in every case *except one.* No deserter was actually shot *except Private Slovik.*

History aside, Slovik was a provocative and enigmatic human being. He was decent, he was sly, he was hard-working and sincere, he was cowardly and he was courageous. After a misspent Michigan childhood that involved periods in reform school, he was able to straighten himself out and obey the exhortation of the warden to "find a good job and a good woman." Assured by his draft board that the Army didn't want him because of his criminal record, he married the love of his life, Antoinette Wisniewski, and settled down into what he assumed would be an uneventful and bourgeois existence.

But on the very day he and Antoinette moved into their new home, the Army changed its mind and drafted him. Outraged and depressed, he was torn from the life he had built for himself and shipped overseas to join a rifle company. At some point, for reasons unknown, he decided that he would never fire his weapon. He deserted, and when he eventually returned to his own lines he was arrested, imprisoned in the stockade, and tried by a general court-martial.

Slovik knew that deserters were punished by confinement in jail; he counted on it. He was willing to serve his time and return after the war to his beloved Antoinette. It was a decision of pure calculation, and given the prevailing circumstances he had every reason to believe that within a year or so he would be safely home.

But Slovik was one of life's eternal losers. Somehow, through a confluence of bad luck and bad timing, his scheme backfired. Instead of putting him behind bars, the members of the court-martial found him guilty of all charges against him and—unanimously—sentenced him "to be shot to death with musketry." The presiding officer, reflecting on the case, later stated that he didn't think a single member of the tribunal actually believed that Slovik would ever be shot. There were too many procedures for review and appeal between the verdict and the firing squad.

Nevertheless, incredibly, Slovik was executed. He met his death in the snowy garden in St. Marie aux Mines and now lies buried in an American cemetery in France. He sleeps in a dishonored grave, surrounded by soldiers who were executed for crimes of rape or murder, and his story was untold and unpublicized until Huie wrote his book.

Perhaps even more incredible is the fact that Antoinette Slovik did not even know her husband had been executed. She was informed only that he died "under dishonorable circumstances"—until Huie approached her in the course of his research.

After we finished work on *That Certain Summer* and the picture was in answer print, our employers in the Black Tower reminded us ever so gently that we had been out of the series business for quite some time.

One-shot TV movies were a nice avocation, but they didn't keep the soundstages humming, pay the salaries of the security police, or put coffee in the coffee machines. We were, were we not, under term contract, and wasn't at least part of our obligation to generate a few bread-and-butter ideas? Bowing to the inevitable, we turned our attention to two new projects, both of them pilots. One was called *Partners in Crime,* starring Lee Grant and Lou Antonio, and the other was *Tenafly,* with James McEachin, the talented black actor who had played the cable car conductor in *Summer.*

Both shows were meant to be escapist entertainment, but each was interesting to us because it went against the tide of traditional industry practice. *Partners* had, as its leading character, a judge—a female judge. Few women had ever carried a dramatic television series,* and it was not until Angie Dickinson starred in *Police Woman* several years later that a series with a woman in the leading role was a success. The Powers That Be were unshakable in their belief that a woman could prop up a sitcom *(I Love Lucy, The Mary Tyler Moore Show,* et al), but not a dramatic series. In any event, *Partners in Crime* aired as a TV movie, but was passed over during the selling season and faded into the limbo of syndication.

Tenafly, however, did become a television series—the first non-comedy series to have a black as its protagonist. Blacks had starred in their own series as far back as the offensive video version of *Amos and Andy,* but always in sitcoms. Again—as with women—the prevailing view held that the audience would accept a black lead only in the context of comedy.

We conceived Harry Tenafly to be a very unexciting private detective in the employ of a large corporation on the order of Burns or Pinkerton. His assignments were usually nothing more than spotting shoplifters in a local supermarket or guarding the presents at a bar mitzvah. He punched a time clock, wore a suit and tie, had a wife and two children, and lived in a suburb with a white man for his next-door neighbor.

For the purpose of the series (it was a ninety-minute show), we

---

* One exception was *Honey West,* with Anne Francis. But in a nervous hedging of bets she was given a male companion. So was Pepper Anderson.

decided that each segment would involve him in two unconnected stories, one major and crime-oriented, the other personal and on a smaller scale. We wanted to present him as an intelligent, upwardly mobile, relatively average middle-class breadwinner, without dwelling on the color of his skin. If any point was to be made it would be made by indirection. No polemics, no scenes involving the issue of race—our hope was that the audience would accept a black as the lead in a genre show without any fuss or fanfare.

NBC took a chance and gave a go-ahead after they saw the pilot. But they tried to repeat the success of the *Sunday Night Mystery Movie* by rotating *Tenafly* with several other series, including *The Snoop Sisters* and *Faraday and Son,* and this time the expected lightning failed to strike. The ratings were tepid and all of the shows were canceled after only a brief run. *Tenafly* did no better and no worse than any of the others. However, with the exception of *Shaft* and, years later, *Paris* with James Earl Jones, there has yet to be another dramatic series with a black lead.

Shortly before we launched the two pilots we made our yearly call to Frank Sinatra's lawyer. Sinatra owned the rights to *The Execution of Private Slovik* and we, doubtless in concert with half of Hollywood, made periodic checks as to their status. They were always unavailable; for years Sinatra had refused to sell. But this time our inquiry brought an astonishing reply: Sinatra no longer owned the property. He had sold it to a New York director of commercials.

The history of the motion picture rights to Huie's book is almost as full of convolutions as the history of Eddie Slovik himself. *The Execution of Private Slovik* was published in 1954, when Dwight Eisenhower, the man who, as Supreme Allied Commander, signed the order for the firing squad, was president. As Huie put it:

> Over the years one film maker after another approached the story, determined to film it. Before the book was published a prominent producer connected with a major studio went with me to the Pentagon. There he was told, "The Army stands ready to cooperate with any reputable producer who wants to make this film as objectively as the

book has been written. All we ask is that Slovik not be
portrayed in the film as any more sympathetic a character
than he is presented in the book." A week later a representative of the White House traveled to California to pass
the word that the White House preferred that no film be
made.

Huie's strong implication is that either Eisenbower or his subordinates felt that a motion picture version of the book would embarrass
the President. Nevertheless, Sinatra finally acquired the rights. He had
decided to make the film with himself as director and with an unknown actor named Steve McQueen as Eddie Slovik. Then he made a
choice that does him credit—but a choice, unfortunately, that triggered headlines all over the world and ultimately forced him to cancel
the picture. He hired, to write the screenplay, a man named Albert
Maltz.

Maltz was a successful novelist who had come to Hollywood to
become an equally successful scenarist. He had written screenplays for
This Gun for Hire, Destination Tokyo, and *The Naked City,* among
others. But in 1947 he refused to answer questions before the House
Committee on Un-American Activities. He became (along with
Adrian Scott and Dalton Trumbo) a member of the Hollywood Ten,
and he was jailed for contempt of Congress. When he was released
from prison he found himself blacklisted, unable to obtain employment at any of the studios. He moved to Mexico and wrote
screenplays anonymously and for little money, selling them with the
names of "fronts" on the title pages instead of his own.

Although Otto Preminger and Stanley Kramer broke the blacklist
by hiring prohibited writers and permitting them to use their own
names, Sinatra's employment of Maltz, as Murray Schumach noted in
the *New York Times,* "marks the first time that a top movie star has
defied the rule laid down by the major movie studios." Maltz was to
receive his first screen credit in almost a decade. When Sinatra was
asked if he was afraid of unfavorable reaction he said: "We'll find out
later. We'll see what happens."

He did not have long to wait. The American Legion, the Hearst
press, and columnists such as Hedda Hopper and George Sokolsky

erupted with fury. Sinatra was more vulnerable than Preminger and Kramer because he was publicly supporting Senator John F. Kennedy for the Democratic presidential nomination. He was also the close friend and business partner of Peter Lawford, who was then married to Kennedy's sister.

After absorbing sufficient abuse, Sinatra moved to meet his critics head-on. At the end of March, 1960, he took a full-page ad in the Hollywood trade papers. Headlined: "A STATEMENT FROM FRANK SINATRA," it read:

> This statement is made by me so that the public will have all the facts before passing judgment in regard to my hiring Albert Maltz to write the screenplay of "The Execution of Private Slovik."
>
> I bought the William Bradford Huie book which tells the true story of the only execution of a soldier by the United States Army since the Civil War.
>
> Since I will produce and direct the picture I am concerned that the screenplay reflects the true pro-American values of the story.
>
> This means that the picture must be an affirmative declaration in the best American tradition.
>
> I spoke to many screenwriters but it was not until I talked to Albert Maltz that I found a writer who saw the screenplay in exactly the terms I wanted. That is, the Army was right.
>
> Under the Bill of Rights, I was taught that no one may prescribe what shall be orthodox in politics, religion, or other matters of opinion.
>
> I am in complete accord with the statement made earlier this week by J. D. Nicola of the Catholic Legion of Decency, who said, "The Legion evaluated films on the basis of art, not the artist."
>
> As the producer of the film I and I alone will be responsible for it. I accept that responsibility. I only ask that judgment be deferred until the picture is seen.
>
> I would also like to comment on the attacks from cer-

tain quarters on Senator John Kennedy by connecting him with my decision on employing a screenwriter.

This type of partisan politics is hitting below the belt.

I make movies. I do not ask the advice of Senator Kennedy on whom I should hire. Senator Kennedy does not ask me how he should vote in the Senate.

I am prepared to stand on my principles and to await the verdict of the American people when they see "The Execution of Private Slovik."

I repeat: In my role as a picture-maker, I have—in my opinion—hired the best man to do the job.

Despite this statement, the attacks in the press continued. Typical was this headline in the *New York Journal-American:* "SINATRA'S WRITER DENOUNCES U.S. LAUDED RED GERMANY IN 1954 LETTER." The *New York Mirror* joined its sister paper with the following: "MALTZ STUCK TO MARXIST LINE."

Less than two weeks after the publication of his advertisement, Sinatra took out another. It read:

In view of the reaction of my family, my friends, and the American public, I have instructed my attorneys to make a settlement with Albert Maltz and to inform him he will not write the screenplay for "The Execution of Private Slovik."

I had thought the major consideration was whether or not the resulting script would be in the best interests of the United States.

Since my conversations with Mr. Maltz indicated that he had an affirmative, pro-American approach to the story, and since I felt fully capable as producer of enforcing such standards, I have defended my hiring of Mr. Maltz.

But the American public has indicated it feels the morality of hiring Albert Maltz is the more crucial matter, and I will accept this majority opinion.

It was rumored at the time that Sinatra bowed to pressure not from the press but from the Kennedy family, who allegedly told him that they did not want this kind of publicity swirling around one of their supporters on the eve of the convention.*

In a blunderbuss postmortem in his column, George Sokolsky likened Sinatra's hiring of Maltz to "the Ford Foundation subsidizing an opera on the Sacco and Vanzetti case." And he concluded, with barely concealed satisfaction: ". . . Sinatra's action outraged a sufficiently large section of the American people to force him to back down. . . . It will not go unnoticed by other Hollywood money-grubbers who committed moral outrages in the name of Art. But is he still to glorify a deserter in war-time?"

Apparently not. Though various producers said they had deals, with Sinatra's permission, to make the picture, he held on to the rights for a number of years—until our annual phone call to his lawyer elicited the information that he had finally sold them.

We spoke to Sid Sheinberg and told him of our desire to do the Slovik story as a television film. NBC expressed interest and Universal's Business Affairs people began the long process—it was to take many months—of purchasing the rights from the New York commercial director who had acquired them from Sinatra.

We were still involved with other work, but we began to set aside blocks of time in which to ponder the best way to dramatize Huie's book. He had told the story more or less in sequence, beginning with Slovik's youth and reform-school days, detailing his courtship and marriage to Antoinette, and then following him into the Army, concluding with his trial and his appointment with the firing squad. The book included letters from Slovik to his wife, as well as observations on his character by people who knew him during various stages of his life. These letters and reflections were far too valuable to exclude, but our problem was how to incorporate them into an ongoing story.

We decided to break the film down into the traditional three-act

---

* Victor S. Navasky, in his remarkable book *Naming Names,* suggests that Sinatra acceded to a private request from Joseph P. Kennedy.

form. The first act, in order to involve the audience immediately, would be the preparations for the execution. The second, a flashback, would examine the reasons for the execution. And the third would be the execution itself. Normally we are not fond of the flashback device because it has become something of a cliché. But in this instance we felt that viewer interest would be dissipated if we started Slovik's story at the beginning.

We also decided to employ a *Citizen Kane* technique, a mosaic approach that would permit people in the present to comment, by voice-over narration, on the events of the past. For example, we wrote a scene in which Eddie and Antoinette are dancing in his favorite taproom when he is home on leave after basic training. As the music of "Tangerine" plays from the jukebox, and the two of them sway together, we hear Antoinette's voice speaking off-camera: "I never saw him again. . . . They told me he had died under dishonorable circumstances . . . but I didn't know until eight years later that they killed him."

The book was so compelling, and we were so mesmerized by Slovik's story, that we did something we had never done before–we sat down and wrote a script before we had even secured the rights to the material. We completed the 124-page teleplay in only a few weeks; it seemed to write itself. Fortunately, a deal was struck, money changed hands, and all legal obstacles were cleared away. Unbelievable as it seemed, *The Execution of Private Slovik* was finally going to be made into a film.

Except–there is always an except–the studio suddenly decided it couldn't afford the excessive costs of the picture. Scores of speaking parts would be required. The story moved from Michigan to wartime France. We had set scenes on Army bases and rifle ranges; there were battle sequences; and there was, of course, the execution itself–ranks of troops, a twelve-man firing squad, a villa, and a coverlet of snow on the ground. *Slovik* was also a period picture, meaning that wardrobe, civilian as well as military, had to be rented. We needed the ambiance of the 1940s, not only clothing but the automobiles and Army equipment of the time. All of this was available, but for a price. And it was a price Universal was unwilling to pay. The network license fee for a two-hour television movie wouldn't begin to cover the expense. Universal expected, in the words of one of the executives, to "eat some deficit," but our projected budget was much too high.

One reason why television films are more limited in scope and subject matter than theatrical motion pictures is the inadequacy of network license fees. Suppliers are always complaining that they are far too low. The networks counter that the money is quite sufficient, providing the suppliers mend their spendthrift ways. Sadly, this perpetual debate all too often manifests itself in periodic campaigns of cost-cutting, and the films that are on the line during these moments of economic hysteria suffer as a result.

For a month or so, *Slovik* was on the verge of cancellation. Pressure was exerted on us to shoot the movie on the back lot, using cornflakes for snow. This was unacceptable. And then someone somewhere had a brainstorm and the dilemma was resolved, typically in a way that was harmful to the picture.

The solution was to sell *Slovik* to the network as a two-and-a-half hour television film. The money for the additional half-hour would give Universal at least some measure of financial relief. The esthetic implications of this were not considered. As it happened, two-and-a-half hours was far more time than we needed to tell the story, but the matter was academic—either the show would be thirty minutes longer or there would be no show at all. Faced with this Hobson's choice we began adding material, some of it extraneous, to our teleplay.

Orson Welles is credited with observing that no film can ever be too short, and in our opinion most motion pictures and television films could benefit from judicious pruning. Perhaps commercials, with their accelerated pace, have conditioned all of us with their thirty- or sixty-second time frames. Ned Sherrin, the British television humorist, has described two ways of telling the difference between a movie-movie and a TV movie. One is that in a movie-movie Ray Milland wears his toupee and in a TV movie he does not. And the other is that in a movie-movie (particularly an old one) characters leave their homes, stroll to their cars, get in, start the motors, and drive off. In a TV movie they are in mid-conversation in a living room, there is a cut, and suddenly they are in their cars rocketing away from the curb.

Making minimal allowance for exaggeration—and setting aside the toupee discussion—there is much truth to Mr. Sherrin's remarks. Film-making techniques have evolved over the years to propel a story at a much faster narrative speed. Audiences have been educated away from the necessity of certain kinds of connective material; the mind fills them in. Therefore padding—the kind we were forced to add to *Slovik*—stands out all the more.

This points up one of the great disadvantages of the television film in comparison with the motion picture. Within rather flexible limits, a movie can be cut to its best length. If something does not play, if there are *longueurs,* they can be trimmed or deleted entirely in the editing room. But a television film has no elasticity; it must be cut to format. The networks provide detailed requirements as to footage and commercial breaks, and there is little room for maneuver. Einstein notwithstanding, an hour is an hour, and it must be filled by sixty minutes of film. This is one of the reasons why television shows, even the segments of a series, may seem long or excessively sluggish. The situation is analogous to a publisher telling a novelist that his book must be 600 pages, and that 599 pages, or 601 pages, are simply beyond the pale.

To counter the problem most producers endeavor to shoot more film than they need. When the picture is completed and editing commences, it is a gift from the gods to be ten minutes or so over-length. This extra footage allows enough latitude to play with the pacing, or to drop entirely a scene that doesn't work. But when the picture is finally down to network format the editing process must stop, even though further tightening would be beneficial.

Once in a while, as in the case of *That Certain Summer,* television films are permitted to come in under footage requirements by what translates into a minute or two. The networks fill in the extra time with public service announcements. But to get a variance is almost as difficult as securing a papal dispensation. This is an unfortunate state of affairs; many if not most television films would show marked improvement if only another few minutes could be shaken out.

Our original intention was to make *Slovik* in France, but since the World Bank was not subsidizing us we began searching for alternatives. We needed snow for the execution sequence, and even the budget-minded executives at the studio could not muster much enthusiasm for their cornflakes-as-snow idea.

We eventually settled on Canada, and after several scouting trips we located a suitable house near Montreal. We also found a remarkable community of talented actors in Toronto, and we decided to use as many of them as possible. Canadians can pass easily for Americans, except for such telltale words as "out" and "about," which they pronounce "ooot" and "aboot." Casting these actors, all of them unfamiliar to American audiences, would give us a leg up on the documentary reality we were seeking. And the Canadians assured us that we would have all the snow we needed.

We hired Lamont Johnson for his third go-around with us, and although he liked the script he needed some persuading. He felt that the Eddie and Antoinette scenes were banal. They were meant to be banal, of course—Huie pointed out that the two of them were deliberately trying to model their lives on the movies and the slick magazine stories of the period. The stereotypical values of the middle class were extremely important to Slovik; after his years of deprivation he had carefully constructed his own small version of the American dream, and when the Army tore him away from this cocoon he was bewildered and resentful.

Even before Lamont joined the project we had pretty much decided that we wanted an acting company of relative unknowns. For the part of Eddie Slovik we had all but settled on Martin Sheen. We asked him to stop by the office and showed him some of Slovik's photographs and letters. Sheen was deeply moved; he said he would do everything he could to hold himself available for our shooting dates.

And then, out of the blue Dustin Hoffman telephoned us from New York. We were familiar with his work, not only on-screen but also in the theater, but we had never met him. He introduced himself and asked whether it would be possible for Universal to change direction and make *Slovik* as a motion picture instead of a television film. If so, he'd be very interested in playing the lead.

We spoke to Sid Sheinberg. After mulling it over he said, "I'm not sure that *The Execution of Private Slovik,* even with Dustin Hoffman, would be a successful motion picture." Sheinberg may have had two films, *Paths of Glory* and *King and Country*, in mind. Both were excellent, both concerned the death of soldiers at the hands of a firing squad, and both were commercial failures.*

Our project had another similarity to these films: the word "downer" was uttered whenever it was discussed. Being a "downer," it had far too great a "downside risk" (surely one of the most oppressive phrases in the show business lexicon) to be considered for a theatrical venture.

We relayed this news to Dustin Hoffman, who digested it and said, "In that case, would you consider me for the television version?" We were startled. So, evidently, was he—he admitted that he had discussed with his psychiatrist the possibility that he might undertake the role of Eddie Slovik for a TV film and had been told, in effect, that he was crazy.

We reminded him that American superstars, unlike their British counterparts, do not risk their careers and their agents' wrath by appearing on television. For that matter, they rarely if ever undertake a run in a play, considering one motion picture a year to be more than sufficient to maintain their prestige and bank accounts. We informed Hoffman that we had a tight shooting schedule, that we had already selected our director, and that, frankly, we couldn't afford him. It was a strange conversation. We were explaining to one of the best young actors in America why he shouldn't do our film, completely forgetting that it was his suggestion in the first place.

He assured us that he was serious about wanting to play the role, regardless of the medium, that he didn't object to the director, and that he would see to it that we could afford him on our budget. He would, however, insist on a suitable rehearsal period and a schedule that would give us enough time to make a worthwhile film. Altogether very reasonable requests, and unlikely to escalate our budget unacceptably. Besides, once NBC knew that we could deliver Dustin Hoffman they'd be only too happy to increase the license fee.

Television people collect Rude Awakenings the way others collect stamps or snuff boxes. We were in for a corker when we met with a group of NBC executives at the network's Burbank headquarters. They greeted the mention of Hoffman's name with what can most

---

* *Paths of Glory* was eventually to recoup its costs.

charitably be described as mild enthusiasm. "If you want him you can have him," one of them said, "but we're certainly not prepared to give you any extra money. Did you see the numbers on *John Loves Mary?* He doesn't mean anything on TV."

Elsewhere in this book we have gone on record with what some might consider a defense of the network mentality. But in the area of casting, all bets are off. For it is impossible to fathom the vagaries of taste, whim, and capriciousness that arise the moment actors are to be selected for a television show.

The Hoffman situation is a case in point. His film *John Loves Mary* had been aired shortly before our meeting with the NBC brass, and it had done poorly in the Nielsen ratings. Ergo, Hoffman could not command a television audience. In addition—and this is another example of network casting doublethink—he was a movie star, and movie stars are not necessarily television stars. Jean Stapleton is a television star. Jane Fonda is a movie star. Therefore, regardless of suitability, the network would prefer Jean Stapleton for a part over Jane Fonda—on TV Miss Stapleton "means more." And Carroll O'Connor "means more" than Laurence Olivier. It would not be wrenching reality to suggest that, from the network point of view, Suzanne Somers is preferable to, say, Diana Rigg. Then too, Miss Rigg is English, and everyone knows that the American audience does not like to listen to a British accent. Proof of this is the failure of a situation comedy that Miss Rigg attempted a number of years ago. The series failed because it was not particularly good, but network people assured us at the time that it was just another example of the "English accent" syndrome.

What complicates things even more is that while Actor A may be in great demand at ABC, CBS won't approve him, and NBC doesn't even know who he is. All of which would be a matter for amusement were it not for the fact that the network has, at a minimum, "consultation rights" over casting, and at a maximum full rights of approval, particularly when it comes to the casting of pilots. Producers must often submit lists of five or six actors for every part to a network executive, who presumably consults the entrails of small animals and then circles the one or two—or none—who are acceptable.

Actually, what the executive may in fact consult are Performer Q ratings, which are popularity indexes complied and furnished by a company in Port Washington, New York. Actors are listed in terms of their popularity and their familiarity. Ms. Fonda, for example, is well known to the audience (or that portion of the audience used as a sample to fill out questionnaires), but she is not well liked. Alan Alda is both well known and well liked.

The very idea of such a rating is deplorable. It is almost a form of blacklisting, and it leads to the low-risk casting of familiar names rather than the use of the best available actor for each part. It also deprives many actors of employment, not only because their scores are low, but because they will rarely be selected over the better-known competition.

The networks, in concert, deny using the Q ratings. And when they privately admit that they do "look them over," they insist that such index systems are only "one tool among many" that may or may not be considered. But even without such Orwellian devices, network casting procedures are a great source of friction between the broadcasters and those on the production line.

As far as *Slovik* was concerned, NBC was not adamantly opposed to the casting of Dustin Hoffman—although we were told that he placed surprisingly low on the index that no one was supposed to read. It was simply that they didn't feel he was worth any special consideration in terms of time or money. They were not particularly avid over the choice of Martin Sheen either, but since they could come up with no one with a blockbuster TV "name" for the part (at the time Sheen was not yet considered a television star) they were inclined to go along with us if we insisted on him.

We called Hoffman's manager and, not wishing to hurt his client's feelings, told him that it now appeared our shooting dates would overlap the start of Hoffman's next film, the Bob Fosse production of *Lenny*. And then we directed Universal's casting department to make an offer to Martin Sheen.

The making of *The Execution of Private Slovik* was a logistical nightmare. In twenty-six days, exclusive of travel time, we filmed in Long

Beach, California, at the prison facilities on Terminal Island, at Camp Roberts (an upstate Army post), at the Fox Ranch, in Pasadena, on the soundstages at Universal, on the back lot, and in Montreal and Quebec City. We shot the court-martial sequence in the Grand Ballroom of the Queen Mary because Lamont fell in love with "all that blond Nazi wood."

If *That Certain Summer* was a writer's picture, then *Slovik* was a director's picture. Lamont worked particularly well with the actors, even to the point of improvising scenes between Sheen and Mariclaire Costello, who played Antoinette. We would monitor these improvisations, write them down, and then polish and distribute them to the actors, who would commit them to memory and replay them with a freshness and spontaneity they would never have achieved by parroting lines of dialogue.

Lamont also grappled with a massive physical production, marshaling troops, deploying cameras, and facing the biggest single disappointment of the shooting schedule, the absence of even a single snowflake in Montreal. While the Canadians clucked their tongues over the "unseasonable weather," we waited in vain for snow to fall. In desperation, we were forced to truck in blocks of ice—literally tons of it—grind it up in machines, and spray it over the trees and courtyard of the Montreal chateau. The ice usually melted overnight and the hapless crew had to snow things in each morning. Fortunately, the air was cold enough for the actors' breath to turn to frost, which added a realistic touch when the cameras were rolling.

There were, as always, mistakes. In one scene Eddie leaves the reform school in Michigan and has a conversation with the warden at the gate. All very well and good—except for a palm tree that loomed over Sheen's shoulder in his close-up. We marched onto the set and inquired about the eyesight of the cinematographer, the camera operator, and the director. When confronted with the news of this inappropriate piece of vegetation in his shot, Lamont decided to brazen it out in true von Stroheim fashion: "There are palm trees in Michigan!" he announced.

It was inevitable that due to the subject matter the filming of *Slovik* would be a gloomy experience. Two excerpts from our journal may give an indication of the day-to-day flavor of the production:

December 4, 1973

Filming in the tower. Crucial scenes between Slovik and the Chaplain. A French Canadian priest is brought to the set at lunchtime to consult with Marty and Ned Beatty. [Beatty played the Chaplain.] His English is not good and their French is nonexistent. Lunch, by the way, is served on the second floor of the garage. Long tables have been set up and there's a serving line. It's much like summer camp–or the Army. In fact, there are moments when we feel we have been transported back to the days of World War II. Jeeps and Army trucks rumble by. Soldiers gather in corners of the courtyard. Rifles. Combat boots and field jackets. Canteens. Privates and sergeants sneaking puffs on cigarettes. Our sense of time has been dislocated. Colonel Burgher, our military advisor, is a hard, trim man who wears a light jacket in the cold. He's been spending his time drilling the firing squad, barking orders at them. He has to break down their Canadian military habits and then instruct them in American procedures. He sometimes forgets he is dealing with actors, not soldiers, but the men indulge him. He is having the time of his life.

We have problems transporting our dailies from America. Given customs and Air Canada's L.A. schedule, we cannot see them for four days. Grumbling, we call them "weeklies." Marty tells us a remarkable thing. His wife has written him a packet of letters, addressed to "Pvt. Eddie Slovik" and signed "Antoinette." As Antoinette she writes about Detroit, their mutual friends, and says how she misses him and longs for his return from the war. Marty didn't read the letters until just before he filmed the Chaplain scene, and when he finally read them he broke down. He is deeply in character now. New York wants to send up reporters but he has asked us to hold off all interviews.

It has grown dark. Trucks stand in the gloom. Ned Beatty, in his Chaplain uniform, crosses in a preoccupied way toward his trailer. Two soldier-actors, as a joke, salute him. For a moment, he doesn't know where he is.

December 11

Filming parts of the execution, all day. This time with the actual firing. Marty is squibbed [a special effects technique where small charges of gunpowder are attached to an actor's body] and wears a bullet-proof vest. The marksmen fire and his chest seems to explode. We all hold our breath, partially from the harsh violence of the moment, partially out of fear that Marty may have been hurt. But he is fine. Our grim day's work is thrown out of kilter because the sun suddenly decides to come out and the sky turns a bright baby blue. We shoot in shadows as much as possible, waiting for the inevitable overcast. Lamont rushes against the fading light. Everyone is freezing.

Now the dead Marty Sheen has been taken from the post and lies, blood-soaked, on the ground. He is waiting for a take. The owner of the house strolls into the yard and glances at him with considerable amusement. "First corpse I've ever seen with his hands in his pockets," he chuckles.

Bill Butler [the cinematographer] looks pale and sick. A doctor is on the set checking him out. Lamont admits that he, too, is coming down with something. It grows too dark to shoot. Reluctantly, Lamont decides he will have to let the assistant director do second unit material in the morning while he gets the reaction shots for the execution. Then Lamont will move up to the Laurentian Mountains for the opening sequence of the picture.

During the day, after what seems like thousands of harried phone calls, some missing dailies have been tracked down. No film lost so far, in spite of all the back-and-forth shipping. We stop by Lamont's hotel room that night to ask if he'd like to join us for dinner. But he looks awful. He is exhausted. He wants to have dinner in his room and fall into bed.

The picture was finished a few days after Christmas and in the expert hands of the editor, Frank Morriss. When he and Lamont completed their cut, and we had made our changes, it was screened for the network. NBC's response was positive, although one high-level executive took strong issue with an aspect of the firing squad sequence. According to Huie, Eddie Slovik was not killed by the first barrage of rifle fire. He sagged against the ropes binding him to the post—there was a hood over his head—moaning while he was examined by a military doctor. There was some confusion as to whether the marksmen should reload and shoot again. Everyone present at the execution was in a state of shock over the fact that he was still alive. Minutes passed. After an excruciating delay, and just before the men readied themselves to fire again, the doctor pronounced Slovik dead.

We included this in the film, although we condensed the time span. The NBC executive wanted it cut entirely; he thought it would be too grim for a television audience. When we mentioned this to Sheinberg he asked, "Did it happen?" We told him it did. "Then deliver the film as is," he said, "and if they don't like it we'll take it away from them and release it theatrically."

We had two other bones of contention with the network. The first was, as Conan Doyle might put it, "The Adventure of the Dirty Words." Very early in the film a soldier refers to Slovik as a "poor bastard." And in one of the middle reels a master sergeant, confronting a sorry group of recruits, informs them that he intends to "kick ass." Naturally Standards and Practices sent us notification that the use of the words "bastard" and "ass" was forbidden. In place of "ass" they helpfully suggested "butt."

The second problem was that NBC, alone among the three networks, would not permit the press to pre-review any of its programs. A matter of entrenched corporate policy. But from our point of view a very definite roadblock. If critics and members of the press could not see the film before it aired, how could they advise the public whether or not to watch it?

Someone once said that television critics are people who describe accidents to eyewitnesses. And it's a truism that a review cannot entice viewers if it is printed after a show has already been on the air. But if it runs in advance, and a particular readership respects a particular critic, then a laudatory notice can be useful. There is no doubt that critical praise for such television films as *Brian's Song* and *The Autobiography of Miss Jane Pittman* was a factor in the massive audiences for each of these shows.

Being naturally disputatious, we decided to fight. One of us boarded the Los Angeles to New York redeye, carrying the twelve-odd cans of *Slovik* film, and the next morning presented himself, with film cans, at Herb Schlosser's office high in the RCA Building. It may seem like a long and quixotic journey to plead a case for a "bastard" and an "ass," but there was also the policy against pre-reviewing to be confronted. Schlosser and his associates ran the film and huddled in debate. Then word trickled out from their screening room in the sky— "bastard" and "ass" could stay. And not only would *Slovik* be pre-reviewed, but a special showing would be held for the press at an East Side motion picture theater.

When the film was in its final form (we had decided against any kind of musical score, employing, instead, several popular songs of the early forties), we showed it to invited audiences. The reaction was all we could have asked for. People emerged from the screening rooms visibly shaken. A friend of Universal's head publicist dropped him a note and he passed it along to us: "Thanks for the invitation . . . Shattering experience. There was dead silence when it finished; none of the usual applause when the credits came on. Obviously people were too overwhelmed by their feelings to react to it simply as a film. . . ."

In the last paragraph of his letter the writer made a point that was important to us: "The other thing that impressed me was the fact that there were really no villains, no nasty sadists. Everybody was decent; all trying to do their duty as assigned. Everybody fitting into the system; only Slovik out of step and too dumb to protect himself. . . ."

Before writing the script we decided we did not want to slant the material, that we would try to the best of our ability to keep our opinions to ourselves and let the audience draw its own conclusions. But true impartiality, though admirable in concept, is almost impossible in practice. While we sought balance, other elements, having nothing to do with the script, came into play—most notably the climate of the times. *The Execution of Private Slovik* was made in late 1973, when the Vietnam War was the central issue on the minds of many Americans. Thus, a contagion of hindsight infected our collaborators, particularly Martin Sheen. He hated the Vietnam War with a great passion, and all too often he was unable to distinguish between it and World War Two. He viewed Eddie Slovik as a martyr, a young protestor (much like the students who decried our involvement in Southeast Asia) whose only sin was to stand up to the Establishment.

He did not want to hear that Eddie Slovik was a deserter in a war that had nowhere near the same moral ambiguities as the conflict in Vietnam. To him Eddie was a hero, and so we were forever reminding him to "show the warts," to let the audience see Slovik's moments of self-serving calculation. Sheen understood our point and tried to be cooperative, but he was all but incapable of delivering these nuances in his performance. He loved the man so much that he tried to make a saint of him on film.

It's been our experience that people usually come away from television with a reinforcement of prior attitudes, and in the case of *Slovik* we seemed to be preaching to the converted. Many of our friends, some of them activists opposed to the Vietnam War, congratulated us for showing the Army as an inhumane killing machine. Others, more conservative, were pleased that we had presented Eddie Slovik as they assumed he really was—a cowardly opportunist.

Perhaps the most typical reaction, and the one that gave us the most satisfaction, occurred during one of our screenings, when we happened to be in the projection booth. Two projectionists were on duty, and as the last reel unspooled they began to argue about the picture. One man said that he didn't understand what all the fuss was about. Slovik had deserted, hadn't he? He had betrayed his buddies. Here was a soldier who wouldn't fire his rifle, who didn't give a damn that the Germans were out to conquer the world. He deserved to be shot.

The other projectionist acknowledged the truth in this. "But thousands of soldiers deserted," he said. "Why didn't they shoot them all? Why just pick on one guy? Was he worse than all the rest?"

By sheer coincidence, Albert Maltz came to one of our last screenings. He had married the mother of a friend of ours, and when we invited our friend we asked if he would extend the invitation to Maltz as well. After most screenings the audience stands around in small groups, sometimes cheerfully tearing the picture to shreds, sometimes full of genuine enthusiasm. But *Slovik* was different–after each showing everyone tended to walk silently to his or her car and drive away. If they liked it, we would hear from them the next day.

Maltz, however, stayed behind for a few moments to speak with us. It must have been a strange experience for him, seeing a film that had embroiled him in so much controversy over a decade ago. He said that he liked Sheen's performance, but other than that he was noncommittal.

Our friend later told us that Maltz disagreed with our approach. He felt Slovik should have come to the belated realization that he had been wrong to desert, that the Army was fighting a just war against the Fascists, and that by attending to his own selfish concerns he had made an immoral choice. With this insight would come peace of mind and, for our drama, catharsis.

Perhaps Maltz's views were being accurately reflected when Sinatra said: ". . . it was not until I talked to Albert Maltz that I found a writer who saw the screenplay in exactly the terms I wanted. That is, the Army was right." Obviously we and Maltz disagreed. In our opinion no one was right, neither Slovik nor the bureaucracy that sentenced him to death. We shared the view of the projectionist who felt that though Slovik committed a crime–understandable in human terms, but a crime nonetheless–the punishment meted out to him was singular and discriminatory. "Why pick on just one guy? Was he worse than all the rest?"

Far from accepting his own guilt, the real Eddie Slovik turned to the men who were preparing him for his execution and said, "They're not shooting me for deserting the United States Army. Thousands of guys have done that. They're shooting me for bread I stole when I was twelve years old."

The night before *Slovik* went on the air, one of us found himself seated directly across from Frank Sinatra in a restaurant. The temptation to speak to him, to ask him if he knew about the show and intended to watch, was considerable. But courtesy–or a lack of nerve—prevailed, and Sinatra was left to eat his dinner without interruption.

The partner who was not dining out was, of all things, watching television. A TV movie, to be exact. As it ended, and the credits rolled, the familiar voice of Ed McMahon came over the airwaves with a list of guests who would appear that evening on the Johnny Carson show. The use of a promotional voice-over, in which an actor or an announcer makes a pitch for the program that follows, is common to all three networks.

And it struck horror into the heart of the homebound partner because *Slovik* ends with a long death march. The body, under a blanket, is carried away, the chaplain by its side. As the final credits roll the witnesses to the execution drift slowly from the courtyard until it is empty. The wooden gates bang shut and the only sound is that of the wind.

We'd had our usual fight with the Technicolor laboratory to keep them from artificially brightening our deliberately muted colors; we'd made absolutely sure that the network technicians would not "correct" either color or sound when the film was transferred to tape for broadcasting. But Ed McMahon had never even crossed our minds. In the middle of our death march we were going to have Ed cheerfully telling the audience to stay tuned for Don Rickles and the Mighty Carson Art Players. Mood-shattering, to say the least.

The next morning we fell on the phone and began making calls to NBC. Finding the right department was like a treasure hunt, and having found it there was the matter of getting authorization to silence the ebullient Mr. McMahon for just one evening. Normally such a request would have required months of paperwork and at least a dozen meetings on the vice-presidential level. But NBC was cooperative and moved with uncharacteristic speed. Just before the network offices closed for the day back East, we were notified that there would be no voice-overs at the end of the program. And that evening, after a year of writing, preparation, filming, and editing—and twenty years after the Huie book was published—*The Execution of Private Slovik* went on the air.

If one believes the ratings (one usually does if they are high and disparages them if they are low), then those who were viewing television that night gradually abandoned the programs they were watching and tuned, en masse, to *Slovik.* By the last half-hour the ratings were enormous.

This was quite possibly the result of advertising. We had strongly resisted the promotional distribution of any photographs of Eddie Slovik bound to the stake, but we were overruled. The network took out full-page newspaper ads, as well as ads in *TV Guide,* that showed Sheen at the penultimate moment, waiting for the firing squad. Thus, in the Monday-morning quarterbacking that followed the broadcast, there was some feeling that people watched the show in increasing numbers because of morbid curiosity. Even the title, which several NBC executives lobbied us to change because it "gave away the ending," was thought, in retrospect, to have been unexpectedly beneficial. For whatever reason, and despite the fact that it was a "downer," *The Execution of Private Slovik* swept the competition.

We had not fared well at the hands of the critics for *Tenafly* or *Partners in Crime,* but the notices for *Slovik* more than compensated. The story itself was so inherently powerful, in a way so much the stuff of legend, that it almost guaranteed an emotional reaction. Some critics felt they had been manipulated, and they resented it. But for the most part the response was gratifying.

Cecil Smith wrote, in the *Los Angeles Times:*

> The last five minutes of "The Execution of Private Slovik" are among the most agonizing I've ever seen.
>
> This is after they've shot Eddie Slovik. We've seen the firing squad march into the courtyard of the chateau at St. Marie aux Mines in eastern France, their combat boots crunching in the thick snow.
>
> Eddie is tied to an upright stake . . . the black hood is over his head. We hear his voice repeating endlessly the Catholic litany of "Hail Mary" and "Holy Mary," the words of the prayers tumbling pell-mell over each other in his desperation to get them said.*

---

* Adding the "Hail Marys" was Sheen's idea. There was no mention of them in Huie's book.

We've heard the order to fire, the crack of 12 rifles.

We've seen Eddie's head fall forward on his chest. We've heard an immense sigh escape from him.

Then it begins. This agonized waiting. The doctor slowly moves forward with his stethoscope. "They did a lousy job," he says, "not one wound in the heart." The nervous Captain asks if his men should reload. "That's right," blurts out the beefy Chaplain. "Give him another volley if you like it so much."

The waiting. The interminable waiting for Eddie to die. . . .

The movie that has finally emerged is worth the waiting. It is a powerful testament told in almost Grecian terms. In a season of brilliant TV movies ("Miss Jane Pittman," "Catholics," "The Migrants"), "The Execution of Private Slovik" is among the best ever made.

Perhaps the most flattering review came from Bill Marvel in the *National Observer.* He said, in part:

> "Slovik" defies all the conventional wisdom about television: that it is a timid medium, that everything on the tube has to be aimed at some kind of lowest common denominator, that made-for-television movies aren't as good as "real" movies. From the warning at the beginning, that young people and others might be disturbed, to the final sequences in which a priest anoints Eddie Slovik's lifeless body, "The Execution of Private Slovik" is as honest as anybody has a right to expect from a work created by human beings.

Marvel's comment about the "warning" referred to a disclaimer that we wrote and asked NBC to include on air just before the start of the film. It cautioned the audience that the story was presented in realistic detail and viewers should consider whether they wished to watch, or wanted to have their children watch.

Disclaimers have become more common over the years. Usually

they are a way of softening the criticism of the docu-drama form; they will often state that some character names have been changed and certain events have been presented out of sequence in the interest of drama. We are in favor of the device because it's one way of alerting the viewer that he or she is not about to see the literal truth—although it does not seem to have molified those who are concerned about the problem of historical falsification. We added a disclaimer to *Slovik* for nonhistorical reasons, however: The ending was graphic and we had an obligation to let the more sensitive viewers among the audience know that it might upset them.

As for the issue of fairness and balance, we were pleased that most critics did not feel that the script was slanted. Cecil Smith said: "The film does not sit in judgment on the judgment of the Army," and Howard Kissel noted, in *Women's Wear Daily*: ". . . the screenplay tries to understand all the participants in this drama . . . it is this unusually broad perspective, this disturbing awareness of the impossible complexity of human events rather than any easy partisanship that ultimately leaves one numbed by the drama."

Lamont and Sheen received much well-deserved praise, and for a week we all telephoned one another with news of reactions from friends and associates. After months of close collaboration none of us wanted to let go. But the reality of television one-shots is that, unlike motion pictures, they do not have a "run." If they are to have any impact it must be immediate. At the end of the week Lamont telephoned and said, half-mockingly and half-plaintively, "Is that all? All that work and it's gone in one night?"

Fortunately, *Slovik* has had more than its share of reruns and it was released theatrically (after we were allowed to cut eighteen minutes from its length) overseas. It also won a number of awards, including nine Emmy nominations (Frank Morriss won for his superb editing) and prizes from various film festivals. Along with *The Law* and *Clarence Darrow,* it won the George Foster Peabody Award for NBC.

Of all the mail we have received on the shows we have done, one letter that came into our office after *Slovik* was aired was the most remarkable.

To understand its effect on us, it's necessary to be aware of several facts that are not widely known about the Slovik case. One of the ironies of the affair is that Slovik may have been shot to "set an example." Yet, after the execution an immediate curtain of secrecy descended. Hardly the expected approach if the military wanted to use Slovik's death as a deterrent. More significant, there were two other deserters who had been sentenced to die in front of a firing squad. For reasons unknown, General Eisenhower rescinded these sentences and they were never carried out, thus giving Eddie Slovik his grim distinction.

The letter we received, addressed to the president of NBC, was from one of the men whose sentence had been commuted. It read, in part:

> . . . I associate very strongly with Private Slovik, as I too was sentenced to be "Shot to Death by Musketry" in Europe, and also to the fact that up to the Point of Execution our lives were uncannily similar.
>
> Court-Martial Justice is not exactly the ideal Forum To Be Tried For Desertion in Time of war. The Awesome Power of the Army, the Phony Patroitism of Rear-Echlon Spit and Polish officers, the Dehumanization of Accused from arrest to Death or imprisonment. To give you an example, after our arrest (there was three of us) we were being detained at Regimental HDQT's, located in an isolated farmhouse. We were stripped of our clothes, all but our shoes, and spent a cold shivering night in fear that we would be shot at any moment. At the Point of Daylight, still naked, we were handed shovels and under heavy guard was taken to a wooded area and bluntly told in the grossest profanity to dig our own graves. I was afraid they were going to execute us out of hand. But I was wrong. This incident was just one of many sadistic events to follow. . . .
>
> Of the two of us to be shot (Slovik or I) it should have been I. Slovik was thoroughly courageous and stuck to his stand right to The Firing Squad. I didn't have the guts to do this, and though I was accused, tried and judged by a

kangaroo courts-martial and sentenced to death I knew that they wanted to hear the cop-out. I wrote to Every General in Europe and finally to President Roosevelt and it worked. My sentence was commuted to life at hard labor. I was sent back to the States in late 1945 and Believe it or Not was walking the streets of Newark, N.J. three years later (1948) with a D.D. in my pocket. In Retrospect I would like to say better they should have shot me. . . .

Two historical footnotes:

1. Eisenhower's only public comment on the case was when he was interviewed for television at Gettysburg by Bruce Catton. Discussing Slovik's execution, he said: "As a matter of fact I approved that one. It was for a repeated case of desertion. The man refused—he was one of those guardhouse lawyers—he refused to believe that he would ever be executed. At the very last moment I sent my Judge Advocate General to see him. He was on the gibbet. And I said, 'If you will go back and serve in your company honorably until this war is over, you'll get an honorable discharge and not the death sentence.' He said, 'Baloney,' or words to that effect. And so he was executed. . . ."

As Huie wrote in his book, "Most puzzling is that Eisenhower thought Slovik was executed by hanging (on the gibbet) and not by firing squad."

2. Antoinette Slovik had seemingly disappeared when we made the film, but after it was broadcast the press located her. She had been living under an assumed name in a Detroit nursing home. Perhaps because of the publicity generated by the production she was emboldened to request payment on her husband's G.I. insurance, plus his accumulated pay and allowances.

In the fifties, William Bradford Huie had tried to help her collect; he felt that Congress could pass a resolution directing the Court of Claims to pay the monies. To that end he approached several senators, but none of them was willing to help. One was told by a White House representative, "Passage of that resolution would look like Congress thinks the President made a mistake. It would be an affront to the President."

Years later, in 1977, Antoinette sat in her wheelchair in front of the White House to petition President Carter. At long last there seemed to be no opposition; the bill appeared to have the support of the President and the Pentagon. Representative Charles Rangel (D-NY) introduced it and the measure was referred to the House Judiciary Committee and then to a subcommittee.

But neither Eddie Slovik nor his widow was to have any redress from the United States government. Although there was no opposition to the bill, Congress was busy with other matters and when it adjourned the bill expired. A staff member explained that the subcommittee "just never had the opportunity of taking it up."

Antoinette Slovik died on September 7, 1979. In 1980, long after we had departed Universal, the studio sent us a telegram from a man who held her co-power of attorney and at whose home she had lived during the last years of her life. He was offering the rights to *Antoinette: The Widow of Private Slovik*. Universal wanted to know if we were interested in writing and producing a television film of her story.

We gave it considerable thought. We had spent a year of our lives with the shade of Eddie Slovik—in some ways we had never been so emotionally committed to a project—but we finally decided that if the story was to be told again, even from the viewpoint of his wife, it should be by someone with a fresh perspective. When Universal called we reluctantly declined.

7 / The Gun

Pressure Groups

In August of 1965, Albert L. Hertz bought a .22 caliber Iver Johnson Cadet pistol for home protection. This was during the Watts riots in Los Angeles.

After his fright had subsided, he passed it on to his married daughter.

She decided the gun was too dangerous to have in the house with two small children, so she gave it to her next-door neighbor, a boy of eighteen.

He sold the gun, he later told police, to a "bushy-haired guy named Joe." Joe's real name was Munir Sirhan.

Somehow, Munir says he doesn't know how, the gun fell into the hands of his brother, Sirhan.

On June 5, 1968, Robert Kennedy was shot to death with Hertz's Iver Cadet.

Our involvement with *The Execution of Private Slovik* was far too time-consuming for us to consider other projects. When a young associate stopped by the office with what he assured us was "an interesting idea for a TV movie," we thanked him but suggested he take it elsewhere. *Slovik* wouldn't be completed for months, our plate was much too full, and we didn't want to be tempted.

Our friend, whose name was Jay Benson and who was an associate producer under contract to the studio, persisted. Ignoring our state of harassment, he settled himself in a comfortable chair and told us his idea. What if (when a television premise is "pitched" it is almost an immutable law of nature that one must begin with the words "what if") a murder is committed and the weapon, a gun, is tracked down across the country by two police officers?

Though we were not rendered speechless by the merits of the idea, we promised Benson we'd think it over and politely showed him the door. But his premise was one of the rare few—television producers will normally hear dozens of ideas a week—that had an afterlife. It kept returning without invitation, nagging at us.

And then one day we inadvertently came across a sobering statistic: There are an estimated 200 million guns in the United States, or about one per person for the entire population.

Strangely enough, when we first came to Los Angeles we had written a half-hour script for a Western series called *The Rebel,* starring Nick Adams, that dealt with guns.

In our story the Rebel rode into an isolated valley nestled in the mountains of the Southwest and discovered a pacifist society. No one carried a weapon as a matter of individual choice. All guns had been freely relinquished; they had been given to the minister, who hung them in the church with the name tags of their owners.

But then one of the guns disapperaed. The townspoeple, in a panic, demanded the return of their own weapons. The Rebel investigated and discovered that a young cowboy had taken his weapon for inno- cent purposes. He was planning to leave the valley and knew he'd need protection in the outside world. The Rebel returned the gun to the wall of the church, but now it was too late. The townspeople had become possessive about their weapons—they had grown to like the feel and heft of them—and they were unwilling to give them up. Eventually, the accidental use of one of the guns caused everyone to come to their senses. One by one, the villagers tossed their weapons into a pile in the street and walked away.

We had wanted the script to be a cautionary tale, but as free-lance television writers we were, almost by rote, rewritten. The minister became a crusty but kindly newspaper editor, the church became his office, and the tragedy at the climax, which was the accidental shooting of a child, was sanitized. The show's only distinction was the work of its director, Irvin Kirschner.*

Benson's visit reminded us of that early effort. We also recalled that for a number of years we had wanted to write a drama on the order of *La Ronde* or *Tales of Manhattan,* in which we could tell multiple stories by having something pass from hand to hand, changing the lives of those who possess it. It occurred to us that Benson's idea might be an interesting point of departure for a teleplay of this nature, but for our purposes we would have to eliminate the murder and the two policemen. Instead, we'd tell the story of the weapon itself—the odyssey of an American gun, from its birth in a manufacturing plant to the moment when it is finally fired.

Benson approved of this approach and agreed to share a story credit with us. We suspected that we couldn't sustain the adventures of an inanimate object for two full hours, so we decided that ABC's ninety-minute *Movie of the Week* would be a better forum than NBC's two-hour *World Premieres.* We called Barry Diller and met him for lunch. He was, as always, decisive. Our thoughts on the teleplay were vague and barely formulated, but by the time dessert arrived he had given us a commitment to proceed with the teleplay. He also quickly agreed to our most radical notion, that not a single actor in the cast would be a "name" or a well-known face.

Diller's support had been essential to the making of *That Certain Summer,* and once again he was willing to go along with us. His attitude reflected a sea change that had taken place in the television industry during the previous decade. There was still an adversarial relationship between the networks and the creative community, but with the ascension of the so-called "hyphenate" to power, it was now possible for the writer to exercise a greater measure of control over his or her material.

---

* Kirschner was to become one of many television directors who moved on to theatrical features. Among his films are *Loving, The Luck of Ginger Coffee,* and *The Empire Strikes Back.*

This was something quite new in the public arts. The novelist had always been sovereign in his field, although encroachment by editors had been on the increase since the days of Maxwell Perkins; the playwright, protected by the Dramatists Guild, had always been first among equals in the theater, although strong directors such as Elia Kazan and Mike Nichols had begun to tip the balance and insist on their own creative prerogatives–but in motion pictures and television the men and women who put words on paper were traditionally relegated to the lowest rung of the ladder. Their work was considered to be nothing more than a "blueprint" or a "roadmap," and they would all too often be replaced by a succession of other writers until pride of authorship or any continuity of vision ceased to exist.

When the power of the major studios declined, feature films came to be controlled in the main by star actors and star directors. And television was the domain of the producer. But by the act of hyphenating, by dividing himself like an amoeba into two parts, the writer could *become* the producer and thus, in the field of television at least, make most of the creative decisions.

The hyphenate concept evolved because it was recognized that a continuing presence was needed to oversee the production of a television series. Given TV's relentless demand for material, why not take the lowly writer, affix a hyphen after his job category, glue on another job category–namely that of producer–and give the poor wretch total responsibility? Whatever the cost, it would certainly be cheaper than hiring two people. And the advantages were obvious. If rewrites were needed to trim the budget, why call in a free-lance writer who didn't know the problems involved? The producer would simply put on his writer's hat and make the changes. Practical and economical. And when the writer was manufacturing expensive mob scenes he would, in theory, put on his producer's hat, cast a cold financial eye at his own script, and run a blue pencil through all those costly extras.

Moreover, many writers who would not otherwise commit themselves to the brutal treadmill of series production could be seduced by a greater salary and the title of "Producer." In the words of a studio executive, "We need them to write so we let them produce." A lagniappe for services rendered, and it worked out well enough to become common industry practice. There are other kinds of hyphenates in television, including writer-directors, actor-producers, and director-producers, but the writer-producer is by far the most prevalent.

Since we have always been of the heretical opinion that the script is the most important single element in the making of a film, we feel the hyphenate trend is a happy one. Producing offers the writer a unique opportunity, not only because he can be relatively autonomous (depending on his killer instinct and his recent track record), but also because he can use the producer's function to extend his work as a writer.

He can write, not only with words, but with wardrobe, with music, with editing, and especially with casting—he's less likely to pick the wrong actor for a part if he's written the part himself. He can be on the set (where, as noted, the writer is often unwelcome), ready to protect or enhance his material. Changes will not be made without his consent, and if changes are called for *he* will make them instead of another writer. If his characters would live in a certain kind of house, then he has only to consult with his location manager and it will be found; if antique furniture, or a taste for minimalist art, will tell the audience something about the people he has created, then he will discuss this with the set dresser. And since he is the man who does the hiring, he can select directors who are compatible and who share his concept of the script. This does not mean surrounding himself with sycophants—if he has picked the right collaborators he should listen to them with an open mind—but he can only listen if he's on the premises, and the producer is the one individual who's *always* on the premises.

Thus, by taking advantage of the opportunities offered by the hyphenate situation, the television writer has at the very least a chance to become the *auteur* of the finished film, be it a segment of a series or a television movie or a mini-series. The terrain is scattered with booby-traps, and the networks still have absolute veto power, but the writer, if he's lucky, need no longer be an impotent outsider, providing he's willing (or able) to move back and forth between the type-writer and the producer's desk.

When we sat down to lunch with Barry Diller we knew we had enough credibility to be frank with him about our intentions. We had been hyphenates for quite a few years, we had worked with him before, and there was professional respect on both sides of the table. Otherwise, what we proposed would probably have convinced him that we had taken leave of our senses.

First, we were suggesting that the protagonist of a television film be nothing more than a hunk of metal. We even wanted to start the picture with scenes of the gun's manufacture and assembly, hardly a conventional beginning if one's goal is to "hook" an audience. Secondly, we had selected a storytelling device that would require the gun to move from one person to another. As soon as viewers became emotionally involved with a group of characters, we'd be forced to drop them as the gun passed on to its new owner. And finally, we not only didn't want well-known actors, but we were adding insult to injury by insisting on the elimination of any makeup and even the slightest hint of a musical score.

None of this came from any perverse desire to be different. It seemed essential that the gun itself should be the star of the film, and to have familiar faces popping up here and there would have undercut the very thing we were trying to achieve. Then too, though the picture was not a docu-drama in the traditional sense, we wanted it to have the look and feel of a documentary. Since what we were attempting was basically a stunt, anything that smacked of artifice, from background music to makeup, would have emphasized the mechanical contrivance of the *La Ronde* concept.

Diller gave us his blessings and paid the check. If he had any doubts he didn't express them. After presiding over literally dozens of television films, perhaps he was jaded and the idea of something even vaguely experimental appealed to him. Or perhaps he knew that he would be leaving the network and our project would be inherited by his successor.

For it happened that the Executive Shuffle, a periodic minuet that sends its ripple effect over networks and studios alike, was in full swing. Soon after our meeting Diller left ABC and went to Paramount, where he eventually became Chairman of the Board. He was replaced by Brandon Stoddard, an ABC executive from the daytime programming division. At the same time, Sid Sheinberg was elevated to the position of President and Chief Operating Officer of MCA Inc., Universal's parent company, where he would be heir apparent and, as a friend of ours put it indelicately, take over "the whole ball of wax." Sheinberg's replacement was Frank Price, a successful writer and producer on the Universal lot. Price would leave in a few years to run the motion picture side of Columbia Pictures just as Herb Schlosser, the President of the NBC network, would be shifted to the videodisc division of RCA to make way for Fred Silverman—but that particular Executive Shuffle was still in the future as we finished up postproduction on *Slovik* and began our research into the world of guns.

There is no question that we had a bias. We didn't like guns. We didn't like anything about them. We had both fired M-1 rifles in the Army, but our fathers had never taken us into bosky dells when we were children and extolled the virtues of shooting at small animals. Colonel Colt's legacy was for others; we did not share in the average American's presumed love affair with firearms. And as we continued with our research we discovered that the vast majority of the public agreed with us. All propaganda to the contrary, the polls indicated that most Americans were in favor of gun control.

Our problem was to keep our anti-gun attitudes out of the script. We did not fully succeed, and in this one film we found ourselves edging close to pure advocacy. The research had hardened our position. Guns were meant to be fired, and the statistics of gun-related deaths in domestic situations, as opposed to the use of weapons in criminal acts, were frightening.

Our other problem was on the craft level. How could we hold the audience, with its notoriously short attention span, with a story that was by nature fragmented and episodic, and without the standard crutches of music, well-known actors, or a seductive "teaser"?

We had already come across the tragic history of the Iver Johnson

Cadet pistol that killed Robert Kennedy—it had passed though the hands of five owners in three years before being fired by Sirhan Sirhan—and we knew that weapons are often sold or exchanged. But we had only ninety minutes of time in which to tell our story (less when commercials were added), and we were concerned that viewers would become disoriented by a constant change of character and locale. Mindful of these pitfalls, we plunged ahead with the script.

The story begins in a factory with the birth of the gun and follows it, by train and truck, to a gun shop where it is purchased by a businessman who has recently been robbed. His reason: "The protection of my home."

He displays it to his wife over dinner and tells her they must both learn how to use it. As the salesman has told him, "Nothing complicated about firearms. They're pieces of machinery, just like an automobile."

But the wife doesn't want it in the house. Reluctantly, the businessman gives it away to his night watchman, who promptly pawns it.

It lies under glass for almost eight months, until a young man in a Brooks Brothers suit comes in to purchase a firearm. He settles on the gun (a .38 Police Special) but is dismayed to learn that there is a five-day waiting period. Unwilling to leave without a weapon, he steals it.

The young man's company is situated in an office building near a modern shopping mall. He goes to work, the gun hidden under his jacket, and finds, as he feared, that he's being laid off as part of an economy campaign. Half-dazed, he goes out to the deserted mall, gun in hand, and waits for lunch hour. Electronic clocks chime and soon the surrounding buildings disgorge secretaries and other office personnel. Soon the mall is swarming with people.

The young man carefully aims the gun and sights along the barrel. He points it at a passing girl and pretends to fire, making the sound of an explosion with his lips. Then he swings it on an older gentleman with a cane who is limping by. He makes another explosive sound, this one louder. Gradually, people realize what he's doing and begin to scatter. At any moment he might pull the trigger.

The entire area is quickly evacuated. Spectators watch from the safety of doorways and windows. The young man sits on a concrete abutment, gently rocking himself, until he is roused from his reverie by the approaching sound of sirens. He gets to his feet, almost like an automaton, and wanders through the mall—people running into shops as he passes—and then, on an impulse, he takes the escalator to the underground garage.

He moves in aimless fashion along the lanes of cars until he sees two black-and-whites pull into the garage. He looks down at the gun, surprised to see it in his hand, and casually tosses it through the open window of a parked car. Then he returns to the escalator and rises toward the sunlight, where police officers are waiting to arrest him.

Two women shoppers get into the car, unaware that the gun has lodged beneath the seat. It's discovered later that day by a young attendant when they drive into a car wash. He debates briefly with himself and then slips it into the pocket of his overalls. His name is Natcho; he's a Mexican-American who lives in the barrio with his wife and widowed father. The three of them occupy a cramped apartment, and Natcho's wife is pregnant. She quarrels with her husband over the fact that there will be little room for the old man when the baby arrives.

The gun is a bright spot in Natcho's life. It gives him a feeling of power and superiority. He never intends to use it, but somehow just having it in his apartment makes the circumstances of his existence more bearable. Both his wife and his older brother want him to sell it or give it away, but he tells them—in an echo of the older business-man at the beginning of the film—that there are crimes in the neighborhood and he wants his wife to have it nearby for protection.

And then the gun vanishes. So does Natcho's father. The two brothers search for the old man with increasing desperation, driving through the streets of the barrio and telephoning their friends. They finally find him in a local cemetery, sitting by the grave of his wife with the gun in his pocket. Unwanted, and fearful that he would be put out on the street when the baby was born, he had come to this quiet place to be close to his wife and contemplate the possibility of suicide. His sons embrace him; it's evident that they have come to an understanding of his needs.

The gun is now repugnant to Natcho and he throws it away in a supermarket trash bin. But he is seen by a young boy, who retrieves it. As is the case with many weapons, the gun goes into the criminal underground. It surfaces when it is purchased, along with several other firearms, by an ex-con named Walt. Walt is serving as the middleman between the gun dealer and two of his friends who are planning a robbery. They intend to steal the nightly receipts from a suburban porno movie theater.

Walt's only interest is his commission. But though he knows his friends are nothing more than rank amateurs, he allows himself to be persuaded to drive the getaway car. The crime itself becomes a comedy of failed intentions. The would-be thieves hold up the theater owner as he is counting money in his office. Instead of being intimidated he is outraged; he yanks open his desk drawer and points his own gun at them. They stare at him, stupefied, as he brandishes his weapon and presses an alarm button. He is so angry he completely ignores the fact that they, too, have a gun. There is nothing for them to do but run—into the arms of the arriving police. Walt is also arrested and their weapons are confiscated.

The gun is used as an exhibit at the trial and then waits for destruction in a police department storage room. Once a year all unclaimed weapons, all knives, rifles, shotguns, and sidearms, are transported to a gigantic shredding machine where they are reduced to scrap.

The gun survives the shredder. Weapons occasionally fall over the side during the process and are tossed back into the machinery by the police. But a young truck driver named Gil, whose job it is to transport the scrap to a factory so it can be melted down and recycled, finds the gun in a heap of rubble and takes it home. It has been mauled by the shredder, but it's still capable of firing.

Gil wants the gun, as he defensively explains to his wife, for no other purpose than recreational target practice. He feels pressured by his work, and some of his friends have told him that they ease their tension by lining up bottles and cans and blasting away at them.

The gun is put away on the top shelf of a bedroom closet. It stays there, forgotten, gathering dust. And then one evening Gil's truck breaks down on the freeway and he calls home to say he'll be late for dinner. His wife takes advantage of this break in her routine to sit down at the kitchen table and have a cup of coffee.

Gil has a young son. With his dinner delayed, the little boy wanders through the house in search of something to do. Eventually he finds himself in his parents' bedroom and remembers that there is a portable radio on one of the closet shelves. Dragging a chair over to the closet, he clambers up and begins feeling around on the top shelf. His searching fingers pass by the radio and touch something cold and metallic. Curious, he takes down the gun.

While his mother continues to sip her coffee in the kitchen, the child settles himself in the chair with his new toy. He points it—he has been taught well by television—and aims it at random around the room. Then he turns it so that the muzzle faces him. He cocks the hammer and stares with fascination down the barrel of the gun.

The camera pans slowly away and comes to rest on a window. There is an attenuated pause—and then the sound of a shot. The screen goes dark.

When the script was finished we had our first meeting with Brandon Stoddard. He was dynamic and full of enthusiasm, and though he was just beginning to feel his way in his new position he gave us an official go-ahead on the project. But not without misgivings. He was concerned that the film would be seen as an anti-gun tract and he cautioned us to refrain, in any discussions with the press, from describing it as such. This, of course, put us in a quandary. It *was* an anti-gun piece. Despite the fact that every event in the script was based on actual incidents, the cumulative effect was clearly a blanket condemnation of firearms. We had knowingly violated those two network shibboleths, "balance" and "fairness."

We returned to the script and reworked it to avoid a heavy-handed stacking of the deck. We also spoke with gun enthusiasts so we could absorb their side of the "right to bear arms" debate. But our belated efforts notwithstanding, we felt in our bones that the possession of firearms should be subject to controls, and *The Gun* was to some extent a manifestation of this attitude. Perhaps pro-gun factions should have had the right of equal time in which to rebut us, although it's a moot point at this late date. And certainly they have not been without their platforms. The gun as an American icon and a symbol of virility has saturated films and television, not to mention radio and comic books, for decades.

Our next task was to select a director, and we were fortunate in our choice. We had been impressed by the work of John Badham on *The Senator* series, and we contacted him and gave him the script. Badham had graduated with a theater degree from Yale, and he had worked his way into directing via Universal's mail room and casting department. He had just finished *The Law,* which we hadn't seen.

He read our script and agreed to undertake the project. He also invited us to a screening of *The Law.* It was a remarkable television film, in our opinion one of the best yet made, and not the least of its many virtues was Badham's direction. He had a cool style, and at our first meeting we all agreed that *The Gun* should extend this even further—we wanted an icy film. Badham seconded our policy of using unknown actors, although it would mean weeks of additional casting time.

In personality he was the opposite of Lamont Johnson. Both of them have a strong visual gift, and both work well with actors, but while Lamont tends to be a charismatic figure on the set, snapping out commands in his resonant actor's voice, Badham gets his way by indirection. And during our helter-skelter production schedule, Badham was never rattled; the greater the crisis, the cooler and more laconic he became. A few years after making *The Gun* he went on to direct his first feature film, *The Bingo Long Traveling All-Stars,* and then he hit the jackpot with *Saturday Night Fever,* starring another graduate from TV, John Travolta.

He had his work cut out for him on *The Gun,* and his calm approach was frequently put to the test. The network license fee was a bargain-basement four hundred thousand dollars and Universal, chafing as usual over the specter of a hefty deficit, had decreed a ten-day shooting schedule. With so little time at our disposal, it would be impossible to deliver a quality film. The script called for fifty-odd speaking parts and almost eighty locations in and around Los Angeles. A more realistic schedule would have been fifteen or sixteen days. We managed to pry an extra day out of the studio but we knew, as did Badham, that we would run over. In the peculiar jargon of the trade, we would "slop."

We had also put ourselves into a corner. By coincidence the Los Angeles Police Department planned to truck out hundreds of unclaimed weapons to the shredding machine, the very situation we had built into our script. It was a once-a-year ceremony and if we could film it, and blend in our fictitious characters, we would greatly enhance the authenticity of the film. The police were not likely to rearrange their schedule to accommodate us, so we had to be flexible enough to gather our actors and equipment at the shredding site on the day when the convoy arrived. But that day was not far off. If we wanted to incorporate the actual event we'd have to limit our preparation time.

There was an even greater problem: finding actors for the barrio sequences. Few films had taken advantage of the Mexican-American community in Los Angeles. It is a teeming and potentially explosive area where cultural pride and harsh poverty maintain an uneasy coexistence. We wanted to photograph the *mercados,* the parks, and the incredible wall murals that were influenced by the works of Siqueiros and Diego Rivera, but most of all we wanted to make use of the available pool of acting talent. Our casting director, who was black, told us that Mexican-Americans shared something in common with other minority groups: since there was seldom any call for them to play parts in films and television, they had not been motivated to develop the necessary skills. The situation had been partially remedied in the case of black actors, but movies and TV were shamefully remiss in the on-screen (or, for that matter, off-screen) utilization of Mexican-Americans. Why should they learn to act when no one ever used them?

We consulted with local theater groups, put out feelers in the community, and availed ourselves of the offices of *Nos Ostros,* an organization that had come into being to increase the participation of Mexican-Americans in motion pictures and particularly in television. With their help—and their occasional hindrance—we were able to cast all of the parts for the barrio sequence with gifted actors and actresses.

But for all its commendable intentions, *Nos Ostros* was still a pressure group, and as such it had many axes to grind. Aside from seeking to generate employment for its constituency, it also fought against the use of stereotypes – the lazy Mexican in the floppy sombrero dozing in the midday sun. All very well and good.

But when we began to deal with the leaders of the organization we discovered that many were actors. In our conversations with them we sensed the faint aroma of a conflict of interest. We had approached them to help us find qualified actors, and we suddenly found that they were – subtly, to be sure – suggesting themselves. There also seemed to be a *quid pro quo* involved: support of the script in exchange for parts. The parts were there to be had, but we wanted an open call, hiring actors on merit instead of by virtue of their positions in *Nos Ostros*.

The situation came to a head when we selected a young actress for an important role. We had not inquired into her ancestry, but *Nos Ostros* was quick to inform us that she was a Puerto Rican, not a Mexican-American. It would be an insult, we were told, if she were to play a *chicana*. The fact that she was the best of the dozens of actresses we had read was irrelevant.

To be fair, *Nos Ostros* at the time was neither monolithic nor did it speak with only one voice, and most of those in charge had no vested interests. And the sensitivity of minority groups, particularly where casting is concerned, is more than understandable. Why should Chinese-Americans, for example, be expected to swallow gracefully the casting of a white actor as Charlie Chan? And why should Indian-Americans (or native Americans, which is the designation they now prefer) accept with equanimity a white man as Cochise in a television series?

It's not a trend that can be easily reversed, and minority nerves have been rubbed raw by years of abuse. Along with most of our colleagues, we try to be open and responsive to pressure groups. But we all resent intrusions into the production process that take the form of manifestos, implied threats, or prior restraint. We signed the Puerto Rican actress on the basis of her ability and found excellent Mexican-Americans for the other roles. After some vague hints of reprisal, the *Nos Ostros* people accepted our decision and there was no further discord.

But *Nos Ostros* was minor league compared to another pressure group that was soon to enter our lives, for as we quietly prepared our film, word of its existence somehow reached the many ears of the National Rifle Association. The NRA, with its highly vocal grass-roots army of gun owners, is one of the most powerful lobbying organizations in the country. Largely due to its relentless efforts, there has been little in the way of significant gun-control legislation in recent years, and this despite crimes, assassinations, and the will of the public. Senators and congressmen, fearing the NRA's ability to influence single-issue voters, have tended to distance themselves from the gun-control dialogue, particularly when they are up for reelection.

Not only does the NRA have the strength of a unified membership, it is also well connected (a flagrant understatement) to the American arms industry. As Robert Sherrill notes, in his excellent muckraking book *The Saturday Night Special,*

> The NRA would doubtless have gone out of business . . . if the gun and ammunition industry hadn't seen that it was a beautiful quasi-official flag to march under. Operational expenses and expenses for conducting many of the early NRA matches were subsidized by DuPont Powder Co., U.S. Cartridge Co. of Massachusetts, Union Metallic Cartridge Co., Hercules Powder Co., Winchester, Peters Cartridge Co., and others. The industry supplied many of the trophies. And it also went to bat for the organization—which is to say, the industry went to bat for itself, for very early in the game the industry virtually became the NRA—in Washington.

We had deliberately kept away from the press to avoid any confrontations with the NRA. The last thing we wanted was an organized mail campaign directed at ABC. More important, we had to find a gun store and/or factory that would be willing to let us use its facilities for the opening scenes of the film.

As we have mentioned, television has the advantage of speed. After many turndowns we found a gun shop that, for a fee (and without insisting on reading the script), permitted us to utilize its premises.

We moved in and out within two days, and evidently just in time. Because Brandon Stoddard, as part of his new duties, was giving interviews.

Though he was speaking to the mainstream press, articles began to surface in gun journals and magazines. The following, from *Gun Week,* was typical of the general tone of the opposition:

> A new television movie on gun control is currently being prepared for ABC. But *Gun Week's* question is: "Is the movie going to be *about* gun control or *for* gun control?" . . .
>
> Brandon Stoddard, ABC vice-president for movies, told a United Press International reporter that the subject of the film will be the dramatized effects a pistol has on the lives of the people who possess it. . . .
>
> "It clearly documents how people's behavior is affected by the possession of a gun," Stoddard said. "There's a funny kind of thing that happens to a human being when he has a gun in his hand. It causes certain problems in a very dramatic way that wouldn't occur if he didn't have one."
>
> What we wonder is what "funny kind of thing" Stoddard is referring to—target practicing, competitive shooting, hunting, or does he mean bank robberies and murders?
>
> *Gun Week* is currently trying to find out more information about the film. If successful, we will pass on such info to our readers. . . .

Scripts, like weapons, can pass from hand to hand. Copies of *That Certain Summer* found their way to members of various gay coalitions and even to one major television critic. *The Gun* was no exception. We began getting calls and letters from gun owners who knew the material cold—and who didn't like it.

But we were finished before the protest could gather any momentum. *The Gun* was completed in twelve days, one day over schedule.

The money had been spent. It was too late now to halt the filming, and if a campaign was to be mounted it would have to come before our air date in November.

In a political context, Walter Lippmann once wrote about "the principles of democracy . . . which assert that the outsiders shall be sovereign over the insiders." The airwaves are deemed to belong to the public, and because broadcasters are permitted access to these airwaves they are charged with programming "in the public interest." But there is no single public; in reality there is a constellation of publics, a stew of conflicting tastes and attitudes, and some of these "outsiders" have become increasingly disenchanted with what they see on their television sets. More and more they have begun to exercise their rights of sovereignty, not only by reaching for the off switch, but also by organizing and seeking out effective ways to make their feelings known. Thus, the pressure group has become a continuing fact of life to the "insiders" who control the industry's decision-making process.

In the late, unlamented days of advertiser dominance over programming, one letter from an unhappy housewife could trigger fear and trembling in executive suites up and down Madison Avenue. Soap was to be sold and the consumer must be kept in a state of passive acquiescence. This was the era of the Lowest Common Denominator and the "bland leading the bland." Ozzie and Harriet were king and queen—anyone who took offense at them was patently un-American.

But as television began to mature and reflect contemporary attitudes, and as the powers of the advertising agencies diminished, pressure groups took on a new and more sophisticated coloration. Instead of the single letter from the disgruntled housewife there would be busloads of mail, all of it curiously similar right down to the same misspelled words. And if that failed there were other avenues of redress. The pressure groups began to perceive that the soft underbelly of the television industry was not the network; rather it was the local station manager and the sponsor whose product paid the bills. The networks, Kafka-like, could send protestors down a thousand corridors until anger would be replaced by floundering and frustration. But the individual station had its license to protect and was vulnerable to local persuasion. And the sponsor, of course, could be driven to frenzy by the mere mention of a boycott of his product.

It seemed—and still seems—that everyone has a complaint. Right-to-lifers. Pro-abortionists. Environmentalists. Gray Panthers. Feminists. Gay liberationists. Religious and minority groups. And the discontent is not only limited to those outside the industry. There are the would-be insiders as well. Why, they ask, are there not more female directors, editors, and composers? * Why aren't more parts being written for qualified actresses who fall in the age range between bosomy starlets and elderly grandmother types? Why aren't there more assignments for black writers, and not only on so-called "black shows"? Why do Mexican-Americans have to pretend to be Anglos in order to get roles?

The grievances are endless. Doctors do not like the way they are portrayed, especially if a segment on a medical series dares to suggest that they are less than perfect. Dentists complain that they are made sport of. Lawyers are unhappy with the inaccuracies of legal shows and psychiatrists insist that their profession is viewed as a simplistic amalgam of Freudian caricature and voodoo. Businessmen grumble that they are often depicted as venal types whose all-consuming passion is the profit motive. And educators are annoyed because they are in competition with the medium itself. To capture the attention of their supposedly nonlinear students, teachers must either sing, dance, or exhibit bionic powers.

All of these groups have a perfect right to make their feelings known. And many of their complaints have merit. The men and women who earn their living in the television industry do not have any particular purchase on the truth. It can even be said that the TV community is a pressure group itself, whose primary purpose is to resist other pressure groups.

However, once the rights of the audience—or of the many audiences—are acknowledged, what then? Are boycotts a legitimate form of protest? Should acting, directing, and writing assignments be par-

---

* According to a Director's Guild survey, since 1949 only .02% of feature films and prime-time TV drama have been directed by women.

celed out on an affirmative action basis? Isn't it humanly impossible for a television show not to offend someone, somewhere, regardless of its content?

If every complaint is heeded, then won't the entire structure become paralyzed? Shouldn't there be an ultimate authority, perhaps the networks, that weighs and balances all of the conflicting claims and counterclaims? But who elected the men who run the networks? Why not vest the powers of decision in Congress, the Senate, in committees and subcommittees? Why not modify the First Amendment? Let the house be burned to roast the pig.

The limits of protest in a free society are a major dilemma of the times. And television, which is certainly one of the most influential of our institutions, was bound to become embroiled in the debate. Those of us who create the entertainment programs for prime-time TV have wrestled with the difficulties presented by protest groups. On any given day we may feel we've had just about enough. How dare they inhibit our creative freedom? We're all good citizens, aren't we? We're nice to our children and we have a sense of social responsibility. Why don't all these noisy people go away and let us do our work in peace?

Then, guilt-ridden, we put our self-righteousness behind us and throw open our doors in an orgy of goodwill. Dammit, let's get some female directors working around this place. No, take out that line, it's offensive to the handicapped. Why can't this veterinarian be played by a black actor? Or an Oriental?

It eventually comes down, as it must, to solutions on a case-by-case basis. Given the nature of the system, there doesn't seem to be a way to institutionalize an across-the-boards response to protest, or at least one that will satisfy the ever-increasing number of claimants. For this reason alone pressure groups are for the most part a necessary goad. Without their complaints, strident or otherwise, the television community would perhaps fall victim to its own parochial interests.

Not that every voice in the wilderness should be heeded. Some years ago the Italian motion picture director Franco Zeffirelli made a television film for NBC called *Jesus of Nazareth*. In a newspaper interview published before the film was broadcast, Zeffirelli casually mentioned that he had emphasized the human side of Christ. Furious over what they took to be a downgrading of Christ's divinity, a group of Southern fundamentalist religious organizations coalesced and mobilized for battle. The sponsor, General Motors, was inundated by mail. So was NBC. The fracas went noisily public and sides were chosen. And yet—*not one of the protesters had seen the film.*

General Motors withdrew its sponsorship. Civil libertarians were outraged; a great American corporation had been bullied into submission. NBC withstood the pressure and broadcast the film. The notices were generally favorable, the ratings were good, and it has been repeated. All without incident. One of the original protesters admitted that the drama was properly reverential and not at all what he expected.

In one rare instance a protest group formed an alliance with the producer of a show against a network. The producer was Norman Lear. He had planned a new series where the character of Maude would go to Washington as a congresswoman, but when Bea Arthur demurred he decided to cast a black actor in the role. When he screened the pilot for an activist group of black congressmen they told him they hated it; it was an embarrassment to Congress and an insult to blacks.

CBS disagreed. Their position was that they alone would be the judge of the suitability of material. But Lear searched his conscience and refused to deliver the show. Talk of contract violation and lawsuits filled the air. The conflict was resolved when the series made a late debut with a white actor playing the lead and a shift of locale to a college campus. Many in the television community felt that Lear had set a dangerous precedent by allowing a pressure group to make what was in effect a programming decision.

The casting process has become a battleground. Finding the right actor for the right part is no longer the only criterion. Perhaps the best-known example of this was the casting of Vanessa Redgrave in Arthur Miller's television film, *Playing for Time,* the true story of an all-woman orchestra, composed entirely of inmates, that was formed by the Nazis at Auschwitz. In an inexplicable lapse of good taste and good sense, the producers signed Redgrave to play Fania Fenelon, a survivor of the concentration camp and the woman upon whose book the film was based.

Redgrave is one of the world's great actresses, but her active support of the PLO and her antipathy toward the Zionist cause is widely known. At the very least, selecting her to play a Jewish woman raised questions of propriety.

Since television does not exist in a vacuum, Redgrave's connection with the drama offended Jews and non-Jews alike. It almost seemed to be a deliberate slap in the face, a bad joke. Even granting her extraordinary ability, was she the only actress in all of Western civilization who could play the part? Fania Fenelon was the most indignant of the protesters. It was her life, after all, and she resented being portrayed by a woman with whom she was in total disagreement.

Angry Jews and their supporters, many of them within the television industry, demanded that CBS should fire Miss Redgrave. But others, to whom *Red Channels* and the McCarthy era was still a recent and painful memory, insisted that actors and actresses should not be denied employment because of their political beliefs.

CBS found itself between a rock and hard place. If the network paid Miss Redgrave off, and allowed another actress to play the role, it would be giving official sanction to a form of blacklisting. But if she were permitted to do the film, what of the legitimate complaints of those who felt she would be insulting the memory of thousands of martyrs who had died in concentration camps?

CBS became the butt of jokes. It was said that they wanted to sign Bruno Hauptmann to star in the title role of "The Charles Lindbergh Story." And Gloria Steinem and Betty Friedan were the top two choices for the life of Phyllis Schlafly. No one could quite understand how the network, with all of its much-disputed but frequently exercised rights of casting approval, had let Redgrave slip by. Actors had been turned down for a hundred reasons, most of them arbitrary and ridiculous, but perhaps the most controversial single piece of casting in the history of the medium had occurred without any network protest whatsoever.

Since Solomon does not have a seat on its board of directors, CBS waffled. The final decision was to let Miss Redgrave play the part, perhaps in the hope that her considerable talents would enable her to give a performance that would transcend her political beliefs. To dismiss her would conjure up that fearful demon, "a dangerous precedent." However, CBS prudently put the finished picture on the shelf so that the passage of time could have its healing effects. The network announced that the show was "as yet unscheduled" and would be aired at a "future date." *

Pressure groups come in all shapes and sizes, but in 1980 something new was added to their company: the government of an entire nation.

In the late seventies a Saudi Arabian princess and her lover were executed for adultery, a capital offense under Islamic law. The princess was shot and her lover was decapitated. The princess was nineteen years old. A British director and producer team fashioned a script taken from the transcripts of interviews and filmed a docu-drama about the event entitled *Death of a Princess.*

After watching a private screening of the program in London, Saudi officials were displeased. The Saudis threatened to break relations with the British government and to suspend oil imports. The film was televised, however, and the Saudis ordered the British ambassador from their country. In Egypt, Anwar Sadat found it necessary to disown the film when he discovered the embarrassing fact that it had been shot within his borders.

When *Death of a Princess* was scheduled to be broadcast in the United States over PBS, a similar contretemps arose. The Saudis protested in a letter to the State Department. With a brief nod to the Bill of Rights, they nevertheless objected to the film on the basis of what they felt were its many inaccuracies.

---

* Due to a prolonged actors' strike in the summer of 1980, CBS found itself short of new product and ran *Playing for Time* early in the fall season. There was a rekindling of protest, but the drama received high ratings and respectful reviews. In a *Newsweek* cover story the magazine's critic, Jack Kroll, said that Redgrave's performance was perhaps the finest ever given on television. Fania Fenelon, however, continued to deplore the casting as a "moral wrong."

Never before had a television program threatened to become an international incident. There were discussions in the Senate, but PBS decided to proceed with the scheduled distribution of the film, although some stations refused to carry it. A spokesman for the South Carolina Public TV Network said, "We made a judgment in regard to the current state of international affairs. We felt the documentary wasn't fair to the Saudis." How the good folks in South Carolina determined this remains an open question.

Complicating the issue was the fact that the drama was to be aired over PBS rather than one of the commercial networks. And one of the chief financial supporters of public television is the Mobil Oil Company, a not altogether disinterested party.

Joseph Sobran, in a *Los Angeles Times* editorial, attempted to deal with this nest of thorns.

> Saudi Arabia [he wrote], better known as Oil Rich Saudi Arabia, can make its displeasure felt, which leaves oil-hungry Americans to argue about whether we should tolerate the showing of TV movies damaging to our national interests. The public-broadcasting folk cry aye, citing the First Amendment. The Mobil Corp., sweating profusely, say yes, but. Some congressmen say hell, no. Consider the argument of Mobil, defender of free enterprise: "We all know that in the United States our Constitution guarantees a free and unfettered press. However, implicit in that guarantee is the obligation on the part of the press to be responsible. Clearly, the people of the United States have the right to expect that the media will not abuse its [sic] privilege."
>
> Now I have held up my copy of the Constitution to the light, and I fail to find any sign that the freedom of the press depends on its acting "responsibly" by standards imposed by the Government. Such a "freedom" would be phony. Any real freedom includes the right (legal, of course, not moral) to act irresponsibly.

However, Sobran focused down to the fact that PBS functions, in part, on tax monies. He wrote:

> To the extent the American people are paying for it, they should be consulted. If NBC were to show a movie that provoked an international incident, it would be entirely within its rights, and our government could refer Saudi complaints to the network. When PBS does so, the taxpayers who may bear the consequences have every right to protest. . . . When a publicly funded enterprise makes trouble for the public, and still claims the same shelter of irresponsibility that privately owned media enjoy, it is time to remind ourselves . . . of the principle that is at stake. PBS wants both the privilege of state support and the common freedom of not having to answer to the state. You can't have it both ways. . . .

Many might quarrel with Sobran's contention that a privately owned network has the right to provoke an international incident. And in the case of *Death of a Princess* the involvement of PBS only serves to cloud the issue. If public funds were not involved, what then? What if the drama had been written by a free-lance writer for Lorimar, or Spelling-Goldberg, or Warner Brothers? Would it be proper for the First Amendment to shield the script and its broadcast when there was a potential oil embargo in the offing? Such questions would give anyone—with the possible exception of the late William O. Douglas—pause.

Death of a Princess did air on PBS and the republic still stands. John J. O'Connor commented in the *New York Times* that with or without the political fuss, the film was an "important piece of television." Saudi crude continued to flow without interruption, although one wonders how the American public would have reacted had the Saudis carried out their threats.

Perhaps mindful of this possibility PBS, in what many considered to be a judicious move, scheduled a follow-up discussion to be tele-vised after *Princess* so that different viewpoints could be expressed.

The Gun was not likely to offend a foreign power. But there was still an internal power—the NRA—to contend with. As the *Dallas Morning News* reported:

> "The Gun" had not even hit the airwaves when gun owners across the country started shooting at it. Fearing that the documentary-style drama . . . would provide un-favorable publicity for them, the individuals have been protesting to ABC . . . A National Rifle Association spokesman said that no official position had been taken, but noted that the group may seek to implement the fairness doctrine if the film is found to put legitimate gun use in a bad light.
>
> As is its policy regarding pressure groups, ABC refused to arrange a special preview for the NRA. . . .

But Universal was not ABC. Frank Swertlow remarked on this in a UPI release:

> . . . Universal-MCA, the overall producers of "The Gun," is in the process of showing the film to the heads of more than 75 gun groups in Southern California, according to a Universal spokesman in Hollywood.
>
> The Universal spokesman added that members of the Los Angeles Sheriff's department, the Los Angeles police chief's department, and the alcohol, tobacco and firearms division of the U.S. Treasury Dept., have seen or will see the film.
>
> In addition, he said the Coalition for Gun Control, an anti-gun group, has been offered the opportunity to view the show.

"We want all sides to see it," the spokesman said. . . .

Although Universal may be mounting a subtle publicity campaign this way, the screenings actually may conflict with ABC's policy on previewing.

"Ultimately it's our air time and our necks," an ABC spokesman said. The spokesman said that ABC and Universal would have to discuss the screening policy.

Our greatest concern was neither publicity nor pressure groups. We were afraid that ABC's Standards and Practices people would not allow us to keep the ending. They had approved the script, but the difference between paper and celluloid is substantial. The accidental firing of the gun by the little boy, even though it happened off-camera, had deeply upset those of our associates who had seen the picture. It upset us as well, but we felt it was essential. We began keeping a file on accidental shootings to buttress our case. Given the incidence of inadvertent gun deaths in America, it was soon overflowing.

As it happened, there was a single piece of profanity in the film. We had left it in place because we had other things on our minds; we intended to take it out when we dubbed the picture. The morning when ABC's censors screened *The Gun* was a nervous interlude for us. We wanted to put the entire day on fast-forward. We sat in our office, wondering what we would do if the network ordered us to change the ending. By noon we were knee-deep in paranoia. We'd go to the press. We'd steal the answer print. Losing all grip on reality, we decided we'd take the picture to PBS.

After lunch a call came in from Charles Engel's office in the Tower. "They saw it," he said, "and they're furious." We clutched our separate phones. "They wanted to know what made you think you could get away with it. It definitely has to come out."

Convinced that our worst fears had been realized we asked the obligatory question: *What* had to come out? Engel could no longer contain himself. He laughed. "The scene where the windowwasher says 'shit.' The word is unacceptable. If you don't remove it they'll do it themselves." And the ending? "No problem," he said. "It's approved."

One of the producer's final responsibilities before a film is delivered to a network is to "spot" the commercial breaks. In a ninety-minute film there can be six or seven of these interruptions. The network's timing and footage format is Sacred Writ, but there is usually some leeway. Producers can either supervise the placement or leave it to the editor. We take a great interest in where the commercials go on the theory that if we're stuck with the damn things we might as well make use of them.

If there are back-to-back talk scenes, for instance, or sequences of an expository nature, it can be a good idea to break them up and give them "air" by inserting a commercial between them. A commercial can also be useful if there's a passage of time, or if the story moves from day to night. But even if there's no esthetic use for a commercial, it should be placed, if possible, where it will not become intrusive. Commercial messages may be mentally tuned out by many in the audience, but if they are poorly positioned they can be an unconscious irritant.

Again, although there are certain restrictive rules, the producer controls the placement of credits and title material. An actor's billing is arrived at by negotiation, and the various guilds and unions have determined where most credits must go (the director, for example, must either have last credit at the beginning of a film or first credit at the end), but the producer has a measure of discretion.

For *Slovik* we held all of the credits, except the title, until the end. For *The Gun* we ran the credits in white against a black background.* The end credits were on a "crawl" that ran from the bottom to the top of the screen instead of on separate cards, and since we had no musical score we replayed the sounds of the factory—another gun was coming off the assembly line.

---

* Titles are almost invariably yellow. This is because technicians in the title and optical departments are forever telling producers that yellow is just about the only color that "reads" well for TV lettering.

We also tried something unusual. Whenever the gun changed hands we superimposed a date on the bottom of the screen to show the passage of time. The story started in the recent past and moved ever closer to the present. The last scene, where the gun, in the hands of the little boy, fired for the first time, had the dateline: November 13, 1974. It was the date of the airing of the show.

The Gun had little impact. It came and went without leaving any resonance—just another TV *Movie of the Week*—and its ratings were disappointingly low. Our friends were almost evenly divided: Some thought it was engrossing, a successful experiment, a well-crafted piece of filmmaking, and others were bored, disoriented, and grudgingly put it in the "Nice Try" category. A woman friend told us, bluntly, "I didn't watch. There are two things I don't want to see on a television screen: snakes and guns."

Perhaps it was just our imaginations, but ABC seemed to breathe a sigh of relief. Its promotion department was then the best in the business, but the campaign for *The Gun* had been (deliberately, we thought) lackluster. Yet even if we were correct, even if ABC had distanced itself from the film, it was painfully apparent that, either because of its form or its content, *The Gun* was not a "must-see" television event. We decided we may have made a mistake by our reliance on unknown actors, yet *Slovik,* also without any stars, had captured an immense audience. For whatever reason, one thing was clear: viewers had no great desire to see the show.

The notices were mixed. Those critics who liked it were quite effusive. The *Hollywood Reporter* stated: "In this year of not-so-outstanding TV movies, *The Gun* stands far and above anything seen so far." Frank Swertlow said: "No one who is sensitive to life and death can come away from this film without being shaken . . . shines the light of truth on a subject that has been ducked by the media for far too long." And Ron Powers wrote, in the *Chicago Sun-Times:*

> The eerie quality of *The Gun* is that the viewer feels a mounting sense of dread as the instrument passes from hand to hand—a dread that the gun will be fired. This is

no small dramatic triumph, considering that prime-time TV is ablaze each night with routine gunfire. *The Gun* will not make the folks at the National Rifle Association happy, but it is a powerful emotional statement and an unusual visual achievement in a medium not known for its visual artistry.

This last remark is a tribute to Badham's work. Even the critics who were unhappy with our script made note of the director's major contribution to the finished film.

Most of the negative reviews complained about *The Gun*'s "episodic nature." As Bill Marvel put it in the *National Observer:* "Since each of the gun's owners could become its victim, the film's suspense rises and subsides so often that by the time the real victim comes along, his fate is curiously unmoving." John J. O'Connor, in the *New York Times,* felt that since our dramatic focus was on an inanimate object the owners of the gun were reduced to quick sketches.

Interestingly, in the light of our concern that we had loaded the show with an anti-gun bias, O'Connor wrote: ". . . the script seems curiously shy about making its point powerfully . . . it is oddly muted, as if Mr. Levinson and Mr. Link were straining to anticipate inevitable objections from the powerful gun lobbies."

O'Connor was right. We *were* straining. Not to avoid gun lobby objections, however, but simply to be fair. Some critics apparently wanted the advocacy drama we originally intended, but none of them thought to address the Fairness Doctrine ramifications of such a naked polemic.

John Carmody, while acknowledging that we "succeeded . . . in conveying the sense of unease and fear that the ordinary, law-abiding citizen feels in the presence of handguns," felt that we had not been daring enough. " 'The Gun,' " he wrote, "is in no way an anti-gun tract." He went one step further than O'Connor, asserting: "Indeed, a fair case could probably be made that the program is actually pro-handgun."

Critics, like everyone else, have political and social values, and sometimes their reaction to a film's point of view may take precedence over the execution of the piece, however artful it may be. The gun lobby, as it happened, did not walk hand-in-hand with the Messrs. O'Connor and Carmody. They neither found the drama "oddly muted" nor "pro-handgun." They thought it was slanted, inaccurate, and nothing short of an abomination.

Witness the following from *Fishing and Hunting News.* Under a thick headline reading: " 'The Gun' Fails the Truth Altogether," the magazine's editor took us to task. He wrote:

> On the evening of Nov. 13th, ABC Television took a swing at many millions of honest upright Americans who happen to be inclined to like and own firearms. . . .
>
> What you saw that evening had little to do with any honest story about guns. It's a yarn about a pistol. Not any pistol—just one pistol. It has nothing to do with fact. It is pure, unadulterated—at times outlandish—and even admitted FICTION. Nothing else. It isn't even particularly good fiction. It contains every cliché anybody has ever heard or written about guns. It makes use of every emotionally pathetic character possible, from the mentally depressed individual to the innocent, unsuspecting child.
>
> It is—whether intentionally or otherwise—a fantasy which, with slick, smooth skill, was aimed at any faction of the public audience that does not know the truth about firearms.
>
> It is, despite any protestations to the contrary, an anti-gun film from the first flick of the switch. . . .

We didn't fare much better in *Guns & Ammo.* The "Letters" column was filled with angry complaints: ". . . I feel every shooter should protest the showing of 'The Gun' to the networks AND the sponsors of that show. . . ," ". . . the movie was a blatant, one-sided and unfair attack on gun-owners and sportsmen. . . ." ". . . We not only have politicians to fight, but also a conspiracy by TV writers, producers, and reporters. . . ." ". . . Every shooter and gun-owner in America ought to boycott the products of the sponsors. . . ." ". . . In fairness to the shooting fraternity, ABC should offer equal time to present the PRO-GUN aspects of firearms ownership. . . ."

Guns & Ammo, in an accompanying editorial, told its readership that "few, if any, of our more than one million readers were happy about 'The Gun.'" Then it placed us squarely in its sights. "It is interesting that Levinson and Link (the producers) have been responsible for other television dramas that do not reflect the general interests of the public at large. These productions have included *That Certain Summer,* a film for television that portrayed homosexuality as normal, healthy behavior; *The Execution of Private Slovik,* a film that unfavorably portrays military treatment of cowardice during time of war; as well as the development of the two popular TV series *Columbo* and *Mannix.*"

We were somewhat nonplussed to find poor old Lieutenant Columbo and Joe Mannix included among our subversive efforts, but *Guns & Ammo* quickly clarified the matter. "A boycott of the sponsors—and the network—may have some effect. . . ." The editorial concluded with a rousing affirmation: "We are the majority. It is our rights that they, a numerical but vocal minority, wish to destroy. It is time for gun-owners to take a positive stand."

Whatever the influence of a single television drama, it pales in comparison with an effective lobbying organization. Anti-gun groups tried to use our program as a rallying point, initiating fund-raising and membership drives and petitioning senators and congressmen. But the NRA, as of this writing, has successfully blocked all efforts to limit, in any meaningful way, a citizen's rights to buy and keep firearms.

The ghosts of Colonel Colt, Bat Masterson, Jesse James, John Dillinger, and Lee Harvey Oswald are not to be exorcised by a television show.

8 / The Storyteller

Violence

A comedy sketch:

THE SETTING: A Senate Committee Hearing Room.

THE CHARACTERS: A Senator and a Nervous Network Executive.

As curtain rises, the network executive is fidgeting on the witness stand. The Senator confronts him, finger wagging.

SENATOR: *"J'accuse!* There is entirely too much sex and violence on television."

NETWORK EXECUTIVE: "But Senator—"

SENATOR: "The situation is intolerable. Think of the harm to impressionable little children. Hour after hour of sex and violence, sex and violence."

NETWORK EXECUTIVE: "Senator, we're talking about two different things. Sex and violence don't always go together."

SENATOR: "No? Then you haven't been to my house lately."

Blackout.

Sex and violence have usually been linked in the public mind, as inseparable as pork and beans, Cheech and Chong, and other all-American partnerships. But in the early years of film, acts of physical aggression were more often than not overlooked as moralists honed in on acts of physical intimacy. Sex, not violence, was the primary concern of the Hays Office, an entity founded to still the outcry over the licentiousness of the fledgling motion picture industry. Gangsters could shoot each other on the silver screen, actors could be drawn and quartered, strangled, stabbed, or tossed off cliffs, and scant attention would be paid. But any indication that a married couple might come within breeding distance of a double bed was strictly verboten, and even the slightest hint that a Fallen Woman might actually enjoy her peccadillos would cause the heavens to open with a plague of locusts. It was an act of courage comparable to walking through fire for Otto Preminger to include the word "virgin" in his innocuous film treatment of *The Moon Is Blue*.

Even comic books fell victim to the sexual censors. Dr. Frederic Wertham, in his book *Seduction of the Innocent,* made a brief nod in the direction of excessive violence, but his true mission was to expose the lust and perversity that lurked between the garish covers of the unsupervised adolescent's reading material. The half-clad jungle maidens and leggy science-fiction nymphs were but the tip of the iceberg, according to Wertham, who rooted out sexual aberrations undreamt of by De Sade. Suddenly, the office of a Comic Book Czar was created, and for a time Sheena, Wonder Woman, and all the other paper sex goddesses were as neutered as capons.

Radio was never much of a problem for the bluestocking mentality—one could not, after all, *hear* cleavage—but television was a different kettle of electronic fish. From Faye Emerson to Dagmar, from nubile Miss Teenage America contestants to the jiggling trio on *Charlie's Angels,* acres of flesh, some of it barely concealed, were flaunted on a daily, if not hourly, basis. And there was no Hays Office or vigilant Czar to speak up for the tender sensibilities of the nation's youth. The only bulwarks against total degeneracy were the network Standards departments and an industry code that was little more than a public relations device.

Again, the preoccupation with sex overshadowed the issue of violence. But gradually, in the late sixties and the seventies, attitudes began to change. The stability of American society was crumbling as students rejected the values of their parents, ghettos burned, and political leaders were assassinated as if the United States were nothing more than a banana republic.

Following H. L. Mencken's dictum that "you must give a good show to get a crowd, and a good show is one with slaughter in it," motion pictures began to reflect the times with films of ever-increasing violence. Cagney and Bogart may well have dispatched their share of villains in the forties, but there was less blood somehow, less of a dwelling on and fascination with the actual moment of extinction than in such films as *The Wild Bunch, Death Wish, Straw Dogs* and *Taxi Driver,* where the killings were all but choreographed into slow-motion ballets of Grand Guignol carnage.

Audiences seemed to love these films—they got off on them—and there were cheers when heads exploded under the impact of bullets. They were either playing along with the filmmakers and didn't take any of it seriously, or else they had developed a newfound taste for gore that had to be fed by ever-increasing doses. Perhaps, at root, they were trying to exorcise the Zapruder film by reexperiencing it.

This new strain of violence found its way, in a watered-down version, into television. And finally parents, educators, psychiatrists, and sociologists took notice. In spite of an increase of "jiggly" and "T and A" on the home screen, sex at long last moved into second position in terms of public concern, and violence began to be seen as a separate and possibly more harmful factor.

Statistics indicate that children watch television on the average of four hours a day. According to *TV Guide,* the American TV set is on for six hours a day. These figures are somewhat misleading, since those six hours do not necessarily represent the viewing time of any single member of the family—they are merely the time that the set, in toto, is operational. But there's no question that the young watch a great deal of television, hour after hour of it, seven days a week.

The influence of television has been a subject of study and debate ever since families first sat mesmerized by Howdy Doody and Gorgeous George. TV has been held responsible for everything from blindness to radiation burns, from providing simplistic solutions to complex problems to turning us into a nation of passive spectators. Its detractors would have us believe that the tube has rendered newspapers obsolete so that we get our information in capsule form from actorish anchormen. It has made a sideshow of the political process. Conversation and social exchange in the home is extinct. The death knell has been sounded for print. And when the new technologies take hold we will never leave our living rooms; instead, we will sit transfixed at our entertainment centers while maurading gangs wander through the rubble of what's left of our cities.

Even allowing for hyperbole, the trouble with all of this is that much of it is speculative and just plain wrong. Until recently book sales have been up. So has attendance at the theater, concerts, and sporting events. As for television's deeper influences, its effect on patterns of behavior, none of these can be measured with any degree of accuracy despite the endless papers, studies, reports, and all the other proddings of the beast. The experts merely add to the confusion by presenting contradictory information.

Whatever the influence of television, it is frequently other than that which is intended. Friends of ours wrote a script in which the heroine of a popular situation comedy spent the night with a man at his apartment. They felt that they were striking a blow for more enlightened sexual attitudes. If this exemplary lady could actually sleep with someone, then obviously sex wasn't so terrible after all.

But we found ourselves wondering what a ghetto child, who quite possibly knows more about sex than the entire production staff of that particular series, would make of such an enterprise. Would he come away with his consciousness raised and a healthier sexual point of view? Or would he, instead, notice the spaciousness of the two apartments on his screen, each of them occupied by a single individual rather than several families, and each with a refrigerator, a television set, and a stereo rig? It may well be that he responded to the show not with a new sexual awareness, but rather with unconscious feelings of envy and resentment at the casual display of opulence, particularly, as is all too often the case, if not a single black man, woman, or child was on view.

There are perhaps millions of people who watched *All in the Family* who did not know, or did not choose to know, that Archie Bunker was a bigot. The neatly fashioned liberal messages in the scripts may well have been overlooked as other, more subtle elements took precedence. A coal miner was quoted as saying: "What I like about Archie is that he has his own chair. And nobody can sit in it but him."

One recalls in this context the Riskin-Capra film, *It Happened One Night.* The picture was quite sophisticated for its time, but its greatest impact was unintentional. Clark Gable removed his shirt in one scene, revealing his bare chest. Shock waves reverberated through the corridors of the underwear industry as sales plummeted. The audience, as audiences do, had chosen to respond to something the filmmakers had not even considered.

Of all the possible influences of television, the depiction of violence and its effect on youthful viewers are perhaps the most controversial. Many well-intentioned people believe that a constant diet of televised violence–those four hours a day the average child stares at the set–is a contributing factor to aggressive and antisocial behavior. And many people, equally well intentioned, believe that it isn't. Although the studies in the field are inconclusive and the statistician's Holy Grail, a direct "causal relationship," has yet to be proven, growing numbers of parents, educators, and social scientists are convinced it exists.

The Surgeon General's Scientific Advisory Committee on Television and Social Behavior, set up in 1969 at the request of Senator John Pastore, released a report that was considered by many to be equivocal, and it was sharply criticized because the networks had input on the committee. Still, when he testified before Pastore at the conclusion of the study, Surgeon General Jesse Steinfeld stated: "While this committee report is carefully phrased and qualified in language . . . it is clear to me that the causal relationship between televised violence and antisocial behavior is sufficient to warrant appropriate and immediately remedial action."

Another major study, conducted by the National Commission on the Causes and Prevention of Violence under the chairmanship of Dr. Milton Eisenhower, stated: ". . . a large body of research on observational learning by pre-school children confirms children can and do learn aggressive behavior from what they see in a film or on a TV screen."

Corroborating Dr. Eisenhower's remarks more than a decade later, two psychologists from the London University of Psychiatry (H. J. Eysenck and D. K. B. Nias) wrote in their book *Sex and Violence in the Media:* ". . . aggressive acts new to [a] subject's repertoire of responses, as well as acts already well established, can be provoked by violent scenes portrayed on film, TV, or in the theatre." The authors concluded: "It can no longer be said that the evidence . . . is ambiguous, or too contradictory."

But the critics of these studies remain unconvinced. By their lights the evidence is *not* consistent, and they counter with questions that they feel have never been answered satisfactorily. Are the children allegedly affected inclined toward aggressive behavior to begin with? What about kids from happy homes with strong parental guidance? Are they so malleable that they turn from Jekylls into Hydes after a few evenings with J. R. Ewing and the Incredible Hulk? How does one quantify aggressive and antisocial behavior, and against what standards is it measured? In fact, why is such behavior necessarily to be discouraged? Aren't there many so-called problem children who are actually far more perceptive than their peers, who rebel, quite properly, against the hypocrisy that surrounds them? Why isn't this kind of aggression beneficial? Perhaps by identifying with a maverick role-model on television, a Jim Rockford or a Hawkeye Pierce, the child does himself more good than harm, easing his passage through the painful rites of growing up by knowing that, like his friends on the TV screen, he's not so different after all.

In the late seventies a variety of pressure groups, particularly the AMA and the PTA, began a concerted effort against what they maintained were increasing and unacceptable levels of violence on television. Armed with the "violence index" compilations of Dr. George Gerbner of the Annenberg School of Communications, and more knowledgeable about the pressure points of the industry's infrastructure, they mounted a highly effective campaign. No longer simple naifs with little understanding of the territory, they were possibly the most millitant and well-organized protestors in the history of the medium. They went to the press, to sponsors, to station managers, as well as to the networks. They brandished studies and editorials. They pointed out that the average American child, by the age of eighteen, is likely to have witnessed more than eighteen thousand murders on television.

All of this coincided, unluckily for the networks, with a cyclical return to hard-action series. While the PTA decried violence, there seemed to be an overabundance of cop and private-eye shows on the air. This was a matter of pure coincidence–medical series and Westerns had reached the saturation point and so the other forms had, as always, replaced them–but it served the purpose of the pressure groups, whose grievances were illustrated nightly by an array of car chases and murders on every channel.

Then, too, there were incidents–isolated and sporadic, but nevertheless disturbing–that seemed to bear out concern about imitative behavior. A gang of children set fire to a man after seeing a similar act on a film shown on TV; an extortionist tried to use the plot device of an early *World Premiere* called *The Doomsday Flight* to intimidate an airline company; * the mother of a young girl claimed her daughter was raped by teenagers who had seen and imitated a rape sequence on *Born Innocent,* another TV movie.

The antiviolence groups made use of all available ammunition, and when the smoke cleared they had managed to score a stunning victory. When the new television season was announced viewers were faced with what on TV executive called "wall-to-wall comedy." Gone were *The Streets of San Francisco, Feather and Father, Cat and Mouse,* and other programs that might have been renewed under different

---

* When informed of this, the author, Rod Serling, is reputed to have said he wished he had never written the script.

circumstances. *Delvecchio* was cancelled. So was *Serpico. Police Story* was reduced from a weekly series to an occasional two-hour special.

The remaining action-adventure shows were given stricter guidelines, allotted so many "units of aggression" per episode, and the producers of one of television's chief offenders, *Starsky and Hutch,* promised they would spend more time exploring the relationship between the two principals, and less time on gunfights and car chases.* The networks took the position that television had never been particularly violent—and even if it was, the problem had been remedied. An attitude guaranteed to delight collectors of corporate realpolitik.

Members of the Hollywood television community, especially writers, were furious at the turn of events. There was much discussion of the *Born Innocent* case. Here was a serious film fashioned by dedicated and conscientious people. The producers, Robert Christiansen and Rick Rosenberg, had made *The Autobiography of Miss Jane Pittman,* among other distinguished television movies. The writer, Gerald DiPego, had done the teleplay for *I Heard the Owl Call My Name.* All of them had attempted, with no desire to be exploitive, to make a cautionary tale about the grim effect of detention homes on young women. In order to point up the potential dangers of such institutions, they had included a rape scene. And now the mother of the girl who had been raped in real life, allegedly by youngsters who had witnessed the program, was suing the network for violating its public responsibilities.

Most writers were firm in their conviction that DiPego had no responsibility whatsoever in the subsequent tragedy. In their view people who committed crimes after watching television shows—and no one seemed prepared to acknowledge that *Born Innocent* was, in fact, the lit fuse that set off the real-life incident—were unbalanced to begin with and looking for an excuse to vent repressed hostilities. Anything, from a gloomy day to a rude salesclerk, could set them off. To neutralize TV programming to the point where it would not

* Only a few years later car chases returned in full glory on series such as *The Dukes of Hazzard* (an imitation of the good-ol'-boy films personified by *Smokey and the Bandit*) and "CHiPS."

influence the mentally unstable would be, even if it were possible, destructive to the medium and discriminatory to the normal viewer.

Then there were the esthetic concerns. Writers contended that violence under its many guises—conflict, action, stress, suspense, jeopardy—was a legitimate tool, a color on the writer's palette, and to outlaw its use would strike a major blow at the very essence of the creative process. Far from being the province of hacks, violence was an important strain in world literature from Swift to Dickens and from Homer to the Gothic constructs of Joyce Carol Oates and Tennessee Williams. The Bible abounds in death and destruction. Fairy tales are filled with decapitations, dismemberments, and other assorted horrors. And Shakespeare piles up corpses in numbers unrivaled by any season of action-adventure episodes on prime time.

But the television community's overriding concern was a deep fear of censorship. This fear (and resentment) was echoed in an *amicus curiae* brief prepared by the Writers Guild on the *Born Innocent* case in which counsel included, by way of a warning, Lenin's ominous remark that freedom of speech and freedom of the press should not be permitted. "Why should a government," he asked, "allow itself to be criticized? It would not allow opposition by lethal weapons. Ideas are much more fatal things than guns."

Though some might consider it presumptuous for TV scenarists to make a quantum leap from their rights to include car chases in scripts to the expression of radical political philosophy, the writers nevertheless saw themselves as a first line of defense against a pernicious brand of censorship. If violence could be suppressed by governmental fiat, then wasn't it only a short step to the manipulation of news, both in print and on the home screen? After all, where is violence more prevalent than on the nightly newscast? Both the Johnson and Nixon Administrations would have been delighted to find a rationale for keeping all those dead bodies in rice fields off America's TV sets.

Those in favor of placing restraints on freedom of expression could argue that the most obvious examples of imitative behavior occur not as a result of dramatic programming, but of news broadcasts. Reports of ghetto riots or the hijacking of commercial aircraft seem to trigger a snowball effect. If a conflagration is featured on the evening news, others are sure to follow. And each hijacking, or bomb scare, seems to beget a spurt of carbon copies. An official panel, empowered to order the network news departments to ignore such incidents, could in all likelihood eliminate the monkey-see, monkey-do repercussions and, as a result, save lives.

This line of reasoning, in the opinion of the embattled creative community, would quickly surface and be legitimized if pressure groups succeeded in telling writers what to leave out of their scripts and how many "units of aggression" were to be permitted. Censorship may begin with mouse bites, but it tends to develop a momentum of its own, and the slightest capitulation would be a dangerous mistake. In the words of Edward Coke, "No restraint, be it ever so little, but is imprisonment."

The antiviolence people found all of this specious and self-serving. They maintained that the airwaves belonged to them, and they had not only the right but also the obligation to protect their children by speaking out. In their view the issue of censorship was a smoke screen. They had no wish to muzzle anyone, but they felt that freedom of expression was not a license for lazy and unimaginative writers, and irresponsible programmers, to pander to the basest instincts of the audience, particularly when easily influenced young people were involved.

The First Amendment, they reasoned, did not protect someone's right to shout "Fire!" in a crowded (and presumably non-burning) theater. To exercise freedom of speech in such a manner would result in harm, just as an interminable cavalcade of TV killings and maimings would do psychic damage to the nation's youth.

They dismissed the fairy tale and Shakespeare arguments out of hand, claiming that fairy tales are not visual, nor is a child exposed to them for literally hours at a time, seven days a week. And they noted that when such stories *do* become visual the results are frequently unsettling—the witches in the film versions of *The Wizard of Oz* and *Snow White* have haunted the dreams of youngsters for generations. As for Shakespeare's theater of duels and corpses, a case can hardly be made that his work is a staple in most households.

Besides, the antiviolence advocates insisted that they were not opposed to the depiction of violence *per se*. What disturbed them was that there had been so much of it and that it was often gratuitous. Their justification for the "so much of it" complaint was Gerbner's Violence Index. But the television community had branded the good doctor's approach as at best quixotic. A comedy pantomime routine in which Shields and Yarnell pummeled each other and that lasted on screen for a few seconds longer than a rape on *Baretta* could well score higher, or more violent, on Gerbner's index. Pies in the face rang the statistical gong along with gunshots and flashing knives, and little note was made of the difference between the two.

Nicholas Johnson, a former chairman of the FCC and a spokesman for the antiviolence cause, defended the use of Garbner's figures at a Writers Guild seminar. He admitted their imperfections, but he added, "They're the only tool we have," inadvertently, one hopes, giving voice to the standard network argument in favor of the rating system.

The president of the Guild fixed him with a cold stare and said, "Some people thought that *Red Channels* was the only tool they had when they tried to drive Communists out of the entertainment industry." Johnson riposted with considerable asperity that Communism was not dangerous according to the Surgeon General. "No," said the Guild president, "the *Attorney* General was the one who said that."

As for the "gratuitous" nature of television violence, the difficulty, of course, was in deciding what was gratuitious and what was not. Any decision would have to be a value judgment, a subjective call. Finally, although the pressure groups conceded that they were not troubled by "motivated" violence, there were those who found this attitude illogical. Wasn't an act of violence, whether motivated or not, still an act of violence, and therefore likely to have an adverse effect on children? Oedipus tears his eyes out. The play is a work of art. But to a five-year-old (assuming any five-year-old precocious enough to be exposed to *Oedipus Rex)* the horrible act of self-injury may far transcend any artistic context.

Anyone who tried to pick his or her way through this forest of pros and cons could be forgiven for turning away in confusion. For every argument there was a persuasive counterargument. And if television was *not* harmful, if children could put it in perspective and distinguish clearly between the reality of their lives and the fantasy of their viewing hours, then all of the hue and cry was pointless. But even if a minority of the studies were correct, what were the ramifications, not only for parents but for those in the business of creating programs for the home audience?

A number of years before the antiviolence groups badgered the networks into a temporary housecleaning we had our own personal debate on the issue. As noted, we had labored in the genre forms of the sixties and had contributed our share of blood and thunder to the airwaves. But the twin murders of the Kennedy brothers made us pause and take stock of our work for the first time in terms of its social and psychological implications. Others doubtless did the same. How much influence did all of us, as individuals, actually have? Was there any connection between an increasing crime rate (with most murders committed by teenagers) and what children watched on their television sets? In short, what were our responsibilities, if any, considering the vast audience we reached?

We eventually came to believe that if television could sell products it could also, by dint of repetition and over a period of years, influence to some degree ideas and attitudes. We had no evidence for this, it was unsubstantiated and purely visceral, but as a result we made a unilateral decision to keep violence out of the shows we wrote and produced. *Columbo* was deliberately nonviolent. So were most of our other series.

Not that our record was consistent. When we made *Slovik* it seemed to us that the horror of the execution had to be presented as graphically as possible. And *The Gun* required the implied violence of the ending, although nothing was depicted on screen. At the time we wondered whether our anti-gun tract, mild though it may have been, might backfire. Was it possible that a child might see the program, miss its point, and instead become fascinated by all the loving close-ups of the weapon itself?

After *The Gun* we made two television movies, one a two-hour pilot based on a novel by Ellery Queen, and the other an original story idea that we asked Peter Fischer to write. Neither show contained any violence. The Queen project was a welcome escape from our forays into social drama—our friends had begun chiding us that our work was becoming too solemn and discursive—and a chance to make a movie just for the fun of it.

We decided to create a valentine to the old-fashioned whodunnit, and so we set the show in a 1940s time frame and borrowed shamelessly from the film techniques of the period: the back-lot look, the optical "wipes" from scene to scene, even the hoary device of pages blowing on a calendar to indicate the passage of time. We deliberately imitated the old Queen radio show by halting our story just before the climax and having Ellery challenge the audience to solve the crime.

We needed a stylish director for this kind of fluff and we were fortunate to get a bearded and flamboyant Canadian named David Greene. Greene had made a number of polished theatrical features, among them *Sebastian, The Shuttered Room,* and *Godspell.* He was also a veteran of *The Defenders* and other New York–based television series, and for one of these shows, J. P. Miller's *The People Next Door,* he won his first Emmy. While constantly protesting that he preferred more serious fare, he had an instinctive understanding of the form. He took a garrulous and expository script and made it into a high-style homage to the films of a simpler and more innocent time. Later, he would win more Emmys for his direction of the first two hours of *Roots* and for *Friendly Fire.*

End of the Line was the title of the Fischer script. It was the story of a down-at-the-heels radio personality who had been reduced to hosting a phone-in talk show in a small California beach community. One of his early-morning callers is a suicidal young girl. He makes sardonic sport of her plea for attention—she's just another one of the "crazies" he has to deal with every day—and he cuts her off. But as other callers phone in expressing their concern, he begins to realize that the girl's desperation was genuine. He enlists his audience and for the duration of his radio program both he and his listeners swap information in an attempt to find her and stop her from harming herself. ABC objected to our title—not, in their view, a "grabber"—and the film, directed by Darryl Duke and starring Robert Culp, was aired under the network-inspired title, *A Cry for Help.*

The *Ellery Queen* pilot sold, and as executive producers we spent most of the following season guiding the series, aided by the invaluable Peter Fischer as our producer. Again, even though we were doing a murder mystery, we kept the level of violence to a bare minimum. The crimes were bloodless and took place for the most part off-stage. Perhaps as a result, the ratings hovered just below a 30 share, not quite sufficient for renewal. An NBC research man, brushing away an alligator tear, remarked on the day of our cancellation: "Too bad—you were just a few share-points away from a four-year run." He neglected to mention that his network had shifted us in midseason to a timeslot opposite the newly reunited Sonny and Cher, who joked about their divorce and pretty much swamped us in the ratings.

Years later, when we had the pleasure of meeting Frederic Dannay (the surviving member of the Queen collaboration), he told us that he enjoyed the show. But at the time we were making it, NBC was not happy. In an effort, as one of the programming executives told us, "to put some adrenalin in your numbers," we were asked to "get out of the camp business and go harder."

By "camp" he meant the forties' humor of the series—admittedly a bit precious on occasion—and by "harder" he was suggesting that we inject more of those familiar standbys, "jeopardy" and "conflict." It was an odd request, considering that the antiviolence forces were already beginning to launch their campaign of protest, and we more or less ignored it.

There's no question that the networks have deliberately exploited violence over the years in their pursuit of ratings. Anyone who has run a television dramatic series has received phone calls—never memos or anything on paper—suggesting more "action" or an increase in the weekly body count. But the situation is complicated because at times a responsible network executive will complain about the absence of "pace" and "tempo," and he may honestly believe that a show could benefit from the addition of a bit more excitement. But all too often "excitement" translates into the PTA's *bête noir,* "excessive and gratuitous violence," and in the case of the request to "adrenalize" the Queen show, it was evident that the suggestion was more pragmatic than creative. Hard-action series usually do better than soft series. Queen was a soft series. Therefore, juice it up.

This particular example of network interference, the first of its kind we had received in some time, started us thinking again about the violence issue. There were also almost daily reminders as we and our story editor met with writers and briefed them on our needs and requirements for the series. Many seemed bewildered when we said that we wanted a nonviolent show.

It's hardly a secret among TV writers that action sequences are easier to come up with than complex plot developments and three-dimensional characterizations. If things are getting dull it requires scant ingenuity to throw in a runaway truck or another killing. To involve the audience without grabbing it by the lapels calls for considerably more effort than creating a chase or a fistfight. This may be why some of the would-be Queen writers bridled at what they felt were our arbitrary restrictions. Others, however, who were quite capable of constructing an excellent script without recourse to violence, were annoyed because they saw our guidelines as a form of censorship.

We finally decided that the best way for us to better understand our own feelings and attitudes toward the influence of television—as well as the violence debate—was to write about it. Early in 1977 we began to seek out opinions on the subject from writers, producers, directors, and network personnel. We also talked with what our colleagues chose to call "the enemy camp," particularly physicians, social workers, and PTA people. We read many of the existing studies, as well as a book that was creating a stir called *The Plug-In Drug*. Written by Marie Winn, its thesis was that the content of television was beside the point—the very act of watching was harmful in and of itself.

We even came across those who wanted *more* violence on TV. They believed it provided a healthy outlet for bottled-up aggressions. Others suggested that the artificiality of television violence was the cause of all the problems. If it were to be presented in realistic and stomach-turning detail, then viewers would soon become revolted and reject it entirely. This theory failed to take into account *The Texas Chainsaw*

Massacre and *Taxi Driver* syndrome–the more violent the film, the more audiences seemed to enjoy it.

We grappled with all of this material, wondering if there was any way of putting it into some kind of coherent dramatic form. Then we began thinking about Gerald DiPego and what his feelings might have been as a result of his experience with *Born Innocent*. How much had it troubled him? Had he lost sleep, or had he decided that the real-life reenactment of his script was a fluke of fate?

Here was obviously a dramatic situation. We were tempted to talk to DiPego, but we realized that since we wanted the freedom of pure fiction it would be better to create a character of our own and let him speak for himself. The more we thought about it, the more enthusiastic we became about telling the violence story from the point of view of a professional television writer. It would have the added advantage of giving us an opportunity to show the audience the world we knew behind the camera.

Paddy Chayevsky had already dissected television in *Network,* but his mordant study had little to do with the reality of the business. From our experience as writers and producers there was little bed-hopping, few tantrums, and none of the surreal activities that *Network* depicted with such relish. Instead, the American TV industry was both more and less horrible than the world of the Chayevsky film. It was by nature prosaic and workaday, inhabited by reasonable people who on occasion did unreasonable things, and by any yardstick hardly glamorous.

Illustrative of this is a story, no doubt apocryphal, about an attractive young actress who offered herself to an elderly producer in exchange for a part in his series. He contemplated her sleepily across his desk and said, "Young woman, let's say I accept your proposition. When can we get together for our little tryst? This week I'm trapped in a dubbing room, and during the nights I'll be rewriting scripts. Next week I have meetings scheduled around the clock with writers and directors. Some of our pictures came in short and the week after that we'll be writing and filming added scenes, all of which have to be edited into various segments. Then I go to New York for network pep talks–they're not satisfied with the ratings. After that, when a new batch of first drafts comes in, I expect we'll have to throw out most of them and start from scratch. So maybe, if you don't mind waiting, we can make an appointment for the week after Christmas."

Our title was *The Storyteller* and our protagonist was Ira Davidson, a man in his fifties and a free-lance television writer. Ira has a comfortable house in a Los Angeles suburb, a loving wife and divorced daughter, and a grandchild whom he adores. Although he was once a would-be poet and a short-story writer, he now sees himself as no more and no less than a skilled entertainer who helps millions of viewers to pass the time agreeably.

Ira has a show on the air one evening, just another of the numberless scripts he's written over the years. This particular drama features several acts of arson as part of the plot, and it's seen by a young boy who lives in Seattle. Late that night the boy leaves his house, goes to his school, and attempts to burn it down. He perishes of smoke inhalation in the fire.

Ira is now confronted by a crisis of conscience. How culpable is he in the death of the boy? At a press conference the next day the producer of the show dismisses the incident—a tragedy of course, no question about it, but an irrational act in no way related to the program. But Ira is not sure. As he ponders the situation he grows more and more disturbed, vacillating between self-justification and feelings of guilt. His attitude is typified by the following sequence, where he is having breakfast with his wife Marian by their pool.

> IRA: Can you imagine writing a scene where a guy is feeling sorry for himself—and he's sitting by a ten-thousand-dollar swimming pool behind a two-hundred-thousand-dollar house.* Drinking fresh orange juice yet.
>
> MARIAN: Doesn't play.

---

* The inflated Los Angeles real estate market has rendered these figures obsolete. Only a few years after those lines were written, Ira's house could have been sold for well over a million dollars.

IRA: Nope. (He picks up a pool net and dips for a leaf on the surface of the water. Then, thoughtfully:) It's funny . . . All my life I've thought I was getting away with something . . . I mean, it's been so *simple*— I make up these little ideas and people actually pay me for them. I'm not a doctor; I don't fly a jet plane with passengers; I'm not a politician sending kids off to war. If I goof nobody gets hurt. I always figured I was an entertainer—show them a good time and try not to put them to sleep. Is there something dishonorable about that?

MARIAN: No. Not at all.

IRA: And no possibility of damage. Just stories. I've been telling them all my life. How can a story hurt somebody?

MARIAN: It can't.

IRA (intense now): Every show I've written—every single show—the good guys always win and the bad guys always lose. Thirty years of happy endings. If I'm so damn influential, why doesn't *that* count for something?

MARIAN (concerned): Ira—

IRA: If I can't change people for the better, how come all of a sudden I can kill them!

Ira finally decides to go to Seattle, seek out the boy's parents and his teachers, and decide for himself the limits of his responsibility. His guide is an on-the-make young newspaper reporter named Tepperson, who is aggressively inquisitive in the Woodward-Bernstein mode. As the two of them munch hamburgers in a drive-in, Tepperson bores in:

TEPPERSON: They make you do it?

IRA: Do what?

TEPPERSON: The networks. If you don't put that stuff in your scripts, are you out of work?

IRA: By "stuff" you mean—

TEPPERSON: You know. Action. Excitement. Jeopardy. The code words for violence. (beat) Look, I'm not trying to pin you down. I'm just curious.

IRA: It's complicated. Anyway, I don't work with the networks, I work with producers.

TEPPERSON: But *they* take orders from the networks.

IRA: Not orders. Suggestions. Nobody gives me a quota of gunshots or corpses.

TEPPERSON: But these . . . "suggestions." Somebody somewhere along the line says—"this is dull—juice it up." Would that be accurate?

IRA: Sometimes. But—

TEPPERSON: Sometimes. Okay. So sometimes somebody asks you—maybe not you but the producer—maybe not the producer, but somebody—to stick in another body, another chase, another fight.

IRA: You're making it sound like a conspiracy.

TEPPERSON: Isn't it?

IRA (annoyed): Tepperson—basics. If I'm doing a detective show, I know there's going to be a murder. If I do a Western, I'll probably have a gun go off. It's part of the form. And it's what the audience wants.

TEPPERSON: And what the audience wants, the networks buy.

IRA: It's called the free enterprise system. And in the process, it moves a lot of soap. And gives jobs to a lot of people.

TEPPERSON: Including you.

IRA: Including me.

TEPPERSON: Something's wrong somewhere.

IRA: The only thing wrong is that you're looking for an easy answer. How old are you?

TEPPERSON: Twenty-nine.

IRA: At twenty-nine, I guess you're entitled.

TEPPERSON: You're forgetting something, Mr. Davidson. I grew up on your stuff. If I'm looking for an easy answer, maybe it's because Matt Dillon and Elliot Ness always solved the case.

IRA: So I didn't give you the real world. Well, you've got it now. How do you like it?

Ira finally has a meeting with the boy's mother. During their talk, which inevitably becomes a confrontation, she leads him into her son's bedroom.

MRS. EBERHARDT (quietly):   On Monday night I came in here. He skipped dinner–I could never get him to eat much. He was watching your show–

IRA (interrupting):   Mrs. Eberhardt–

MRS. EBERHARDT: If you'll let me finish–

IRA: I'm sorry, I can't. *My* show, the *director's* show, the *actors'* show, the *network's* show–

MRS. EBERHARDT: Did you write it, Mr. Davidson?

IRA: Yes.

MRS. EBERHARDT: Did it start with you?

IRA: Yes, but–

MRS. EBERHARDT: He was watching your show. I asked him if he wanted something to eat, but he was very involved. He said he'd get something later. What I saw on the screen was a burning building. . . . Later that night my husband and I went to bed. They called us at two in the morning to come down and identify the body.

IRA (sympathetically, but with mounting frustration): Mrs. Eberhardt, thirty million people saw that show—

MRS. EBERHARDT: *Your* show.

IRA: Thirty million people saw it. Now I can't believe—I really can't believe—you're seriously suggesting that a play, a piece of film, a make-believe story, got your son, out of all those people, to go out and set a fire. There had to be something else.

MRS. EBERHARDT: There wasn't.

IRA: There *had* to be. Look, you're new here. I'm sure it wasn't easy for him to start all over at a different school—

MRS. EBERHARDT: Mr. Davidson, you may not want to hear this, but he wasn't having any problems readjusting. He was making friends.

IRA: Then why?

MRS. EBERHARDT: Because you caught him when he was tired. Or feeling pressured. I don't know. I *do* know it would have passed, it would have gone away. But then he saw something on television—the fire you built—and at two o'clock in the morning our phone started to ring.

> IRA: Look, I know how you feel. At least I think I do. But it's not that simple. And I have to tell you that I resent all this talk about *my* show, *my* fire—
>
> MRS. EBERHARDT: You come into people's *homes,* Mr. Davidson. The homes of people you don't even know. Is that on your mind every time you sit down at your typewriter?

That evening, as Ira prepares to return to Los Angeles, he is visited by the boy's father, who apologizes for his wife's behavior. He admits that his son was troubled.

> MR. EBERHARDT: He was bright, he was alert—he was a very sweet boy—but I don't think either of us could communicate with him properly. There was some part we couldn't touch. We were told four years ago that he'd benefit from psychiatric counseling. We said we'd look into it but we never did. . . .

When Ira arrives home in the early hours of the morning, he finds his wife waiting up for him. He begins to undress without comment. She studies him and then:

> MARIAN: Aren't you going to tell me about it?
>
> IRA: Not much to tell. (beat) I met his parents.
>
> MARIAN: Oh?
>
> IRA: Seems their son had problems. A lot of problems. (pause) Isn't that terrific?
> (She looks at him sharply. It's a curious thing for him to say.)
>
> IRA (flat): I mean, now I'm off the hook, aren't I?

At this point we stopped writing. Our last scene was to be a meeting between Ira and a producer on a new action-adventure project, a scene that would resolve his personal conflict and end the film in a satisfying manner.

Unfortunately, we hadn't the vaguest idea what the ending should be.

We requested an appointment with Frank Price, then the head of the television department, and made a trek to the twelfth floor of the Black Tower to let him know that we wanted to stir up the violence controversy at a time when the networks were disposed to let sleeping pressure groups lie.

Price was a rarity in the industry, a production chief whose background was in writing and producing rather than in law or the agency business. He had worked his way up from a reader on the *Matinee Theatre* to executive producer of such Universal staples as *It Takes A Thief* and *The Virginian*. As a youngster he had been a voracious reader, and in our encounters with him we had traded nostalgic reminiscences about the Oz books and Albert Payson Terhune's noble collies. Unlike many studio and network executives, he was well grounded in the techniques of script construction.

His response to *The Storyteller* was immediate—he disagreed with us completely. He held to the traditional view that violence, on-screen or in print, was nothing to be concerned about, and as our meeting ran well beyond the allotted time he launched into literary precedents from D'Artagnan's swordplay to Mary Shelley's sad but murderous monster.

He had obviously given much thought to the subject. The Gospel According to Price was that blaming the ills of society on television was like blaming a mirror for its reflection. TV does not exist in a vacuum; there are countless other variables, and to say that one has a more profound effect on children than any of the others is scapegoat-mongering in the extreme. He mentioned the inordinately high violence level on Japanese television and asked why, even when population differences were taken into account, the Japanese had a lower crime rate than the United States. The same was true of other countries.

His secretary buzzed him. Appointments were stacking up like jets over a socked-in airport, but Price was oblivious. He moved on to cast doubt on the existing studies. Who funded them, and with what biases? When statements were issued under the imprimatur of the PTA or the AMA, did they really reflect the thinking of the total membership, or did they come from a vocal minority? And why, if parents were so upset by violence on television, did the ratings indicate that some of the most popular shows were the very ones condemned by the PTA, Gerbner, Johnson, et al? The off switch was the ultimate censor, and parents didn't seem to be using it.

Finally, Price pointed out that by making a film on the subject, we'd be placing ourselves in a no-win position. If we were faithful to our material we'd have to examine the problem rather than offer any pat solutions. This wouldn't make for very satisfying drama, and it would probably open us up to charges of coming down firmly on both sides of the issue. Depending on how we resolved Ira Davidson's dilemma, we'd either be whitewashing the networks or else we'd be giving aid and comfort to the enemy.

When Price had finished we asked whether his talkathon was a thinly veiled—or, more accurately, thickly veiled—attempt to persuade us to abandon the project. "No," he said. "I think you'll be making a mistake if you do it. But I can hardly take a position against censorship and then censor you. By all means go ahead. We'll give you our support."

He was as good as his word. The Universal development list, an in-house compilation of every television show in whatever stage of preparation, now included: "L & L 2-hr. violence film." Misnomer it may have been, but at least we had official sanction. Not that Price relented in his efforts to cause us to see the light. At every opportunity he chatted with us about the issue; somehow he always had new evidence in hand that refuted the PTA's figures or disparaged Gerbner's techniques. Actually, we were fortunate to have him as a devil's advocate; by challenging us to constantly reexamine our premises he led us to include a rather unusual device in the film that served to point up the complexity of the debate.

Borrowing the idea from Jean-Luc-Godard, we wrote a series of Man (and Woman) in the Street interviews and inserted them at pivotal moments in the script. There were five of these, in which people from various walks of life—a TV journalist, a police officer, a psychiatrist, and two housewives—expressed their views on television violence to an unseen interviewer. We hoped that these brief set pieces wouldn't interrupt the flow of the story, but instead would serve as a useful counterpoint.

There was still, of course, the problem of the ending. When Ira meets with his producer in the last scene he has just returned from a voyage of conscience. And although he has been "let off the hook," as he wryly remarks to his wife, he has nonetheless undergone certain changes that preclude a return to business as usual. Yet here he is, ready to pitch another story and write another script.

We finally concluded that Ira's response should be similar to our own. He would continue with his work, but he would find a way to fashion his entertainments without the use of violence. As a corollary to this, and just as important, he would make clear that his choice was a personal one and that he would not presume to impose it on anyone else.

It seemed to us that this was the only possible solution, not only to the climax of the script but also to the violence debate itself. All concerned had to recognize that it was a matter of personal responsibility. Parents had to exercise control over their children's viewing habits. If the antiviolence pressure groups would express their objections by turning off the set, then the shows they found objectionable would quickly vanish, always assuming that their opinions were shared by enough of their fellow citizens to cause a significant decline in the ratings.

The writer's responsibility, on the other hand, should be to consider the implications of what he puts on paper. Is a given scene of violence necessary or is it merely an easy way out of a structural trap? Is he supplying what he wants, or what he thinks the network wants? Finally—does he give his own children unlimited viewing privileges, or does he share with his critics the feeling that everything on the air is not appropriate for the young?

Once we completed the script, we met with Brandon Stoddard to see if ABC would be interested. There had been enormous changes at the network since we had made *A Cry for Help*. In less than two seasons it had apparently learned how to transmute base metal into gold and had elevated itself from its perennial position in third place to shoulder CBS aside as the undisputed leader in the ratings. Under the direction of Fred Pierce, and with Fred Silverman in charge of programming, ABC turned the Family Hour to its own advantage by slotting bubble-gum sitcoms such as *Happy Days* and its spinoff, *Laverne and Shirley,* both of which captured vast audiences. The network also made shrewd use of the Olympic Games (spiced up by Roone Arledge's technological gimmickry) to promote its schedule. And then, of course, there was *Roots,* a supposed white elephant that Silverman played off during the course of one week to get rid of it.

ABC's new eminence was to have unfortunate repercussions for years to come. Goaded by a press that had turned the ratings race into headlines, the three networks scrambled with increasing desperation to compete, and as a consequence there was little risk-taking and virtually no support for marginal shows. Series came and went through an accelerating revolving door, and at NBC in particular there was an orgy of "stunting." * The competitive hysteria eventually led to that infamous evening when *Gone With the Wind, One Flew Over the Cuckoo's Nest,* and a TV movie based on the life of Elvis Presley were scheduled opposite each other, giving viewers an acute case of electronic frustration.

When we entered ABC's modernistic new offices—the reception area, with its ceiling of inlaid wood, never failed to remind us of a Dansk cheese tray—we could almost smell the pure oxygen of success. No one was making jokes anymore about putting the Vietnam War on ABC so that it would be canceled in thirteen weeks. Now NBC was sulking at the bottom of the ratings ladder and CBS had been rudely awakened from its patrician air of superiority. Incredibly crisp young men and women were moving through ABC's wide hallways with a new sense of purpose. They were on top, they had rocketed to the moon, and there they intended to remain.

---

* Stunting is the preempting of regular programming for special shows. Its purpose is to deliver rating points.

All of which did not bode well for our project. It was certainly not a flashy script; at best it might make for thoughtful drama. But since ABC was now fully committed to the business of razzle-dazzle and high numbers, "thoughtful drama" was not likely to appeal to the mood of the moment. We knew why we wanted ABC–they could give us the advantage of heavy promotion on hit shows–but the question was: Would they want us?

Stoddard was cordial, but he saw at once *The Storyteller* would have problems in terms of mass appeal. We could hardly tell him that in this case we were not particularly interested in mass appeal–we simply wanted to make the film. He told us he'd think it over, but there was little enthusiasm in his voice and we suspected that our prospects were dim at the number-one network.

Another meeting was called several weeks later in the office of Steve Gentry, a personable young ABC executive. Also present were Frank Price and Marvin Antonowsky from Universal, Lou Rudolph, ABC's man in charge of television films, and Stoddard, who made the introductions and discreetly vanished. We launched into a description of our story, trying to make it sound as exciting as possible, but the only nods of approval came from Price and Antonowsky. As the home team, this was expected of them; they were there to give us moral support.

When we had finished, Gentry looked thoughtful. He was obviously pondering and perhaps tempted. Rudolph, however, had no doubts. He didn't want the show. He was the most perfectly tailored human being we had ever met, and as he turned us down we found ourselves in awe over the impeccable cut of his suit.

Rousing from our survey of his apparel, we defended *The Storyteller* on the basis that it was worth doing simply because it was worth doing. This tautological sales pitch seemed to have no effect whatsoever. Then we pointed out that television had not examined itself sufficiently, and here was a rare opportunity to do so. Rudolph was unmoved. Finally we tried our ace in the hole–we said that since ABC was the acknowledged champion it could afford, unlike the other networks, to have at least one TV movie that didn't deliver stratospheric ratings.

Rudolph smiled. "We want good films," he said. *"And* we want good numbers. We don't see why we can't have both."

It was an irrefutable argument, and there was little we could do to counter it because we suspected that *The Storyteller* would probably not deliver the Nielsens to which ABC had become accustomed. Speaking from his frame of reference, Rudolph was only doing his job. Our disagreement, as was usually the case, was with a system that made it difficult for anyone in a position of authority to take an occasional flier.

As soon as the meeting broke up Rudolph drew us aside. All, apparently, was not lost. He said he might reconsider if we would make certain "changes" in the story. We should open with an exciting sequence in which the boy sets fire to his school. The audience should actually *see* the conflagration instead of only hearing about it. The boy should not perish, but should be hunted down and arrested. Ira Davidson should become a peripheral character–the public would never empathize with a rich television writer–and should be replaced as the protagonist by a flamboyant lawyer who would defend the boy. We'd still be permitted to incorporate some of the pro and anti-violence material, but it should be condensed and delivered in the guise of a climactic courtroom speech.

We thanked Rudolph, told him we'd give serious thought to his approach, and drove at top speed back to the studio–where we made an immediate call to NBC and asked if they'd be interested in meeting with us about a two-hour television film called *The Storyteller.*

NBC's response was favorable and to our surprise they gave us an immediate commitment to write the script. Since it was already finished we waited for a suitable period of time and then sent it over to their Burbank headquarters. Final approval, we were told, was assured; it was only a matter of "touching base" with New York.

We were in the midst of discussing casting and a director when Charles Engel, then Universal's liaison with NBC, called to relay the unexpected news that our script had been rejected. Paul Klein, the network's head of programming (he had replaced Marvin Antonowsky, who had replaced Larry White) had turned it down for reasons unspecified. He had overruled his own TV film department, whose members had approved the script, so now we had lost our second network.

Our faith in the project was somewhat shaken, but we decided to try CBS, the last of our potential markets. CBS usually paid less of a license fee than its rivals, and we had never made a film under its auspices, but we were hardly in a position to pick and choose. We requested a meeting with Paul Monash and his associate, Donald March. Monash was a well-known film and television writer-producer whose presence at CBS was somewhat unusual. Under normal circumstances network executives are promoted from within and have seldom written or produced on their own, perhaps on the theory that such experience would make them unduly sympathetic to the blandishments of the creative community. Monash, however, had major-league credentials, and when we sat down with him and March we got the impression that he had taken the job as a lark and was just passing through. As a profit participant in such films as *Carrie* and *Butch Cassidy and the Sundance Kid,* he obviously didn't need the money.

He listened attentively as we described what we wanted to do with *The Storyteller* and without hesitation said that he liked it. Both he and March made some constructive suggestions, and when the meeting adjourned it appeared we finally had a patron.

All too often those of us who work in television find ourselves spending more time putting projects together than we do in the actual writing and making of the films. Just getting to the starting line requires so much wasted energy that creative resources may be spent at the very moment when they are needed the most.

It had taken us much longer to position *The Storyteller* ("position" being another favorite word of the trade meaning, Webster notwithstanding, to maneuver something into a favorable spot for ultimate launching) than it took to write the script. But events had not quite played themselves out. There was still the matter of Paul Klein's breakfast.

Charles Engel had been annoyed by NBC's rejection, and when he heard that Klein was coming to Los Angeles for what *Variety* calls "network confabs," he alerted us to hold ourselves in readiness. Shortly thereafter we received twin midnight calls—Engel instructed us to appear in the dining room of Klein's hotel at eight the following morning. Instead of telling him that the matter was settled, that we were making our film for CBS, we agreed to show up at the appointed hour.

We were fully prepared to dislike Klein—after all, he had summarily turned us down—but when we invaded his morning meal under Engel's cheerful supervision we found him to be rumpled, sleepy-eyed, and gruffly engaging. He had drifted in and out of various network positions for years, but he was perhaps best known for contributing the phrase "Least Objectionable Program" to the language. It was his theory that viewers would not watch something because they liked it, but rather because it was the least offensive of the programs available.

He had also speculated over the deterioration of quality in television, suggesting that it was a result of cheaper prices for the average TV set. Only those with college educations had the means to purchase sets in the early days of the medium, but as costs came down and the distribution of sets became more democratic, programmers found they had to appeal to less discriminating audiences.*

We discussed these conceits with Klein as he attacked his cantaloupe, pointing out that they were elitist, cynical—and probably true. We were getting along famously and the vibrations at the table seemed to augur well until he set down his spoon and said, in an abrupt change of subject, "You're here to convince me to do your script. Well, I don't want to. It isn't junk, like most of the stuff I read, but the damn thing is too cerebral, too didactic. It isn't a television film, it's an essay."

Since we were sitting there with an almost guaranteed CBS commitment in our pockets, we chose to differ with him. With absolutely no regard for the nuances of power politics involved, we told him

---

* Perhaps Klein was a student of De Tocqueville, who wrote: "When only the wealthy had watches they were very good ones; few are now made that are worth much but everyone has one in his pocket."

bluntly that he was wrong. It was *not* an essay, it was a drama. Moreover, it was the kind of drama that NBC could certainly use to upgrade its faltering image. The network was not likely to go into receivership if *The Storyteller* was put on the schedule. Admittedly the show was a loss leader, but even if we made it poorly it would be no worse than the glut of B-movie programs they had been running lately, and considering its subject matter it deserved a shot over one more pretty-girl-in-jeopardy epic. We continued in this fashion—giving the project a hard sell had become second nature by now—until the dining room was almost empty and Klein was casting desperate glances at his watch.

He finally threw up his hands in surrender. "All right," he muttered. "I'll do the damn thing just to shut you up."

He beckoned for the waitress, signed the check, and rushed off to a meeting. And several days later a work order arrived from NBC, officially committing the network. We suddenly found ourselves in the embarrassing position of having sold the same project to two competing buyers.

In our zeal to make the picture we had foolishly—and improperly—given something to Klein that we had promised to Monash and March. Egg-faced, we called CBS and explained our predicament. They were somewhat nonplussed, but they were kind enough to relinquish their claim. Now all we had to do was shoot the film, which was a far simpler matter than getting a network to finance it.

Ironically, we had not encountered our series of rejections because of the "controversial" nature of the material. We had assumed from the start that our subject matter would be the sticking point, but in fact it was never an issue. By the time we began making our rounds violence had been surgically excised from the airwaves—for all intents and purposes it had ceased to exist—and the networks no longer considered themselves sitting ducks. What bothered ABC and NBC about our script was its "softness" and its tendency to deal with "ideas" rather than "emotional situations an audience could identify with." There was concern that a quiet film on a complex subject with an odd protagonist (a *television* writer, for chrissake!) would not get ratings. Still, it should be noted that despite its misgivings NBC gave us upward of a million dollars, left us alone, and doubtless hoped for the best.

With Martin Balsam playing Ira and Patty Duke in the role of his daughter, we began filming. Patty did us a favor by lending her name to the project–the part was relatively small–and it was a pleasure working with her again. Things had changed for her since the troubled days of *My Sweet Charlie;* she was now married to John Astin and she presided over a household of children. Our director was Robert Markowitz, whose work we had admired on Ernest Kinoy's indictment of violence in pro hockey, *The Deadliest Season.*

By an extraordinary coincidence, the Zamora case broke on our first day of production. A young man named Ronald Zamora had killed an older woman in Miami Beach, Florida, had stolen several hundred dollars and her car, and had gone on a spree at Disneyworld. Defense counsel introduced a novel and bizarre explanation for the crime. He contended that Zamora, a minor, was the victim of "television intoxication," that his addiction to television shows had all but hypnotized him and rendered him unable to stop himself from committing murder.

While we were filming our fiction, the real-life parallel made headlines across the country and refueled the violence debate. Zamora was eventually convicted, but on his behalf his parents filed a suit against the networks for damages. The complaint alleged that the plaintiff had become "completely subliminally intoxicated" by his extensive viewing of television violence and had developed a sociopathic personality that was desensitized to violent behavior. ABC, NBC, and CBS stood accused of failing to use ordinary care to prevent Zamora from being "impermissibly stimulated, incited and instigated" to duplicate the "atrocities" he viewed on television.

A U.S. District Court judge found for the defendants. In his opinion he observed: "The plaintiffs ask the Court to determine that unspecified 'violence' projected periodically over television (presumably in any form) can provide the support for a claim for damages where a susceptible minor has viewed such violence and where he has reacted unlawfully.... To permit such a claim ... would give birth to

a legal morass through which broadcasting would have difficulty finding its way. . . ."

Embroidering on this theme, the judge continued: ". . . I suggest
that the liability sought for by plaintiffs would place broadcasters in
jeopardy for televising *Hamlet, Julius Caesar* . . . and indeed would
even render John Wayne a risk not acceptable to any but the boldest
broadcasters."

Having struck a blow for free expression, however, the judge added
a caveat that left the issue, if not the case, clouded. "Without question, television programming presents problems and the study of
these continues," he wrote. "One day, medical or other sciences with
or without the cooperation of programmers may convince the FCC or
the Courts that the delicate balance of First Amendment rights should
be altered to permit some additional limitations in programming."

Thus, even though the case was a victory for the networks, such
phrases as "with or without the cooperation of programmers" and
"additional limitations" were very much present, like worms among
the roses, as possible harbingers of battles yet to come.

The Storyteller was completed and aired. It was not a success. That is, it
was seen by millions of people instead of *many* millions of people. As
one critic remarked in his review: "Unfortunately, few viewers will
watch the show. Most of the audience will be tuned to ABC, which
will be offering a piece of 'legitimate' violence, the important NFL
clash between Baltimore and Miami."

When the national ratings were in, with our drama registering a
mid-twenties share, an ABC executive called Frank Price and said,
"You see? We told you so."

Surprisingly, we got some of the best notices we'd ever received.
Mike Drew, of the *Milwaukee Journal,* wrote: "One of TV's chief
advantages over movies and theatre is the speed with which it can
treat current issues. Often it does this exploitively, sometimes en-
grossingly. But almost never has it analyzed itself with the clear-
headed perception displayed here." After lavishing justified praise on
Martin Balsam's performance, *TV Guide* called the film "a serious and
suspenseful drama that dares substitute ideas and matters of con-

science for the buckets of blood and screeching of brakes that are the more usual TV-movie staples." And Cecil Smith wrote, in the *Los Angeles Times:* ". . . it's a marvelous film, an absorbing film that couldn't have been made anywhere but on television. . . . never before has the whole process of television been more vividly dramatized."

Even John J. O'Connor of the *New York Times,* who had not been particularly sanguine about *The Gun,* was pleased. He found that the film had "remarkable dramatic weight," and he noted that "television is notoriously reluctant to deal with its own problems, [but] 'The Storyteller' carefully examines a phenomenon that the medium too often seems determined to ignore." *Broadcasting Magazine* began its review by saying: " 'The Storyteller' may have been the most penetrating network depiction of the complex spectrum of interests and responsibilities that the television industry comprises," and ended with, "The show came in third in its time period, beaten by Monday Night Football on ABC and a circus special on CBS."

Our own feelings about the film were mixed. We were glad we had made it and we took pride in the overall craft level of the production, but we also had to admit that it was a rather peculiar piece of entertainment, slow-moving at times and without much dramatic fire. Although the show seemed to have little impact, it was nominated for both an Emmy and a Writers Guild Award for best original script, and it brought us the greatest in-pouring of mail of any of our television films. The majority of letters were from parents who had considerable difficulty keeping their children away from the television set, and they seemed to want to share this with someone.

To us, the most important piece of correspondence came from Gerald DiPego, the author of *Born Innocent.* He wrote: "Thank you for 'The Storyteller,' an honest, thoughtful film on a subject that concerns us all."

The Storyteller was our last project at Universal. For several years we had been thinking about leaving; we had been under a corporate roof for more than a decade, and although the relationship had been happy and productive, we had begun to feel an underlying sense of stasis, an itch to move on. Universal was no longer alone in the business of making films for television. Now almost every major studio, as well as most of the independents, were suppliers of this particular form, and many of them had been calling us about books and projects that seemed exciting. The entertainment industry is a haven for transients, and it was time we joined their number. Our contract was coming to an end and we decided not to renew.

On our last day a small party was held for us in our offices. Some of the better pieces of Jules Stein's antique furniture we had acquired (stolen from other offices) was parceled out to covetous associates, our Rolodexes were tucked away in the trunks of our cars, keys to the underground parking garage were dutifully relinquished to the studio security guards, and our secretary arranged a lavish spread, consisting of domestic champagne, Cheese-Whiz, and Ritz crackers.

Nothing like a classy show-biz farewell.

Epilogue

During the several years we worked on this book we came to realize that it was impossible to take a biopsy of the television scene, freeze it, fix it on a slide, and make any observations that would hold for a few months, much less any longer periods of time. The creature under our microscope refused to stand still.

If we noted a burgeoning trend on page 20, it would quickly peter out by the time we reached page 38. If we stated in our introduction that television was getting better a new season would come along to contradict us, more often than not characterized by replications of Xeroxes of previous carbon copies.* Sadly, the only constant seemed to be the audience's refusal to support some of the better efforts, the *Paper Chases*, *Lifelines*, and NBC's commendable attempt to bring regional theater into the home.

Television has entered into a major period of transition, and definitive statements are almost instantly rendered obsolete by the increasingly fluid nature of the medium, much of it a result of ABC's recent competitive posture and its attendant claim on the advertiser's dollar.

---

* As soon as *Real People* became a ratings success it followed as the night the day that viewers would be subjected to *Speak Up, America; That's Incredible; Games People Play;* and a slew of other imitations.

And some of the decline in quality can be traced to the fact that the Lear brand of issue-oriented comedy, tremendously influential for most of a decade, finally ran its course. Then too, many of the better writers and directors, the Alvin Sergeants and Steven Spielbergs, joined the Chayevskys, Lumets, and Altmans of a previous era by moving exclusively into the motion picture field. Theatrical films remained more prestigious, and many talented young people tried their best to bypass television entirely.

On the credit side, hard-won breakthroughs in the depiction of more mature subject matter could not be reversed (even *Happy Days* did a touching episode on an autistic child) and movies made for television remained a viable and rewarding form for audiences. As the industry moved into the eighties there was still much that was worthwhile to be seen—providing, as always, that viewers were selective.

After we left the safe harbor of Universal we continued to make television films, either on our own or in affiliation with various production companies. Our first was *Murder by Natural Causes* (originally titled *Natural Causes* until CBS, fearful that viewers wouldn't know it was a mystery, appended the *Murder by* to nudge them into enlightenment), starring Hal Holbrook, Katharine Ross, and Barry Bostwick, and directed by Robert Day.

Causes was an independent production, meaning, among other things, that we had no studio to absorb our deficits. If we ran over our license fee the additional costs would be taken out of our personal hides. This led to a preoccupation on our part with such life-and-death matters as investment tax credits, back-end sales potential, and what to feed thirty extras for lunch on location, steak being too expensive and chipped beef too parsimonious. Suddenly we had a queasy sense of *déjà vu*—we were back in the Wharton School poring over balance sheets in Accounting One.

Obviously an adjustment was required, both for a better picture and for reasons of sanity. We turned over the business end to our associates (not completely; we had no desire to mortgage our houses) and concentrated on the film. This made for a schizophrenic experience—whenever we demanded greater expenditures, much as we had at Universal, we were rudely reminded that we were no longer under a financial umbrella and that the dwindling cash reserves were our own. It was a balancing act between overages on one side and necessary production values on the other, but the compensation in terms of almost total creative control, without the usual layers of opinion between ourselves and the network, made the risk worth taking.

Still, we learned that there are obvious dangers to independent production. When one's own money is being spent there is a temptation to cut corners, a tendency to hire the cheaper rather than the better actor, editor, or cameraman. Happily, some independent companies (Grant Tinker's MTM Productions is a notable example) have a respect for quality and are willing to pay for it.

Another such company is Time-Life Films, a division of Time, Inc., which has expanded the old Luce empire into television and motion pictures and has presented such TV movies as *Amber Waves* and *The Bunker,* as well as James Costigan's and Daniel Petrie's superb miniseries, *Eleanor and Franklin.*

It was for Time-Life that we wrote and produced our second post-Universal film, a drama about the 1957 Little Rock school integration crisis. Starring Joanne Woodward and directed by Lamont Johnson, *Crisis at Central High* was a complex undertaking that was filmed entirely on location in Dallas and Little Rock, with hundreds of extras and dozens of local actors, and it was our misfortune to have our shooting schedule coincide with record-breaking heat waves in both cities. As a result the picture went over budget, but at no time were we pressured to make damaging compromises.

Critics of the television industry—ourselves included—often ridicule the motives of the production companies and the networks. It has been said that a cynic is an accurate prophet, and whatever broadsides are leveled against TV, no matter how outrageous, are apt to be correct. Money, not a desire for art, lubricates the system.

But what sometimes makes the game worth the candle are the occasional surprises, the goings against the grain, and it should be noted in fairness that these moments do occur. One such grace note centered around the screening of our rough cut of *Crisis* for CBS.

Time-Life was committed, and paid, to deliver a three-hour film, but when it was edited to the required running time we were disappointed with the result. The picture was slow; there were too many funereal walks down hallways and enough pregnant pauses and lugubrious looks to set one's teeth on edge. Hidden away in the footage was a leaner, better film, but we were unable to chip away and find it because of our contractual obligation to hand over three hours, nothing less.

During the screening there was a constant creak as people shifted in their seats. When the lights came up all of us (our line producer, Bob Papazian, Time-Life's supervising producer, Freyda Rothstein, and Lamont) repaired to the office of William Self, CBS's executive in charge of television movies.

Self was flattering; he liked the film. But he admitted that he found it "a bit slow-moving in spots." One of our group, in a misplaced attempt at gallows humor, suggested that a solution to our problems would be to throw away a half-hour of footage. Instead of smiling, Self nodded. "That's what I was thinking." His tone was such that we realized he was serious. "Let me get into this with Bob Daly," (at the time the president of CBS entertainment) he added, "and I'll be in touch."

To our utter astonishment we were notified several days later that we would be permitted to deliver a two-and-a-half-hour picture, and that we could go back to the editing room and recut the film. Within a week, after extensive tightening, we were able to present the network with a vastly improved version.

CBS's decision, based purely on Self's creative judgment, cost the network hundreds of thousands of dollars. It was one of the rare and refreshing cases where good taste and good sense prevailed.

Viewed from almost any perspective, television has failed to live up to its potential, a condition it shares with most of our institutions. Yet however imperfect, it cannot be ignored, and in spite of our ambivalence we continue to regard it with a perverse affection. It may well be a sometimes thing, but there are moments, admittedly few and far between, that justify its existence.

Whether such moments will become the rule rather than the exception may be determined over the next few years. As we have noted, the medium is in transition. Television has always evolved, always been in a state of flux, but it seems to us that it's been changing recently at an accelerating rate. There's a feeling in the air that the network system of broadcasting as described in this book, and as America has known it, is terminal. We have been told that we are on the brink of a new epoch in mass communications. A nation that has always been infatuated with technology has a new and glittering assortment of toys, and despite inflation and recession people are laying down their dollars for videotape recorders and cable hookups, for cassettes of old film classics (and new pornographic epics) and some of the large-screen systems.* Videodiscs are already on the market, and if the prognosticators are to be believed, we will be able to summon up via computer and information banks anything from TV games and language lessons to grocery price lists and airline schedules.

The networks insist that all of this will "supplement" rather than replace advertiser-sponsored free TV, and as they bravely maintain this stance they scurry to co-opt the new technologies with cable product of their own and subsidiary companies to manufacture whatever equipment will be in vogue.

For those of us who provide "software" for this "hardware" (two new terms to affront the ear) the delivery system is the least of our concerns. A story is a story and a film is a film, whether brought into the home by satellite, cable, disc, cassette, or carrier pigeon. We are told that diversity will liberate us. The proliferation of access—a phrase disturbingly reminiscent of the deployment of nuclear warheads—will set us free. No longer need we be at the mercy of the mass audience; we can make films for the more discerning and sophisticated minority. And since there will be no sponsors we will not have to concern ourselves with the foibles and follies of Madison Avenue. Best of all, censorship, standards and practices, and worries about Bible belt backlash will be things of the past.

---

* According to one estimate, over 50 million homes will have cable hookups by 1985, and 70 percent of these households will subscribe to some form of pay TV. Also by the mid-eighties, consumers will have purchased from eight to ten million video cassette recorders.

Our view of this is admittedly somewhat skeptical. Perhaps an entertainment Utopia lies just over the horizon, but it's more likely that if new corporate structures replace the old, then new limitations and restrictions are sure to follow. As long as there is still a bottom line—a product to be sold—there may ultimately be little difference between the presently constituted rating system and the keeping track of dollars at a home box office. Both measure audiences, and if someone is counting, then numbers will call the tune.

On the other hand, as Tevye would say, one has only to look at the neighborhood newsstand to see specialty magazines (one-subject publications dealing with everything from hot rods and home decoration to food and the pleasures of the bath) coexisting with *Time, People,* and *Newsweek.* Will enough opera aficionados purchase videodiscs of *Manon* to make the production costs worthwhile? Will young filmmakers forge a distribution chain that can bring their works, however uncommercial, to the homes of viewers who would be interested, and willing to pay? If such efforts are financially feasible, then the technology may serve the artist, rather than the other way around.

It is, of course, entirely possible that the much-touted media revolution may fizzle. America, as pundits are fond of observing, must reorder its priorities. When jobs are scarce and energy costs are high, people may no longer be fascinated by the difference between a stylus or a lasar beam for videodiscs, or the merits of the Beta system versus the VHS.

In that event they may turn for their view of the world to those old familiar warhorses, the networks, and they may even suffer the commercial breaks with more equanimity. After all, the damn thing is free, and it's cheaper than going to a movie or buying some new gadget to plug into the wall.

And so we will all be back in the company of the devil we know, complaining about it, vilifying it—and watching every day.

Index